HOW TO PREPARE A HISTORIC
RACING MINI

HOW TO PREPARE A HISTORIC
RACING MINI

CLASSIC CARS OF KENT LTD

WITH DANIEL H. LACKEY
WITH CONTRIBUTIONS BY JEREMY WALTON

THE CROWOOD PRESS

First published in 2018 by
The Crowood Press Ltd
Ramsbury, Marlborough
Wiltshire SN8 2HR

www.crowood.com

© The Crowood Press Ltd 2018

All rights reserved. No part of this publication may be reproduced or transmitted in any form or by any means, electronic or mechanical, including photocopy, recording, or any information storage and retrieval system, without permission in writing from the publishers.

British Library Cataloguing-in-Publication Data
A catalogue record for this book is available from the British Library.

ISBN 978 1 78500 381 3

Classic Cars of Kent Ltd is grateful for the contributions to this book made by Jeremy Walton

Photography © CCK Historic

Typeset by Jean Cussons Typesetting, Diss, Norfolk

Printed and bound in India by Replika Press Pvt. Ltd.

contents

acknowledgements 6

foreword 7

1 introduction and regulations 8

2 sourcing a Mini and body preparation 27

3 safety first 39

4 subframes, suspension, steering, brakes, wheels and tyres 57

5 gearbox, differential and drivetrain 75

6 engine specification and guide to assembly 85

7 fuel system and carburettors 111

8 wiring loom, instruments and switch gear, safety, engine electrics 124

9 setting up, HTP application and race preparation 138

10 testing and racing 152

useful contacts 171

index 174

acknowledgements

From the very start of this project we all agreed on what we wanted to achieve. We wanted this book to target the grass roots competitor and unpack all of the regulations that define pre-1966 Mini racing and in particular those in the FIA's Appendix K. We wanted to show exactly what it takes to build and compete in a historic racing Mini so that we might inspire a new generation of historic Mini racers. We decided we would build and compete in our own car and use it to illustrate this book. We wanted to showcase the parts, manufacturers and suppliers we believe in and highlight some of the businesses and individuals who help to support a thriving Mini racing industry. We could not have done any of this if it was not for the huge amount of support we received.

First and foremost, a very special thanks to Chris Harper of Mini Sport. Chris has championed this project from the very start and provided the impetus to really get it going. His support is what made all of this possible. He's one of the hardest-working individuals I've had the pleasure of working with and his relentless commitment to the classic Mini industry is truly commendable.

A special thanks also needs to go to Jeremy Walton. His initial contributions helped to set the tone and the format of the book. His wealth of experience in both motor sport and journalism has given him a unique insight and his style and sense of humour are always appreciated.

We'd like to thank Nick Paddy and Bill Sollis for believing in the project and for supporting our endeavour to appeal to the grass roots Mini racers. Their help and support at the circuit was invaluable. Nick's done more for the international Mini community than anyone else and his support of this book has been most appreciated. Bill's contributions in testing and setting up the handling of our car were tremendous. There are not many racers out there with Bill's level of experience or success, so we really appreciate the time we spent with him.

We are truly grateful to photographer Gary Hawkins. A true gentleman and one of the best motor-sport photographers in the UK. We've known Gary Hawkins for many years and worked with him many times. His professionalism and the quality of his work are second to none. All of the action photos taken at Brands Hatch during testing and racing were taken by Gary.

I'd like to acknowledge the hard work and dedication of Mark Forster, particularly for his contributions to the Mk1 Mini community and the racing history of the Mini. He has kindly contributed to this book his knowledge, expertise and historical fact-checking. His passion and commitment are rare and cannot go without mention. Also to some individuals from the group of Mk1 Mini enthusiasts at www.mk1-forum.net. Ed Dickson, for making his 850cc Super Deluxe available for photographs and Pete Flanagan and Stuart Watson for kindly providing some additional historical photos and some current club racing photos. I'd also like to give mention to Barry Hawkins, a pivotal member of Downton Engineering from 1962 and a pioneering Mini racer. We've used some wonderful photographs of Barry racing his Mini back in the 1960s.

Every Mini racer in the world has a debt to pay to the legendary 'Smokin' John Rhodes', the charming hooligan who took immense pleasure trashing the pants off of Mini Coopers throughout the 1960s. His devastation of Dunlop tyres inspired the thousands that came to the circuit to watch him and continues to inspire Mini racers and enthusiasts today. Thank you, John.

foreword

MINI MEMORIES THAT LIVE ON TODAY

Although I was an established single-seater driver before racing a Mini and went on to drive other saloon and sports cars at Le Mans, it is the Mini Cooper S era that sticks in the memories of motor-racing followers. I am grateful for the seasons of satisfying success with Cooper Car Company. The 1300cc class wins we recorded together in the British Saloon Car Championship from 1965 to 1968 live on in many memories, together with images of our Racing Green Cooper S types with their distinctive white bonnet stripes.

Millions watched my appearances in TV rallycross with Abingdon-prepared Minis, but it was very hard to tell which Mini was winning under thick layers of mud!

The Mini was a popular car all round the world, so that I also won a European Touring Car title with the Cooper S in 1968. I enjoyed our outings in Europe with the legendary Mini at circuits such as the equally legendary Nürburgring, for racing remained a pleasurable sport on and off track. It was a joy to drive for John Cooper; his success in Formula 1 ensured my car would be competitive.

I should explain my unique driving style, aiming to get the fastest cornering speed from tyres with little adhesion. The car was set up to induce oversteer on lifted throttle, so it would oversteer at the apex of a corner with reduced application of the accelerator. Quickly flooring the throttle to prevent a spin would pull the Mini around the corner in a drift with tyres ablaze, hence my nickname 'Smokin' John Rhodes'.

I called Ginger Devlin, my team manager, 'Ginge'. He would say: 'Don't bother changing Rhodes' brake pads – he doesn't use them … only the tyres.' I thank Ginge for all the other efforts he made to get the success we achieved in the Mini Coopers.

All that was some fifty years ago, so it gives me equal pleasure to see that the Cooper Minis are still out there earning crowd applause in classic racing events. I think it still gives spectators huge pleasure to see a Mini jostling for track position against the bigger cars, embarrassing even the large American V8s when it is wet. David is still a winning spectacle against Goliath!

I think we owe a vote of thanks to outfits like CCK Historic in Sussex who keep the faith, preparing such excellent examples of the Mini that this book could be based on their knowledge and expertise. The recreation of my 1966 Mini, beautifully built by Shaun Rainford and his team at CCK, has incorporated many key period parts with generous help from my old team manager. Having driven many of Shaun's cars at the Goodwood Revival, I know his future success is assured.

My best wishes to CCK and readers of this book, and long may the Mini continue to amaze us all with its exploits! I hope you all have as much fun and racing pleasure as I did with that very special little box of tricks…

John Rhodes, circa 1967.

Minis competing at Goodwood's Members' Meeting.

1 introduction and regulations

RULES OF ENGAGEMENT

Although more than five million Minis were sold between 1959 and 2000, their legendary status was founded in sport, not sales. The global fame of the earlier Mini rests on its David versus Goliath competition achievements during the 1960s in Cooper S guise. Today, just as they did back then, spectators thrill to the spectacle of the best Mini aces battling with appropriately large American V8s at venues such as Goodwood in the West Sussex countryside.

Motoring history records multiple Mini wins in Monte Carlo, the world's most famous rally: the French score it at three victories, Brits at four, but when did we ever agree? Class or outright winner of Touring Car races from Australia back to Britain, via the prime prestige events of

Racing Minis in the early sixties quickly became very popular.

introduction and regulations

Downton Engineering's Barry Hawkins' Mini versus a Lotus Cortina.

Current Appendix K Mini racer.

the European Championship, Mini has done it all. This tiny tot beat the might of some of the world's wealthiest and most creative automotive rivals.

We are not here for the history, which is thoroughly documented elsewhere. Yet the rules governing the advice given in this book date back to Mini's competition heyday some fifty years ago in the mid-sixties. Certainly the safety requirements are pure twenty-first century, mostly evident within. Otherwise the themes running throughout our guide will produce a Mini that – at a casual exterior glance – could have harked back to life in a 1964 paddock.

Why have we chosen to construct such a period piece? There are a bewildering number of competition formulae that a Mini could tackle around the world, but a pre-1966 Appendix K is the original and purest form. To build a

Engine bay of a current Appendix K Mini racer.

introduction and regulations

publié le / published on: 24.06.2016, application au / application from: 24.06.2016 (dernières mises à jour: en rouge / latest updates: in red)

ANNEXE K AU CODE SPORTIF INTERNATIONAL
APPENDIX K TO THE INTERNATIONAL SPORTING CODE

RÈGLEMENT TECHNIQUE POUR LES VOITURES PARTICIPANT AUX COMPÉTITIONS HISTORIQUES INTERNATIONALES

1. PRINCIPES ET ABREVIATIONS

1.1 La FIA a créé le règlement figurant dans l'Annexe K afin que les voitures historiques puissent être utilisées en Compétition selon des règles préservant les spécifications de leur période et empêchant la modification des performances et des comportements pouvant naître de l'application de la technologie moderne. La compétition historique n'est pas simplement une formule de plus dans laquelle il est possible de remporter des trophées ; c'est une discipline à part, dont l'un des ingrédients principaux est l'attachement profond aux voitures et à leur histoire. Le sport automobile historique permet une célébration active de l'histoire de l'automobile.

1.2 La présente Annexe K s'applique aux voitures qui sont soit des voitures de compétition d'origine, soit des voitures construites exactement selon la même spécification que des modèles dont l'historique de compétition internationale est conforme aux règles internationales de l'époque concernée.

Les seules variations autorisées par rapport à la spécification de période sont celles autorisées par l'Annexe K.

Les voitures sans historique de compétition internationale, mais possédant un historique de compétition dans des Compétitions de championnat national ou d'autres Compétitions nationales significatives d'un statut équivalent peuvent aussi être acceptées.

Si un modèle n'a pas participé en période à des courses internationales, les PTH des voitures correspondantes doivent être présentés à la CSAH avec la preuve provenant de l'ASN concernée que le modèle possède un historique de compétition dans des Compétitions d'importance nationale.

1.3 La présente Annexe K doit être respectée dans toutes les Compétitions internationales pour voitures historiques et est vivement recommandée pour toute autre Compétition historique.

1.4 Le Conseil Mondial du Sport Automobile de la FIA («CMSA») a pleinement approuvé l'application du principe visant à autoriser tous les Concurrents et les voitures en sport automobile historique à courir dans le monde entier dans le respect de normes et de règlements communs.

1.5 De plus amples informations sont disponibles sur le site internet de la FIA : www.fia.com.

1.6 **Abréviations**

	Titre complet
PTH	Passeport Technique Historique de la FIA
LPVRH	Laissez-Passer pour Voiture de Régularité Historique
CSAH	Commission du Sport Automobile Historique de la FIA
BDVH	Base de Données des Voitures Historiques de la FIA
Homologation	Fiches d'Homologation et Fiches de Reconnaissance approuvées par la FIA

2. DISPOSITIONS GENERALES ET DEFINITIONS DES VOITURES

2.1 Dispositions Générales

2.1.1 Les Compétitions internationales ont été régies par la Commission Sportive de l'ACF de 1906 à 1921 et par la FIA (dénommée AIACR jusqu'en 1947) de 1922 jusqu'à aujourd'hui. L'Annexe C pour les voitures de course biplaces a été introduite en 1950 puis intégrée à l'Annexe J en 1966. L'Annexe J a été introduite pour les voitures de Tourisme et de Grand Tourisme en 1954. L'Annexe K exige que toutes les voitures de compétition historiques soient préservées sous la forme dans laquelle elles ont couru selon ces règles, sauf si des modifications sont rendues nécessaires pour des raisons de sécurité.

TECHNICAL REGULATIONS FOR CARS COMPETING IN INTERNATIONAL HISTORIC COMPETITIONS

1. PRINCIPLES AND ABBREVIATIONS

1.1 The FIA has created the regulations in Appendix K so that Historic Cars may be used for Competitions under a set of rules that preserve the specifications of their period and prevent the modifications of performance and behaviour which could arise through the application of modern technology. Historic competition is not simply another formula in which to acquire trophies, it is a discipline apart, in which one of the essential ingredients is a devotion to the cars and to their history. Historic Motor Sport enables the active celebration of the History of the Motor Car.

1.2 Appendix K applies to cars which are either original competition cars, or cars built to exactly the same specification as models with international competition history complying with the International rules of the period.

The only permissible variations to the period specification are those authorised within Appendix K.

Cars without an international competition history but which have a competition history in national championship Competitions or other significant national Competitions of equivalent status may also be accepted.

If a model has not taken part in period in international races, HTPs of corresponding cars must be submitted to the HMSC supported by evidence from the relevant ASN that the model has a history in period of competition in Competitions of national significance.

1.3 The present Appendix K must be respected in all international Competitions for historic cars and is highly recommended for any other historic Competitions.

1.4 The FIA World Motor Sport Council («WMSC») has given its full approval for the enforcement of these principles, which allows all Competitors and cars in historic motor sport to compete world wide to common standards and common regulations.

1.5 More information can be found on the FIA www.fia.com web site.

1.6 **Abbreviations**

	Full Title
HTP	FIA Historic Technical Passport
HRCP	Historic Regularity Car Pass
HMSC	FIA Historic Motor Sport Commission
HCD	FIA Historic Cars Database
Homologation	Homologation Forms and Recognition Forms endorsed by the FIA

2. GENERAL PROVISIONS AND DEFINITION OF CARS

2.1 General Provisions

2.1.1 International racing was governed by the Commission Sportive of the ACF from 1906 until 1921 and by the FIA, which was known as AIACR until 1947, from 1922 until the present day. Appendix C for two-seat racing cars was introduced in 1950, becoming part of Appendix J in 1966. Appendix J was introduced for Touring and GT cars in 1954. Appendix K requires that all historic competition cars will be preserved in the form in which they raced to these rules, except where safety considerations may enforce changes.

FIA's Appendix K 2016 document.

introduction and regulations

pre-1966 racing Mini shows an inevitable interest in motor-sport history, plus the world of historic motor sport has boomed in popularity in recent years and there are more people than ever looking to find their way in. The primary set of regulations that we work to in this book are the most widely accepted, allowing an owner/driver the largest choice of international and premier national events with a decent chance of racing reliability. In some areas of the sport the rules are so relaxed that anyone with ambition can build a Mini that is unrecognizable from the production model, for example one redeveloped around tubular subframes and clothed by lift-off flyweight panels.

The regulations we are building to are issued by the international governing body of motor sports, the Fédération Internationale de l'Automobile (FIA), which has more than 230 member clubs or National Sporting Authorities (ASNs) around the planet. Our ASN in the UK is the Motor Sport Association, or MSA. The regulations we use as our benchmarks are formally called Appendix K to cover overall competition rules for all historic vehicles and the FIA's homologation form number 1300, which covers the detailed specification of the Mini Cooper 1275 S. The purpose of Appendix K is so that:

> Historic Cars may be used for Competitions under a set of rules that preserve the specifications of their period and prevent the modifications of performance and behaviour which could arise through the application of modern technology. Historic competition is not simply another formula in which to acquire trophies, it is a discipline apart, in which one of the essential ingredients is a devotion to the cars and to their history. Historic Motor Sport enables the active celebration of the History of the Motor Car.

The homologation form is effectively the formal recognition and detailed description of a vehicle approved for FIA international competitions. It applies to the Austin or Morris Cooper S types that continue to be prepared in the twenty-first century for historic motor sport. The homologation form for the 1275 S was originally stamped on 11 April 1964, with production of the model having started in February of that year. However, the first Cooper S model to be released was of course the 1071, which was homologated for international competition a year earlier in May 1963. There are very few 1071s racing today, as the in-class advantage of the 1275 S rules out any real chance of a competitive drive. Hence the 1275 S has become the standard in historic events today. Also homologated in March 1964 was the tiniest terror of the breed. The 970 S

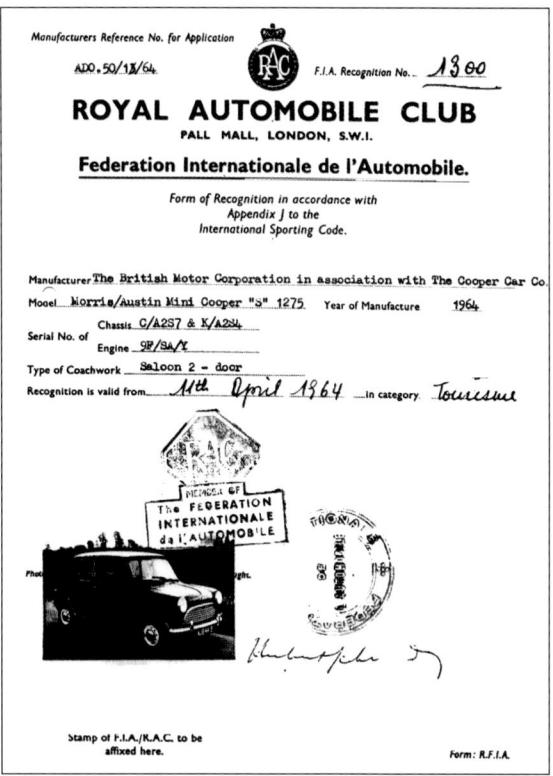

FIA homologation form 1300 for the Mini Cooper 1275.

was an aggressive competitor in the under-1000cc class. The original 848cc Austin 7 or Morris Mini Minor was the first Mini to gain international recognition, approved during 1959, the first year of manufacture.

Additional homologation papers were granted at later dates for subsequent models, keeping the Mini alive for international competition. These included 1966 Group 1 homologation for the 1275 S and 998, with the 970 S getting another lease of competition life after production ceased in August 1964, with a March 1968 second homologation. This was necessary as it was an effective British Touring Car Champion for Gordon Spice (1968) and Alec Poole (1969), both using Arden engineering: Mini remains a rare 1-litre class choice in historic events today as the rear-motor Imp in the UK and continental European rivals have reaffirmed their supremacy.

Aside from the stringency of Appendix K, there is potential for some flexibility within historic motor sport here in the UK. The Historic Sports Car Club (HSCC) runs a championship for pre-1966 Touring Cars with the Historic Racing Saloons Register (HRSR). The championship is open to Appendix K vehicles, as well as vehicles built to the HRSR's own set of rules. Much of the preparation

BUILDING A HISTORIC RACING MINI

CCK HISTORIC, YESTERDAY AND TODAY

CCK started with a bang, literally. Founder and co-owner Shaun Rainford recalled, 'I did my City & Guilds apprenticeship for a well-known Triumph classic car specialist (then trading as Cox & Buckles, now Moss Europe Ltd) for some years. I had a golden opportunity to go for a job in Aachen on the German–Belgian border, but on the way there in my TR4, which I had restored from the ground up, I was involved in an accident.'

Unexpectedly back in Britain, Shaun's mum made it clear that he was not to 'sit around moping'. Fear not; Shaun's TR4 was repaired and sits in the small fifteen-car and memorabilia CCK Museum today.

'So I bought an MGB GT cheaply, kitted it out with tools, jacks and stands, and became a mobile mechanic around my local Kent area.' Enterprising, but not the total answer to his self-employment problems, as Shaun explained, 'It got too cold working by the kerbside lying on cold concrete in winter, so I looked around for some premises.' Warming to his work, progressing from lock-ups to more usable workshops and sales facilities, Shaun returned to his classic business roots.

The CCK name originally stood for Classic Cars of Kent. 'We did fine until the early 1990s,' Shaun remembered. 'Then the money just was not around from City bonuses and the like. It just was not adding up, but I was lucky enough to meet Cheryl Sowerby, who was used to high-finance deals. She came in as a partner and we got back on our financial feet.'

It helped the recovering business that Shaun was respected as a racer, one gathering national championships. Shaun has always prepared and often raced an unusual variety of basic cars converted for track employment, for example a 1961 Riley 1.5 and a very rapid Austin A40 in the Top Hat series. There is also considerable expertise within CCK with the Frogeye and MG Midget-based racers, all using variants of the A-series engine that is also at the heart of Mini power.

'As Classic Cars of Kent is no longer located in Kent, we usually work now under the CCK Historic name,' explained Shaun. The boss then showed us some of the resources he shares with half a dozen employees and occasional freelance skilled labour. These resources enable CCK to offer: 'a fully comprehensive one-stop' historic racing car service under a sprawling collection of tidy ex-farm buildings. That means Shaun and company have

Shaun Rainford balances the Nash Metropolitan through Goodwood's Woodcote corner.

Mini Sport's premises at Padiham, Lancashire.

the in-house skills and hardware to do: 'complete ground up restoration, panel fabrication, body repairs, respray and painting, machine shop, rolling-road tuning, corner-weighting, suspension set-up, engine building, car storage, car transportation and recovery, race preparation, race support and much more'.

There is also the packed museum to browse, containing a famous 1960s competition Cooper S, a scattering of motorcycles, emotive memorabilia and models, plus a low-mileage Ferrari 328 GTS, a 500cc Cooper F3 car and a unique Nash Metropolitan racer.

In British historic racing circles, nobody asks who CCK Historic are. The creative company's prodigious output of mainstream and distinctly individual saloons and sports cars speaks for them, especially at Goodwood Revivals and Members' Meetings' featuring appearances for their front-running Volvo PV544, Lenham GT 'SS1800', the Nash Metropolitan, plus all of the customers' cars they spend the racing season taking care of. The Rhodes Mini lives in the reception area of CCK to remind us of just how far this company goes in the recreation of time-warp Minis. That very special racer was constructed around some original parts with the assistance of former Cooper Car Company engineer Ginger Devlin and lead driver Rhodes.

The tartan red example that illustrates this book has been built by the team at CCK with support from a number of parts suppliers, most notably Mini Sport. The high-quality parts supplied by Mini Sport have been instrumental to the build.

MINI SPORT

A backbone of the Mini performance and competition cottage industries, Mini Sport of Padiham in Lancashire was founded in 1967 and remains a Harper family business in the second decade of the twenty-first century. They have an enormous spread of stock and services, some operated through subsidiaries such as www.paddyhopkirkmini.com. What concerns us is the extensive engineering and product knowledge they bring to period Minis today.

Founder Brian Harper bought his first 850 Mini in 1960 and used it from shopping trip to circuit racing, sprints and hill climbs. Appreciating the versatility of this family friend, a move up the Mini speed ladder to a 997cc Downton-tuned Cooper came naturally. Brian and wife Heather were now severely bitten by the motor-sports bugs, particularly rallying. That meant a constant need for parts, both replacement and modified, crammed into the Harper garage business.

An advert in the weekly *Motoring News* brought astonishing results and by the late 1960s, Mini Sport had become a significant commercial enterprise. They moved into Padiham town in 1969 and now have a redeveloped site to keep pace with their growth.

The first exclusively engineered product became a rigid throttle linkage and today they offer sophisticated developments from 7-port cylinder heads to major engine components and five-speed gearboxes through their subsidiary, Motorsport Advanced Developments.

A 30,000sq ft complex has a tenth of its floor space devoted to a showroom, but the same site also houses fast-fit and service centres, a rolling-road facility and body repairs and restoration, supported by a paint booth and specialist body finish areas.

introduction and regulations

Alec Poole's Equipe Arden 970 S.

We have emphasized racing rather than rally formats as that is what we have practical experience of, but many of the basics naturally apply to both disciplines and we are grateful to Mini Sport in the UK for their input into the preparation of historic rallying Minis. You can also hill-climb or sprint (autocross in the USA) our tiny terrors, but you may be up against more radically re-engineered vehicles. So, enjoy a taste in these branches of the sport where (almost) anything goes from road car to ex single-seat formula warrior, but expect to need a purpose-built vehicle for competitive results, unless the event has a classic connotation.

UNDERSTANDING THE REGULATIONS

The regulations that will govern your build on first glance may appear complicated. There is a lot in Appendix K that will not apply to you. The trick is knowing where to look and finding which rules are relevant to your Mini build. By approaching the regulations in a logical way, you can build an understanding of the definitions and the applications of the rules.

The first and most basic definitions will define the model of car, the historical period it is from and the regulation class or group in which you wish to compete. Owners for an HSCC vehicle will be the same, but under their rules there is a little more freedom; for example, brakes are free. This means that you can use aluminium calipers and vented discs instead of the original cast-iron calipers and solid discs. Other freedoms include free wheel widths, provided they do not protrude from the body, and gearbox internals, as well as the choice of carburettor, which includes the use of the infamous Weber DCOE carburettor.

Minis racing in the HSCC's Historic Touring Car Championship.

introduction and regulations

Engine bay of a Group S Mini with an 8-port head and fuel injection.

of the August 1959 to October 1967 first-generation Mini, as well as the industry, use the 'Mk1' designation to define the first generation of the Mini and it is this Mk1 model that is required for any pre-1966 Touring Car race series. The 1275 Mini Cooper S came out in 1964, which places it firmly in period F. The FIA defines this as running from 1/1/1962 to 31/12/1965. In this period, the British Saloon Car Championship (BSCC) ran to Group 2 regulations, as defined in the FIA's Appendix J, the sporting code of its day. Group 2 allowed limited modifications and placed certain restrictions on vehicles. For example, cars had to run to their factory track width and engines had to retain their original cylinder heads and homologated carburettors. It is this specification that defines pre-1966 Historic Touring Car racing today.

Factory Minis also ran in the later period G (1/1/1966 to 31/12/1969). Within this period, the BSCC made a change to Group 5 regulations that allowed more extreme modifications. A wider track width was allowed with wheel-arch extensions, while cylinder heads and induction were free, which allowed for the development of the wild fuel-injected 8-port cylinder heads from the likes of Arden. The cars were very fast, but the complexity and expense of running these vehicles defeated even factory funding back in the day. With this book, we are only concerned

John Rhodes in his Group 5 Mk1 Mini Cooper S circa 1966.

introduction and regulations

with the Group 2 heyday of the Mini and the FIA's period F: 1962 to the close of 1965. This was the most popular period in Historic Touring Car racing and a sensible and competitive specification that is still capable of serving up Goliath-beating results today.

There are two important points to clarify with regard to the Mk1 body and period F. First of all, you do not need an original Mini Cooper S as the basis of your race-car build. Any Mk1 Mini will suffice. Most of the Mk1 Mini Cooper S race cars seen on the circuit would have been built from the lowly 850cc derivative rather than from a genuine factory-built Cooper S. Secondly, you can still use a 1966, 1967 or 1968 registered Mk1 Mini to build a race car for pre-1966 competition. Regardless of what year it left the factory, the important fact is that it is a Mk1 Mini and built to the 1964 homologation form.

Use of the Mk1 body is compulsory, so it is vital to make this Mk1 distinction. That means we also refer less frequently to the officially dubbed Mk2, a short-lived October 1967–70 facelift Mini with larger rear screen and tail lights: in Cooper Mini terms, just the 1275 S and 998 Cooper adopted the Mk2 bodyshell. The final plain 998 Cooper was made in November 1969, leaving just the 1275 Cooper S to make it into the Mk3 body, which is distinguished by the deployment of concealed door hinges. Neither Mk2 nor Mk3 bodies are recognized for FIA historic motor sport in the designated 1962–6 period F that is our benchmark for this book.

The Mk3 Mini debuted at the October 1969 Earls Court Motor Show and appeared alongside the unloved Clubman with extended snout. The Clubman 1275GT featured a single carburettor 1275cc, fundamentally different to a twin carburettor 1275 Cooper S, which offered a distinctly more expensively and durably engineered motor. The last UK-assembled 1275 Cooper S is recorded as leaving the lines in July 1971. According to 1990 Rover factory statistics, almost 100,000 (99,281) Cooper 997cc and 998cc models were made in the UK, fewer than half that number (45,629) of Cooper S, with the smaller capacity 970 S and 1071 S distinctly rare.

It is worth noting that the Hydrolastic suspension system was a Mini feature that appeared on various models from October 1964 to 1971, when all Minis returned to the original rubber cone layout, assisted by the telescopic shock absorbers, front and rear. The Mini Cooper 1275 S was homologated with the rubber cone suspension in 1964 and by building your race car to the 1964 homologation it is not necessary to retain the Hydrolastic suspension even if it was originally fitted to your vehicle.

DETAIL STUDY REQUIRED

All motor sports, from Formula 1 to the grass roots, require extensive examination of their regulations to ensure that you at least compete on level terms with the opposition. If that prospect bores you to tears and you just want to pick up your tools and get started, then renew your acquaintance with the classmate/work colleague who did pay attention to the detail, ad nauseam. You may find them in accountancy, Inland Revenue, divorce law or property development, because you need that kind of devious mind on your side. Working with your newfound Unfair Advantage, get reading yourself. Ensure that you at least have an idea what the law-makers and technical inspectors (scrutineers, or 'scrutes' in racing parlance) are likely to look for in your addition to the grid.

We start with the FIA Appendix K document, which can be downloaded from the FIA Historic Database on the Internet. For your own hard copy of FIA Appendix K, apply to Britain's Motor Sports Association (MSA), which has the advantage of offering a back-up phone number (01753 765000) for specialist advice. Such K-papers cost £14 from the MSA, but downloads are free. You will also need a copy of the Mini's homologation papers that we referred to as well. From the MSA these cost £42 in 2017 from the address and contacts within our 'Useful Contacts' section at the end of the book. However, you may be able to find a copy online.

The object of Appendix K is to ensure that historic cars compete, 'under a set of rules that preserve the specifications of their period and prevent the modifications of performance and behaviour which could arise through the application of modern technology'. The FIA sees it as part of its mission to celebrate and preserve the history of the motor car, but inevitably the human competitive spirit results in progress even within tightly regulated sports – look at Formula 1 – and your Mini will be up against others prepared at least precisely to the performance limits imposed by the homologated parameters.

That means your Appendix K Mini in 2018 and later will be a lot faster than even the aces could manage with similar technical rules applied in 1964. With the sheer knowledge accrued in more than fifty years of competition development for the astonishing A-series motor, common sense decrees that the lap times set around an unaltered track – say, Thruxton in the English west country – will be faster than top men like John Rhodes set back in the day. That does not mean you are more talented than the Mini legends. They were the very best men that BMC/Cooper Car Company, Broadspeed, Arden and others could find to hurl their 'Minibricks' around each corner at improbable angles. Aces like Johns Rhodes and Handley had the added incentive of factory funding and cash bonus schemes, but you are hopefully doing all this for the sheer pleasure. Enjoy …

APPENDIX K

At first glance, the FIA's Appendix K document may appear somewhat overwhelming. There are ninety-four pages to it, which include twelve appendices covering all aspects of safety, as well as permitted and restricted modifications within every discipline. Much of this document will not apply to us, but we need to be able to find the areas that do. The main section is titled 'TECHNICAL REGULATIONS FOR CARS COMPETING IN INTERNATIONAL HISTORIC COMPETITIONS'. This section applies to all historic vehicles and includes date periods and all definitions, as well as safety regulations, modifications and restrictions universal to all disciplines. We already know that our car will be period F (1/1/1962 to 31/12/1965) and the following definition for Competition Touring Cars includes those cars homologated before 1966 in Group 2:

FIA Appendix K 2017
2.3.5.1 Post 1946 Competition Touring Cars are either:
(a) Models of limited series production of Periods E till I (1/1/1947–31/12/1981) derived from a model of series production Touring Car and upgraded within the limits of period Appendix J and including cars homologated by the FIA in Group 2 before 1966.
(b) Models of 1/1/1966 onwards which were homologated in Group 2 or Group A and conforming to the period Appendix J.

So now we know that we are dealing with a homologated Group 2 Competition Touring Car in period F. This will help us to find the specific areas of Appendix K that apply to our race-car build. As well as the General Technical Regulations of Appendix K, there are some Appendices that deal more specifically with permitted modifications. The following helps to point us in the right direction:

FIA Appendix K 2017
7.3 General Technical Regulations for Production Road Cars
7.3.1 Touring, Competition Touring, GT and GTS Cars of Periods E, F and G1 (1/1/1947–31/12/1969) will comply with Appendices VIII and IX of Appendix K.

This paragraph states that you must comply with both Appendix VIII and IX. Appendix VIII of Appendix K is titled 'Modifications authorised for cars of Periods E, F and G1 for Series Production Touring Cars and Standard Grand Touring Cars'. Appendix IX of Appendix K is titled 'Modifications authorised for cars of Period E, F and G1 for Competition Touring Cars and Competition Grand Touring Cars'. Appendix VIII covers the modifications for what in 1965 became Group 1. Your Mini must comply with these, as well as the rules set out in Appendix IX for Competition Touring Cars. However, where there is a conflict in the rules Appendix IX will apply over Appendix VIII. Just because you are not building a Group 1 car, do not skip Appendix VIII, as there are permitted modifications in this section not covered in Appendix IX. The specifics of these Appendices will be covered in the relevant chapters of the book, but it is important to read and understand both of them, as they will answer most of your questions as to what is allowed and what is not.

As you would expect, the FIA rules ban any modifications that were not homologated in period or defined within Appendix K. Basically, 'Period Specification is defined as the configuration of the model, proven to the satisfaction of the FIA or the stewards, to have existed in the period in which it is classified.' That implies you either get your pet demon tweak recognized in advance of competition via reference to the FIA, or you have a race-day decision from the stewards: the latter can mean heartbreak if your vehicle is deemed ineligible to compete in an overseas event for which you have already paid entry fees and transported crew/car and equipment.

The message is clear – it really is worth reading regulations carefully and getting any technical queries clarified beforehand. A specific paragraph in Appendix K spells out the FIA attitude and reads:

FIA Appendix K 2017
3.3.3 Generalities on alternative components:
Alternative components to the original manufacturer's specifications can only be used if it is proven that these components were either homologated, or allowed by the period Appendix J and used in that model of car in a Competition entered on the FIA International Sporting Calendar in the period. …

Freedoms granted in period by Appendix J do not now confer complete freedom but rather authorise the use of modifications and/or components actually and legally used in period on the particular make and model as a result of those period freedoms.

17

introduction and regulations

Our Mini in the scrutineering bay at Brands Hatch.

Officialdom reserves the right to make a final judgement on precise equipment utilized – and the final arbiter of any FIA ruling is usually taken from the French language original, not the English translation. Arguing with officials in France or French-speaking Belgium can be frustrating in the extreme if you are not fluent. Our experience over the last thirty years is that the time spent studying regulations in advance, or clarifying that which really is not clear to you or marque experts (rare on such a well-known competitor as the Mini) avoids such raised-voice experiences. Attend classic race meetings at least in the season prior to your debut to see how the scrutineers are interpreting the regulations in practice. For most potential competitors, a look over the engine bay and interior, plus a wheels-off peek at the leading Minis, will tell you what is actually happening out there.

The regulations continue:

FIA Appendix K 2017
3.3.4 The period, alternative components, and the extensions of the homologation form to be considered will be specified on the HTP (Historical Technical Passport) applicable to this specific car.
3.3.5 Unless otherwise specifically authorised by these regulations, any component of a car must have identical dimensions and material type must be the same to the original part. Evidence of this must be provided by the applicant.

Quite simply, unless the component is on the homologation form or allowed under the Appendix J of the period, it can't be used. Further to this, any component utilized must be made of the same material and made to the same dimensions. This applies to any part of the car. For example, aluminium rear radius arms are not allowed, nor are aluminium rear hubs. Back in the 1960s, if BMC wanted to use an alternative component, it would have had to be homologated before being added to the back of the homologation form as an amendment. There are a number of optional equipment items that were added to the back of the homologation forms in 1964–5. Included in these recognized additions was an oil-cooler option with an alternative six-blade radiator fan, plus an alternative camshaft (8.08mm max lift versus 10.01mm) and a three-branch exhaust manifold. A closed-circuit system for the oil-breather layout was passed on the basis that it was for intermittent use in the USA export models. Critically, the factory also ensured a 'High Traction Differential' (read limited slip) and steel flywheel with a 5.03kg (11.09lb) weight were (optionally) admitted by the FIA, saving on the production 6.8kg (15lb) item.

A second 25ltr fuel tank brought total capacity to 50ltr in the trademark twin-tank layout with two external fillers on opposite sides of the rump. More mundanely, the 1965 Model Year Hydrolastic suspension was added to the 1275 S homologation in November 1964. BMC competition engineers corrected some vital

introduction and regulations

carburettor information at the same date, including the HS2/H4 choices, flange diameters and the fact that SU carburettors feature variable choke diameters.

The appearance of your historic racer and its structure are strictly regulated. Appendix K defines the silhouette and chassis as:

FIA Appendix K 2017
3.7.1 The silhouette is the shape of the car viewed from any direction, with body panels in position.
3.7.2 The chassis is the overall structure of the car around which are assembled the mechanical components and the bodywork including any structural part of the said structure.

In the Mini's case it is structured as part of the overall bodyshell rather than a separate chassis. You could argue that the subframes are literally subchassis as they carry 'the mechanical components and the bodywork including any structural part of said structure', as demanded in FIA Appendix K.

You do get some important metallic freedoms. Appendix K states under 'General definitions':

FIA Appendix K 2017
3.7.3 The term «material type» indicates the same material, but not necessarily to the same specification.
3.7.4 Thus, for example, «aluminium» is metallurgically aluminium but may be of a different grade and contain elements not present in the original component to the exclusion of aluminium beryllium. Magnesium may be replaced with aluminium.

This means that if an original component is made from steel, then any modern replacement must also be made from steel; however, it can be of a different grade of steel. In practical terms, this allows the use of higher grades to make components stronger. Components such as driveshafts can be made from stronger steel. Strictly speaking, even the smallest components such as valve spring caps or clutch arms must be made from their original steel material, although you will see some get away with alternative metals in areas that are not easily visible.

Another area where the cunning competitor-engineer might expect to gain an advantage is with tolerances, especially on a kerb weight that was homologated at flyweight 620kg (1,367lb) for 1964 1275 S. All preparation specialists will examine motor and suspension allowances. Unless the Mini official homologation form states otherwise, the FIA decrees tolerances as: 'all machining, excepting bore and stroke: [plus or minus] ±0.2%'. For all unfinished castings (such as the cast-iron cylinder block or head for Mini), the allowance is ±0.5 per cent. Practically, for the 1275 S you will find that a rebore of 0.020in, delivering 1293cc, was the maximum allowed within the 1300cc class limit of the day. Stroke had to remain unaltered. We have a separate chapter detailing engine preparation and specification. Today, just understand that the old BMC creators of the competition Cooper S at Abingdon did not walk past any opportunity to speed the aged A-Series into a more competition-friendly output, such as a brace of piston shapes pictured and homologated, the familiar 9.75:1 compression ratio (CR) dished design, or a high-octane friendly 12:1 CR domed piston.

You are restricted to nominated fuel suppliers, but these do depend on the obvious practicality of availability of suitable branded petrol at each venue. Alcohol and other trick fuel mixes are confined to formula cars, especially Indianapolis machines from 1940–60. There are some get-out clauses for non-homologated cars, but the Mini definitely does not qualify for anything other than FIA or organizer-specified fuels. In the UK that officially indicates 102 RON octane (90 MON), including 'freely available' commercial lead-substitute chemicals – and no more than 2 per cent lubrication additives. Oxidants, aside from atmospheric air, are specifically banned.

The best valve intake and exhaust diameters for power output were specified on the original homologation form with the additionally typed proviso 'blended and polished'. So painstaking handwork across the port profiles was, and is, permitted, provided that the maximum tolerances are not exceeded. The 1964 Abingdon BMC competition department also ensured that you could employ either HS2 or H4 SU carburetion.

Percentages for likely suspension tolerances and dimensions cover +1 per cent on the front axle widths and track. Similarly on wheelbase, tolerance is set at ± 1.1 per cent.

SAFETY FAST

The most common non-historic updates cover safety issues and the safest working practice is to check out what has been specifically allowed or FIA-stamped, especially with regard to the roll cage. We will look at specific safety moves in a subsequent chapter, but here is a general guide to what the FIA requires as a preview of the detail we apply to the historic racing Mini. Perhaps the first generality is the one that hits hardest in the practicalities of racing any production-based Mini: rust! The authorities broadly state:

introduction and regulations

FIA Appendix K 2017
5 SAFETY PRESCRIPTIONS
Competitors should be aware of the possibility of corrosion and/or ageing of components and the consequences thereof, and must take measures to ensure the integrity and safety of these components while respecting the original specification.

It follows that you present the car in clean condition – just as you should for an MoT in Britain – and that you absolutely do not ask any stress-bearing component to take to the track without being sure of a new part or inspected and tested pedigree.

Areas of safety that the FIA and any sensible organizer insist on inspecting highlight electrics from battery to ignition and the fuel systems. The regulations state: 'Protection of the battery terminals against the risks of shorting is mandatory. If the battery is retained in the cockpit, it must be of the dry type, be securely fixed, and have an insulated, leak-proof cover.' A simple but vital move is the installation of a circuit breaker, meaning that all circuits – bar those for any automatic fire extinguisher – can be interrupted, closing down engine and associated electrical systems. For Minis and any closed car, there must be an external switch for the circuit breaker clearly marked with a red spark symbol within a white-edged blue triangle featuring a minimum 120mm (4.7in) base. This will usually be adjacent to the windscreen pillars on a Mini.

Safety pull cables and identification stickers on the front wing.

Inside the cockpit, another circuit-breaking switch also needs to be clearly marked and within reach of a safety-belt-trussed driver. Confusingly, these circuit breakers are often referred to as the master switch in English. All race cars will need the master clicked to 'on' before any electrical activity will be heard in the cockpit, such as whirring fuel pumps. Many a driver's race has been spoiled by a flurry of arms and elbows leading to accidental activation of the master switch, followed by comparative silence and creative combinations of Anglo-Saxon oaths, before the intrepid pilot realizes what has happened.

Equally important are safeguards for fuel, oil and brake lines. You are allowed to protect external pipes and we

The cockpit of our Appendix K Mini.

introduction and regulations

would advise that you do this. It usually means some form of hard-case braided lines. However, within these otherwise strict rules, it is mildly surprising to find that the regulations weakly offer: 'If the series production item is retained, no additional protection is necessary.' Please do not save money running 1964 rubber brake pipes or plumbing for fuel feeds from the same era!

Fuel and hydraulic lines can run within the cockpit and although the regulations state that they do have to be protected, a metal braided line or a solid copper type will satisfy scrutineers. These can pass through a sealed bulkhead or utilize bulkhead joints, which can only be, 'screw sealing joints or vehicle manufacturer approved joints'. Now we start to appreciate why so many competitors opt for at least some elements of professional preparation, as interpreting rules for which the final arbiters are within the French language has led many an English speaker into vigorous technical inspection disputes, from the Abingdon Mini era onwards.

Chapter 7 will specifically detail Mini fuel systems, but the Mini can have either a production steel tank or a racing fuel cell. If you rely on the production steel tank, some overseas officials may want to see that the tank itself is filled with foam cubes, which guard against fuel vapour fires: suppliers such as Demon Tweeks stock such versatile tank fillers in cubes, balls or layers from A.H. Fabrications, ATL or their own-brand stock.

One big difference in safety standards between road and race cars is that fireproof bulkheads are a normal requirement and how this is to be achieved will be explained in a later chapter. Similarly, a fire extinguisher must be carried. A simple hand-held extinguisher will suffice for UK events, but even in the early 1970s effective on-board systems covering the engine bay were com-

Raydyot style lightweight racing mirror.

mon in race-prepared saloon cars. Drivers or marshals can speedily activate on-board systems via pull cables connected externally, or within the restricted reach of drivers wearing safety harness. Drivers in closed cars learned very painfully that standard tanks, unsealed bulkheads and lack of an extinguisher could soon lead to life-changing burns with a high chance of death.

Separate oil catch tanks should be of 2ltr capacity. There is a let-out clause in Appendix K that allows you to keep the production closed-circuit breathing, venting from steel rocker cover tube to carburettor, should originality be your thing, but we wouldn't recommend it.

Other less obvious safety moves covered by an Appendix K cover throttle return springs and the requirement for two external rear-view mirrors. Back in the sixties, Cooper Car Company's entries were seen with just an internal mirror, whilst multiple Mini championship-gatherer Richard Longman ran the BTCC and won the title in 1978–9 with one external and a single interior mirror.

More common-sense safeguards include the official Appendix K requirement for front lamp glasses to be taped – usually served by an asterisk-pattern of black sticky tape in period. The front windscreen has to be laminated: a safety glass option, which crazes on impact and thus obscures vision, was common on the production lines of the sixties.

Another nod to the passage of time is that you can now use a quick-release (detachable) steering wheel of different diameter and style to the original black plastic bus driver's two-spoke design.

A further apparently obvious safety measure was that of the internal rollover bar. In the Group 2 era the likes of John Rhodes and John Handley raced with no rollover protection whatsoever, but later cars eventually utilized

Lifeline fire extinguisher mounted to the rear of the passenger side floor.

introduction and regulations

Black vinyl tape helps to hold the glass if it gets cracked or broken whilst racing.

Leather bonnet strap.

simple hoops made by John Aley. In this book, we will detail the much more sophisticated and complex cages that are common practice today, for which the FIA lays down a detailed specification. The basic regulatory attitude is that competitors should move with the times. Today's cages not only enhance driver protection, but also deliver a boost in body stiffness that is welcome when wheeling a sixty-year old design into another 100mph corner with steel crash barriers lining any run-off

FIA-approved roll cage in our App K Mini.

introduction and regulations

John Rhodes' Mini wearing the now famous Cooper bonnet stripes.

Driver names and nationality flags on the wing.

The regulations also try to preserve the period appearance of vehicles. Period livery (paint and contrasting colours) is encouraged. Mini examples are the Cooper Car Company white bonnet stripes and dark green paint, or Broadspeed's Crimson with Silver roof. The driver's name and relevant nationality flag are compulsory on each side of the car.

There are constraints on commercial advertising logo dimensions, while content such as old race stickers and personal messages is ruled out, along with cliché schemes like shark's teeth and flame patterns, unless it can be proven that they are part of a period livery. It is a given that at least one space attached to the competition numbers will display the event organization's advertising.

HISTORIC TECHNICAL PASSPORT

Another mandatory requirement is to get your Mini's twelve-page HTP (Historic Technical Passport) papers, which replaced the FIA Historic Vehicle Identity forms in 2004. If you are in France they will ask for the PTH (*Passeport Technique Historic*). You will not be able to race in FIA international status events, or those conforming to FIA rules, without HTP papers.

This is what FIA HTP papers look like.

areas. Similarly, safety belts (today more truly described as harnesses with four or six attachment points), replacement race seats and associated headrests are of a totally different design than were sported in the Mini's factory racing heyday.

Ancillary regulatory body requirements mean that bonnets must be modified without production catches, secured by external 'safety fastenings'. In practice, this meant a leather strap, superseded by the ubiquitous bonnet pin layout in the later seventies. If you check the old race pictures of the Cooper Car Company S types in 1964–5 race action, no securing devices are visible, but the factory rally cars always sported straps or other obvious bonnet back-up security and that remains general practice today.

You might not think it worth stating, but the authorities do demand that rear brake lights work. Devious top competitors often rendered brake lights inoperative so that rivals could not see their late braking points!

introduction and regulations

HTP documents serve to set the parameters for technical/scrutineering inspections and queries. For organizers, they are vital to set the class structure to their events and final classification. The British MSA defined the HTP's purpose clearly in 2013:

> The HTP is essentially a sporting document and its purpose is to allow a car to take part in International competitions. An HTP says nothing about the authenticity, provenance, origins, etc, of a car. It is concerned only that the car's specification is that of the particular model it purports to be, the whole purpose of the HTP is to try to ensure that cars accord with the authentic specification and can therefore compete with one another fairly.

Whether the car is wholly original, partly original, assembled wholly or partly out of period components, or is a copy or replica built recently, is not relevant to the issuing of an HTP. The prime criteria to be granted an HTP is that the car represents a provable specification and type that competed internationally in period.

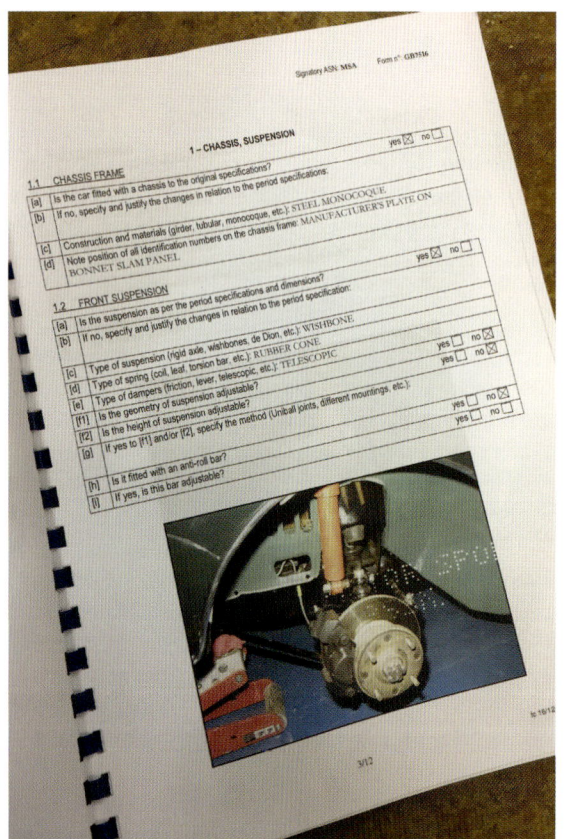

Inside the FIA HTP papers.

You can apply for an HTP through the national motor-sport authority (MSA in UK) and the British authority does offer a very helpful PDF download document, FIA Historic Technical Passports (HTPs), to guide you through the process and prices (see 'Useful Contacts'). In Britain, the MSA registers and files an HTP electronically at a cost of £340 including VAT upon application, with an additional fee of £231 to be paid when the HTP is ready to be issued. It is also vital to note that an individual registrar is subject to an additional £210 fee plus 45p per mile to carry out the inspection of each vehicle. In Britain, the Touring Car technical inspection names are frequently familiar to any regular competitor from race weekend scrutineering bays.

Fine if all is in order, but the HTP can deliver a lost racing weekend. If your Mini Cooper is found not to conform to some aspect of the HTP, there can be dire consequences. It may be something that you can remedy on the spot; if the problem is too fundamental to fix at a circuit, you face the possibility of exclusion from the event and the stewards forwarding an explanation to both the FIA and your ruling body (MSA in the UK). Similarly, a car can fail to get a race even if it complies with the HTP, but not with Appendix K.

Less seriously, a red dot may be placed on the opening page of your HTP. This means that a minor irregularity has been discovered, but FIA officials can allow the car to race – usually because the infringement does not improve performance – with a note beside the dot explaining what must be rectified before the next appearance. More serious is a black dot placed on your HTP form, because that marks a safety failure, which will mean no race unless the problem can be remedied rapidly. Even then, you will still have to find an FIA official in order to obtain a written certificate confirming that you are no longer a black dot miscreant.

Lost HTPs can be replaced (at a price!) and have to be recognized by each national body should the Mini be sold to another country. There is a central FIA database that holds details of any HTP disputes and dot markings, plus each country's supreme motor-sports national body will also hold HTP data. When you receive your HTP papers, the homologation papers are usually bound in with them.

This may seem to be rather basic, but all of us have fallible memories – speaking of which, do ensure that all of your race kit (helmets, boots, socks plus fireproof inner and outer race wear) is in FIA date-stamp accord with the rules for the events you tackle. Most circuits have a racewear shop for emergencies, but not all …

introduction and regulations

HSCC Mini on Weber carburettor.

ALTERNATIVE NON-FIA REGULATIONS

As well as the FIA route, we will also be considering some less restrictive regulations like those from the Historic Sports Car Clubs (HSCC) Historic Touring Car Championship. Safety prescriptions as defined by the MSA and the FIA's Appendix K will still comply, but the range of suspension, brake and engine modifications allowed will vary significantly. For example, alternative carburettors such as the Weber DCOE may be allowed as well as aluminium 4-pot brake calipers and vented brake discs.

Those who would like to push the modifications a little further, or those who just want a more relaxed approach may find the HSCC or CSCC (Classic Sports Car Club) more to their taste. Although the cars may appear to be very similar, it must be noted that unless running in Appendix K guise entry into the more prestigious events will not be available. For those who want the relaxed approach of club racing but still wish to apply to the stringent FIA regulations, there is an Appendix K class that is run within both of the above mentioned clubs.

WHERE TO RACE

Knowing where you want to race and what your racing budget will be may influence what direction you choose to go in when building your Mini. Take a look at all clubs offering races for pre-1966 Touring Cars and take the time to attend some race meetings, speaking to both the organizers and other competitors. Check out the individual regulations for each of the clubs and get an idea about what you would like to do in your Mini. It is much easier to build a car to a set of regulations than try to adapt it afterwards. Below are some of the main organizations you will come across, followed by a small description. Contact details for all clubs mentioned will be in the 'Useful Contacts' section at the end of this book.

This list is by no means definitive. There will be other clubs, individual events and countless regularity rallies, hill climbs and sprints for which your racing Mini will be eligible. Keep an eye on the historic motoring press for up-to-date information on alternative events, from Hill Climbing at Prescott to Brighton Speed Trials, and if you are lucky enough to be a GRRC (Goodwood Road Racing Club) member, the Goodwood Sprints.

Masters Pre-66 Touring Cars

Masters Pre-66 Touring has everything from the mighty V8 Yank tanks to humble Minis, all raced spectacularly in mini-endurance races with pit stops for one or two drivers. With a class structure broken into engine size, Ford Falcons take on Mustangs, Lotus Cortinas tackle the BMW TiSAs and Minis' super Coopers three-wheel their way to success.

In 2015, Masters held seven races at: Catalunya, Spain; Brands Hatch, UK; Monza, Italy; Donington, UK; Zandvoort, Netherlands; Spa, Belgium; and Dijon, France.

The Mini is a popular choice for club racers.

U2TC

U2TC is a series for pre-1966 under 2-litre Touring Cars. It claims to visit all the best tracks in Europe, enjoys a high standard of race preparation and high driving standards. It is an invitation series and cars are expected to conform strictly to Appendix K.

In 2015, U2TC held seven races at Donington, UK; Spa, Belgium; Dijon, France; Silverstone, UK; again at Spa, Belgium; Paul Ricard, France; and Portimão, Portugal.

HSCC Historic Touring Car Championship

The Historic Touring Car Championship is for saloon cars that were in series production before 1966. Cars can be developed in line with period modifications and a separate class is run for cars complying with FIA Appendix K regulations. With Mini Coopers taking on Ford Anglias, Lotus Cortinas, Ford Mustangs and Ford Falcons, the racing is always exciting.

The HSCC had a big calendar in 2015, with ten events held in the UK at Thruxton, Silverstone, Donington Park, Snetterton, Cadwell Park, Brands Hatch, Croft, Oulton Park and again at Brands Hatch and Silverstone.

CSCC Swinging Sixties and Classic K

The Swinging Sixties Series is for all Sports, Saloons and GT cars originally produced in the 1950s and 1960s. Compared to the Classic K Series, the Swinging Sixties allows modifications to cars and splits them into two separate groups for smaller- and larger-engined cars, with a total of eleven classes. It is a very popular and long-running series.

The Classic K series is for pre-1966 GT and Touring Cars running to Appendix K (no sports racers). A series of one-hour races for one or two drivers represents great value for money, in what has become an increasingly expensive area of motor sport. The organizers claim to have a refreshingly common-sense attitude to eligibility and scrutineering.

Races in 2015 were held at Snetterton, Silverstone, Brands Hatch, Rockingham, Mallory Park, Donington Park and Oulton Park in the UK, with one race at Spa in Belgium.

HRDC Allstars

With an ethos of recreating the 'Allcomers' races of the 1950s and 1960s, the Allstars series is open to Sports, GT and Touring Cars and aims to offer competitors an easy access route into historic racing. With an emphasis on Appendix K regulations and all cars running on Dunlop CR65 historic race tyres, it aims to provide an accessible and accommodating format.

2015 saw five races all in the UK at Silverstone, Brands Hatch, Oulton Park, Mallory Park and Donington Park, with a track day at Goodwood in March.

Mk1 Mini road car.

2
sourcing a Mini and body preparation

BUYING THE BEST FOUNDATIONS

Racing an economy car conceived in the 1950s is bound to get tricky. Just how difficult it can get starts right here with the classic Mini bodyshell of the August 1959–October 1967 first series, which we refer to as Mk1. For authentic appearance and proper compliance with the target regulations, the foundations to a historic competition Mini must be based on the first series Mini body.

Racing, rallying, roadrunner or pure show car, two subjects will never be far from our lips in the initial stages: rust and cost! If we had written this book back in the days of cheap second-hand original Minis, we would probably only have discussed rust and a full-scale assault on its wretched presence as the priority to tackle before all else. As you will have seen in the first chapter on regulations, the authorities list this as a priority in preparation, but that ignores one fact of twenty-first-century classic car life.

Baby Boomers and collectors from the UK and around the globe now value the Mini, especially the 1959–67 Mk1, to an extraordinary degree. Both 'barn finds' and properly restored 850 Minis were attracting strong bids at auction and doing fine business for dealers in 2016. In 2013, we saw an example of an £8,250 sale price for a 1963 Cooper (997cc) barn find. We have seen ordinary 850s go at this sort of money and more when restored. Any hint of 1959 provenance, or 'earliest known example', outside the official Heritage museum exhibit, could well power bidders to £30,000 frenzies, whatever the condition. However, there are mitigating circumstances.

We are not bothered about the rare and desirable 1959 model, while Cooper and Cooper S types have had their own strong financial following for longer than the 848cc originals. At the time of writing, 'ordinary' 998/997 Coopers were £10,000, or more if in usable condition, and the Cooper S types could easily double that. All we want is a sound basis for a race car, so how can one be found without exhausting the budget almost before starting? We have tackled this increasingly difficult task many times. There are some distinctly different paths to pursue, depending on your circumstances and the depth of preparation required. As clarified in the previous chapter, a genuine Cooper S is not necessary. Any Mk1 Mini, including the lowly 850, will suffice as the basis for a historic race-car build.

The first thing to remember is that you must find an original Mk1 Mini of that 1959–67 run. There are no simple short-cuts, such as buying a complete replacement shell from British Motor Heritage. British Motor Heritage only manufactures a complete body for a much later Mini than we require, because the company uses the original tooling, which was successively modified to stamp out every major modification. Thus Mk1 outside door hinges, smaller rear screen and myriad more details would not be present – and our project period racer would not proceed beyond technical inspection. You can get complete panels for some items from Heritage – and other sources that we talk about later – but our advice would be to look for the best complete Mini you can find in the UK, as there are plenty around still. But, and as time goes by, it is becoming a larger BUT by the year, original and early Minis are appreciating strongly. At the time of writing, that would most likely be an 850 or possibly a 998 Cooper selling for £5,000 to £10,000 and you would be spending that kind of money looking for the absolute best body you can find.

Of course, it may be attractive to save £3,000 on the purchase price for a less tidy or rustier example, but if you plan to have the car professionally prepared, £3,000 will not cover the cost of turning a rustier example into the foundations for a race Mini. For example, our company would charge in the region of £15,000+VAT to restore and paint a substandard body. However, for racing, a car's body does not have to be seam-welded, so buying a restored vehicle with a sound body can save the cost of expensive body restoration and paint. Starting with a restored example may also have the added benefit of many new or restored parts, which will also save on costs later on.

It will cost you a lot less to prepare an existing sound vehicle for racing, but the downside is that the body will have an unknown quantity of filler in it, which might make it difficult to build it to the homologated weight limit of 620kg (1,367lb) for the 1275 S. If, however, you intend to go to much greater lengths in preparation and plan to seam-weld the shell, it should be possible to take a body that may need more work. If you are building a car from bare metal, you can make it strong and light with good-quality panels. If you end up with a race car that is underweight, you then have the luxury of adding ballast exactly where you want it in order to improve handling. This is the route that the top teams will always take, as it gives them that slight advantage over the competition.

Buying a complete car rather than something in bits will ultimately be beneficial, even though much of the original components, such as suspension and brakes, will be replaced. Items such as door latches, wiper motor, heater and even subframes, if in good condition, will all be utilized and sourcing them individually may be more costly in the long run. That said, there are often bare bodyshells or incomplete projects available and they may offer good value, so it is always worth considering every option.

FIT FOR PURPOSE?

Now that we have searched the world and come up with a suitable 1959–67 Mk1 Mini, one that you probably found locally – or dragged in from a back lawn in a wheelbarrow, as we did! So, what happens next to the two-door shell and what will be required if you are an ambitious and talented DIY racer?

If you are starting your race-car build with a complete and sound bodyshell from a restored or well-maintained vehicle, there will be little body preparation required. At the very least, you will need to weld reinforcement plates in the floor for the roll cage, details of which will be covered in the next chapter. Seam-welding the door or window apertures will burn the paint, so this may have to be skipped. If you are building to Appendix K specification, you must retain the steel doors, bonnet and boot lid. However, if you are planning to race with the HSCC's Historic Touring Cars, fibreglass or aluminium closing panels are allowed. You may, on the other hand have chosen to restore a bodyshell and, like the top teams looking for ultimate competitiveness, may want to start with a bare metal shell.

Looking at the tools required specifically for bodywork, anyone tackling this level of competition preparation will already have an extensive set of tools. So far as body preparation is concerned, the primary item that may be outside a DIY experience is the use of a MIG welder; suitable machines cost from £110–150. While a MIG device can cost all the way up to £1,000, with more power and

sourcing a Mini and body preparation

Our Mk1 was found abandoned in a field with extensive rust.

Rust has destroyed much of our Mk1 Mini, but most panels are available to restore it.

Scrutineers will look for good-quality welds, especially on the roll cage.

double the number of heat settings, this is not really necessary for the thinner panels. Scrutineers will look at the quality of welding, so unless you are a competent welder or wish to put in the practice before working on your race car's bodyshell, it is best to leave this work to the professionals. Other tools you will need are a set of hammers and dollies, metal shears, a variety of welding clamps, a drill and an angle grinder with cutting discs, grinding discs and 36grit linishing discs.

One key use for your MIG welder other than in restoration will be for seam- or stitch-welding. Seam-welding the shell in certain areas will boost body strength and increase its rigidity. A MIG welder would also be needed to affix the mandatory reinforcement plates that support the roll cage footplates. If welding is not your thing, there are a number of specialists who can do this work for you. More detail on roll cages and their fitment will be covered in the next chapter.

sourcing a Mini and body preparation

Example of seam welding along the outer sill.

BODY: LITTLE DEVILS IN THE DETAILS

Like us, you may be starting your project with the restoration of a Mk1 bodyshell. Ours was extremely rusty and for many would have been too far gone. We would not recommend starting with a shell quite this bad, but with our in-house body shop facilities it did not make a lot of difference. It is worth mentioning that although cheap body panels may be tempting, they will generally fit poorly and putting this right will cost more than buying the best panels in the first place. We will take a look now at what panels are available and how best to go about preparing your Mini body for historic competition.

Our first port of call for any panel work is M-Machine Ltd in County Durham. They make many panels for the Mini and source anything they do not make from British Motor Heritage. We use M-Machine primarily because we believe they make unmatched quality panels, especially for the Mk1, many of which are not available elsewhere. For example, they will modify many Heritage panels such as the boot floor and the front panels to replicate more accurately the original Mk1 panels. There are cheaper replacement panel sources that you might research, especially where a panel is not under obvious stress, or availability is a problem from regular quality suppliers. However, for more critical panels good fit may become an issue.

We will start with the floor. In the Mk1, this was a single pressing from front to rear, including tunnel and

Our Mk1 Mini left much to be desired.

sourcing a Mini and body preparation

Our Mini received a complete new floor from M-Machine.

cling the rear side glass and the door. There is no supplier of this complete Mk1 panel, although they can occasionally be found for sale on eBay. Today, all you can buy is the rear quarter panel, which will run from the bottom of the rear side window down to the sill and from the rear edge of the door back to the rear seam. Also available is a lower quarter section, with the lower section of the doorstep/sill to extend below the doors. The lower doorstep is available on its own, as are the inner and outer A-panels. The door and side window apertures are not available, but rarely require any attention anyway.

Do not ignore the rear floor/back seat area. With all the trim stripped and the rear seat removed, any deficiencies in welding and rust intrusion will likely be apparent. If your shell is really bad, like ours was, then you may need to replace the rear bulkhead. You will often find cars with late rear bulkheads fitted, as for many owners this was not an important detail. The rear bulkhead is specific to Mk1 and Mk2 and without a rear seat fitted is visible and

Repair panel for the bottom of the rear quarter, including the doorstep.

inner sills. If you are reworking an original 850cc tunnel, remember that the cut-out for the gear lever differs from remote (Cooper and S) to the forward location of the magic wand that commands an early 850's gear selectors. You will need to cut a new hole for the remote gear selector and fit a cover to the original opening. When restoring the floor there is enormous flexibility in panel supply that allows you to buy anything from a single front or rear, left or right floor section, to a complete floorpan including cross member, tunnel, rear subframe mounting panel and outer sills. At the time of writing, this complete floor was available exclusively from M-Machine at the very good value price of £540 +VAT. It is often quicker and easier to replace the entire floor and sills in one go than attempt localized repairs.

It is very rare today, but the earliest Minis had foam filling applied in the sills to overcome production water-repellent deficiencies. If you find such items and the rest of the car matches a 1959–60 production date, maybe you should rethink racing plans: it is probably worth a lot more money as an early collectible!

The original Mk1 Mini side panel stretches from the rear seam to the front seam. This is a large expanse of sheet steel running from the roof down to the sill, encir-

The rear bulkhead and boot floor were rusted through.

sourcing a Mini and body preparation

New modified boot floor from M-Machine resembles the original Mk 1 item.

should be correct. The Mk1/Mk2 rear bulkhead panel is available from M-Machine, as is the rear seat pan/boot floor.

The boot floor and rear seat pan form one complete panel. M-Machine modify a later panel to make it look like the original Mk1 panel. If you purchase this panel from an alternative supplier, it will have an extra bump on the left-hand side, which was added in production to clear the fuel pump on the late fuel-injected models. Aside from the boot sheet-metal rust, the box that surrounds the battery will usually have rusted as well if the car has been neglected. The sensible approach is to buy, at less than £20, the rectangle that encases the battery from a quality supplier.

The rear panel can have a tendency to rust just above the bumper. This, like the side panels, was once supplied as a single pressing, but is no longer available. Occasionally coming up on eBay, a new old-stock item can easily cost £800, so repairs for the lower portion of the rear panel will be the requirement. The rear valance beneath is also a popular rust spot, but these are cheap and easy to replace.

Rusty front bulkhead with inner and outer wings and front panel removed.

sourcing a Mini and body preparation

A closer look at the rusty bulkhead cross member.

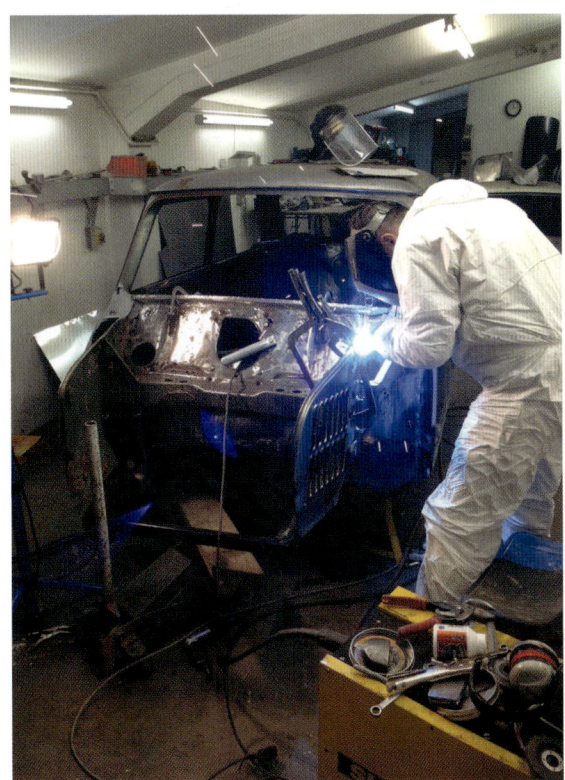

Welding new inner wings.

A front subframe has been fitted in order to line up the bulkhead crossmember repairs and the new inner wings.

The bulkhead cross member has been repaired and a new inner wing has been fitted.

New front panel and wings fitted.

sourcing a Mini and body preparation

1in square tubing is used to brace the bodyshell before the floor is cut out.

Moving up to the front of the car, it is highly likely that the wings, scuttle and front panel will have some excessive rust. It is general practice to replace all of these panels. The front bulkhead for a Mk1 is not available, although repairs for the cross member are. You will often find rust in the front bulkhead, which will require careful restoration.

Complete inner wings are available from M-Machine and are very good. Front panels are Heritage, unless they have been modified by M-Machine to represent more accurately the Mk1 item. There are a number of subtle differences that most won't worry about; these include smaller indicator plinths and, for pre-1964 models, a full-width skirt under the bumper. Front wings and scuttle are Heritage items and fit fairly well.

A common-sense basic is to be aware that major surgery – indeed any major cutting of a modern monocoque body – requires you to brace surrounding panels first, in order to ensure accuracy for the surrounding panels and subsequent refitting. Our pictures show the type of bracing we used to keep the shell honest without a floor. You must have reference points and the easiest way to ensure they are preserved is by bracing.

Safety is paramount when restoring or preparing a bodyshell, especially bearing in mind what you are going to be asking from this body in motor sports. This simple shell, initially developed to deliver economy motoring to the post-Suez petrol-starved masses, will now be repeatedly asked to take corners beyond 100mph on high-grip surfaces, tarmac that develops seriously aggressive G-forces. It is also possible that – like the rest of us – you may run out of talent on a slippery surface and slam into solid objects at speed, or be attacked by a rival. Overall, we suggest you have the best in metalwork around you. Panels should be straight and strong and your welding should be of the highest standard. Watch out for brazing on older restorations, as well as excessive amounts of

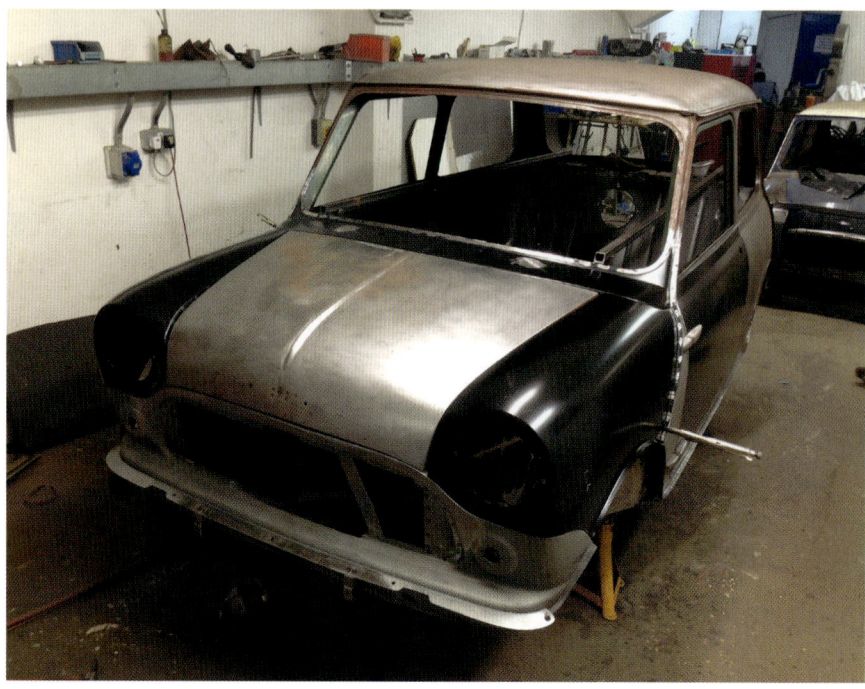

Restored Mk1 bodyshell nearly complete.

sourcing a Mini and body preparation

filler, poor welding or poor panel fit. Your Mini's bodyshell may have to save your life, so make sure it is up to the job.

PREPARATION

There are some critical areas in the body that take particularly high stresses in a racing application – and some steel sections that are surprisingly complex for such an outwardly simple design. There are a number of external seams on the classic Mini and except for the seams that surround the roof panel, the obvious seams are usually covered up after body preparation. The lower seams are best seen in chrome strip and the vertical seams by body-coloured capping strips, both of which will be required for an acceptable factory-finish appearance. The rear valance seam will be covered up by a bumper, which is required on today's FIA racers in our FIA project period F (1962–5). From 1966 (FIA Period G of 1966–70), the more radically modified Group 5 Touring Cars could run without bumpers. With all the Mini's seams being originally spot-welded, additional seam-welding – as elsewhere on the body – will boost the overall rigidity of the shell. Time-consuming, but worthwhile.

The inner sill rises upwards from the floor to meet the 'doorstep' on each side and where it meets what would be the outer sill in a conventional layout, the box section folds back down to double up on that upward floor

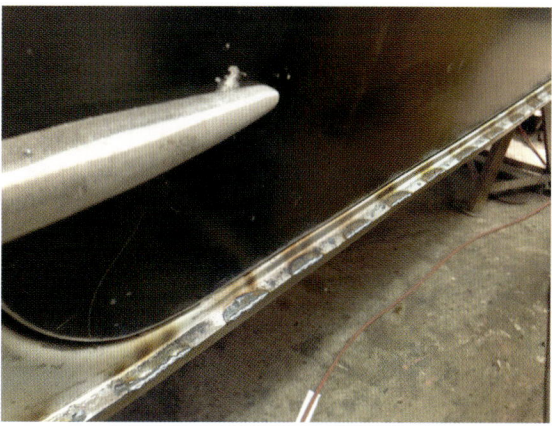

Seam-welding along the sill of our racing Mini shell.

incline. This overlap of the outer sill and floor should ideally receive seam-welding too. If there's a body join that you can see, the advice seems to be, if in doubt, weld it. However, the roof panel and surrounds are left alone, because of the difficulties in welding access. There are some tricks of the Mini flooring trade that are particularly common in rally-car body preparation. For example, the cross member that runs beneath the seats can be removed and a smaller and additional member slotted inside for additional strength.

Staying with the steel bodyshell, the seam-welding

Seam-welding the windscreen aperture.

sourcing a Mini and body preparation

A wheel-arch-to-bulkhead stiffener was introduced in 1965.

Rear-wheel-arch-to-boot-floor reinforcement and rear subframe mounting point.

process has been found to be effective in some less obvious corners. Aside from the obvious external seams on the original Mini, seam-welding should be applied to the front and rear screen surrounds, around the door apertures and the surrounds to the three-quarter side windows aft of those doors. Seam-welding these areas will benefit local torsional strength. More complexities are discovered behind the rear bumper, a meeting point for three panels: namely the under-bumper valance; the rear single panel from roof to floor; and complete boot/back-seat floor, simply known as the boot floor. It is well worth stitching them together, again particularly to resist the torsional twisting forces that a Mini generates.

Inside the boot, you will find that later (1965–6) Mk1 Minis had a small box section that reinforced the rear bulkhead to the boot floor and to the inner rear wheel arch. This uprate is allowed as a retro fit on earlier Minis that lack that small steel panel, one now catalogued as a wheel-arch-to-bulkhead stiffener. We recommended fitting such triangulated wheel-arch-to-bulkhead stiffeners, as they brace the rear wheel arch and the shock absorber, and the rear bulkhead and the boot floor, against the extra forces of motor sports.

A secondary small steel-stiffening item located to the rear of the inner wheel arch braces the rear of the arch to the boot floor. This panel is also the upper layer in a multiple-layered reinforcement for the rear subframe mounting. Especially prone to rust, that vital connecting bracket is available from M-Machine.

Beneath the boot floor there is a flat reinforcement plate followed next by the rear valance closing panel. The rear valance closing panel folds around to form the lower-most layer in the reinforcement of the rear subframe mounting. Including the boot floor, there are four

Rear subframe mounting reinforcements seam-welded for extra rigidity.

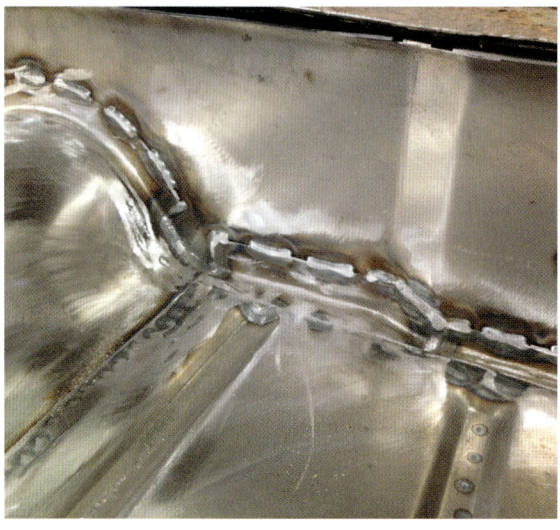

Seam-welding along the subframe mounting panel.

sourcing a Mini and body preparation

FIA Appendix K 2017
5.6 Bulkheads
5.6.1 From Period F onwards, fireproof bulkheads must be installed. They are recommended for other periods.

MSA Yearbook **2017 (J) Competitors: Vehicle**
5.2.2. … have a protective bulkhead of non-flammable material between the engine and the driver/passenger compartment capable of preventing the passage of fluid or flame. Gaps must be sealed with suitable flameproof material that completely closes any gap at all times.

MSA Yearbook **2017 (Q) Circuit Racing: Technical Regulations**
Chassis
19.1.1. Have a bulkhead between any fuel tank and filler and the driver/passenger compartment sufficient to prevent the passage of flame or liquid. …

This is achieved by blanking off larger apertures with alloy sheet and petrol-proof sealant. A necessary measure on a Mini is a half-inch production gap, where the assembly line soundproofing is removed. This is found in the vertical sections of the rear bulkhead and around the rear parcel shelf. Once a cardboard template has been made, alloy sheet of 1 to 1.2mm stock can be cut and secured via petrol-resistant silicone sealants. Smaller circular holes can be welded or filled with rubber blanking grommets.

Front damper mounts.

layers of steel spot-welded together. Stitching these layers together will further help to improve rigidity.

Where the rear subframe attaches to the rearmost floor is another key zone for concentrated reinforcement. This panel is often referred to as the subframe mounting panel and can be seam-welded along the floor and boot floor.

At the front, the subframe layout is a complete wheel-away assembly on a Mini, making it easy to implement complete power-unit and integral transmission changes. That leaves the inclined shock absorbers as a freestanding unit with conventional mountings bolted to the body. If your model started life as a Hydrolastic car, there may be no front shock mounts. These are readily available from all good suppliers. Check the front bulkhead carefully and make sure that the cross member is sound and free from rust. This area is the main structural support for the front subframe and engine and can be stitched to the bulkhead and inner wings.

A mandatory and sensible regulation demand is that the bulkheads front and rear be sealed off from the driver's cockpit. Although this is a safety concern, it also falls within the remit of body preparation so should be considered during this process.

1.2mm aluminium sheet used to seal the rear bulkhead and parcel shelf.

sourcing a Mini and body preparation

The rear bulkhead hole is covered with an aluminium plate.

Both the front and rear bulkhead on the Mini, as well as other BMC vehicles of the time, have one large hole in the middle. These holes were used to carry the bodyshells through the production line in the factory. The standard treatment for the hole in the rear bulkhead was a cardboard-like material screwed in place. This is not fireproof, so will need to be replaced ideally in aluminium with sealant and rivets to hold it in place. The hole in the front bulkhead will also need to be covered.

Almost ancillary in comparison with the stressed items we have discussed, the official word on bonnet, boot lid and roof is that these simpler steel pressings should be left strictly in standard factory trim. That means no fancy lightweight hole drilling for the bonnet and boot, no substituting thinner gauge metal or trick carbons in the sheet-metal roof panel. Yes, we remember an entire BMW factory team of World Touring Cars being removed from a dominant result because of trick flyweight roof panels. And that was after the outright winning Ford Sierras had already been disqualified. They have long memories at the FIA, as do their technical inspectors/scrutineers. If a fancy factory team did not get away with flyweight unstressed panels, neither will you!

For Appendix K, all closing panels must be made from steel; aluminium door skins are not allowed. If, however, you plan to race with the HSCC, you may substitute the steel panels for aluminium or fibreglass, provided that your car is not under its allowed minimum weight.

There is more on basic body lore to come in the next safety-linked chapter, covering items such as roll cage installation and security of the bonnet and boot lid. Back in their day, these often depended just on the production catches, which is not a good idea today. A bonnet flying open at 100mph will most certainly ruin your race.

Throughout bare-body preparation and assembly respect the fact that this is a design that is fifty years old which was intended to provide economical transport for the masses. Yes, it was a work of genius and you will get maximum fun per pound/hour spent, but never forget that the Mini's basic body is your foundation to ensuring that high-stress questions are safely answered out on the track.

Cooper S versus the large American V8-powered Mustang.

3 safety first

INTEGRAL SAFETY STEPS AND EQUIPMENT

Constructing a bare body that you know has had the best in basic strengthening is not just the foundation to your racing ambitions, but will also serve to embrace many more moves to enhance your safety. Even so, safety should never be taken for granted. We have witnessed the deadly consequences of a racing Mini colliding with a larger car and the premier Goodwood or Silverstone classic annuals have seen plenty of wonderful David and Goliath struggles between front-running Minis and heavyweight American V8 iron, especially in wet conditions and poor visibility. While this may be tremendous for spectator entertainment and driver ego, we want it to stay fun. The fact is that such battles see the larger car's driver absorbed in balancing limited grip against big power and they may miss that pesky Mini, the one in hot pursuit within one of the many blind spots that exist on every racing saloon.

The opposition outside your Mini will almost always carry more bulk: biffing larger vehicles at speed usually leads to the departure of the smaller car from track limits. So we need to give ourselves the best possible chance when track battles turn turtle: yes, co-author Walton has been upside down in professionally prepared 1300cc saloons without injury.

So here is how to tackle the headline safety details, beyond building the best Mini bodyshell your resources can command.

ROLLOVER PROTECTION (ROPS)

Before we get into the cage-preparation choices, here is a valuable general observation taken from professional advice: how you instal equipment is as important as the equipment itself. Today, such obviously life-or-death safety-related components have to be made to meet exacting standards, but back in the day standards

safety first

Safety Devices bolt-in roll cage.

of installation or absence of basic equipment could be deadly.

Roll cages and safety belts arrived in wider racing through the 1960s and there were Minis and rivals racing without cages through much of that decade! The Americans and their 150mph stock cars helped to spread the word, especially when Jaguar's domination of UK and some European saloon events was ended by the arrival of 7-litre 'Yank Tanks'.

In Mini terms, this example illustrates the point. Back in the 1960s even the professionals would mount seat-belt anchor points to the rear bulkhead. That would result in a production rear bulkhead crumpling forward in a heavy accident, forming a crushed V-shape under impact. It does not bear thinking about today, but Mini legend John Rhodes experienced just that accidental consequence in 2009 and proved it will result in your (helmeted) head striking something solid. Hard. Best avoided.

The rollover bars forming a cage within the cockpit are absolutely the heart of our defences. A proper roll cage serves not only to preserve our person, the integrity of the body in protection and possible faster repair, but also aids competitive speed. How can a spider's web of internal scaffolding weighing around 25–35kg (55–77lb) lower lap times? Basically, because current roll cages uprate and brace the Mini's fifty-year old body design against twenty-first-century racing demands, delivering a stable foundation of stiffer resolve than could be realized fifty years ago.

Frankly, there are some liberties taken in roll-cage design versus the strict technical interpretation of the FIA international regulations. We will only publish what you should do and not encourage infringing the rules, but please also use your eyes and common sense to examine front-running Minis. Understand what passes through the scrutineering bay without hindrance, especially where 'new' racing Minis hit the historic tracks from professionals.

You can buy a perfectly satisfactory roll cage off the shelf from some suppliers. It will usually have been constructed by Safety Devices, an East Anglian firm originally founded by Mini racer and winning driver John Aley. Proprietary is easiest and it can all be bought from Mini Sport. Expect to pay around £700 +VAT for the complete cage when it has the now mandatory diagonal rear bar and compulsory door bars. The Safety Devices roll cage is a good cage. It is FIA certified and will be adequate for most, especially if you are on a smaller budget. It is a bolt-in cage made from the compulsory 2.5mm thick 38mm cold-drawn seamless steel tubing. It is a little heavier than some other options and of course there will not be the added benefits of a custom roll cage that has been built around your height, leg length and seat position.

There are a number of firms that make custom roll cages. We have the facilities in our workshop and often make cages for vehicles where no alternative is available. If you are a taller driver and want to ensure you have a little more room, a custom cage may be something you wish to consider, although the cost is likely be significantly higher than an off-the-shelf item, for example around £1,600–£2,000.

One of the most popular choices for the front-running teams is the Historic Mini T45 roll cage from Custom Cages. It is an FIA-certified weld-in cage that can be supplied as a kit for your own installation, or it can be installed by Custom Cages. We chose this roll cage for our Mini, but we have the benefit of a professional workshop for installation and welding. Home installation would not be recommended at all. The Historic Mini T45 roll cage is the most comprehensive cage available and it is also the lightest due to the use of T45 steel tubing. T45 is stronger and with only 1.6mm wall thickness is also much lighter.

You might wonder how a roll cage can be made legally with thinner-walled tubing than what is allowed by the regulations. When a roll cage is certified by the FIA it has to pass physical impact tests. A cage can be designed to use thinner-walled tubing as long as it passes the tests and is successfully certified; this means that you cannot simply use T45 tubing at home to build your own cage. The Historic Mini T45 roll cage includes a dash bar, roof bar, double door bars, two diagonals crossing at the back and a bar between the feet of the main hoop. With all these extra tubes the overall cage still weighs around 10–15kg less than a standard steel cage. This cage is lighter, but it is also safer, which is why it is the number one choice.

Detailed Construction Specifications

It is your responsibility to ensure that your roll cage meets all of the demands of the FIA/MSA. We will outline some of the main regulations here, but we must stress that if you are doing any of this work yourself, you *must* familiarize yourself with the regulations as they are set out by the FIA/MSA. The last thing you want is to be sent home from a race meeting because the scrutineers were not happy with your roll cage.

FIA Appendix K 2017 Appendix VI
1.1.5 Specifications
The specification of the structure installed must be detailed on the Roll Over Protection Structure Description document which must be attached, as an appendix, to all HTPs issued after 1/1/2014.

For T, CT, GT, GTS and GTP cars of Period F onwards
The minimum specification is a ROPS in conformity with drawing K-3 as detailed in K-8, K-9 and K-10 with a compulsory diagonal (orientation optional) and door bars complying with Appendix V.
…
Tubes through the front bulkhead or attached to the body/chassis within 10cm of the front suspension pick-up points are not permitted unless this is a period or homologated specification.

Although popular with many Mini racers in other disciplines, for a historic racing Mini of period F you cannot attach the roll cage to the front suspension pickup points and you cannot run your tubes through the front bulkhead. The thinking here is that such duties for a safety cage stray into the realms of a tube-frame body structure; one that becomes the primary chassis of the car, while the body serves as mere cladding.

The FIA details minimum requirements for the type of internal safety cage to be constructed in the Appendix K regulations, right down to the bolts employed and the cold-drawn seamless steel tube dimensions set at a minimum of 38mm diameter with 2.5mm wall thickness.

Just six primary mounting points are allowed on the Mini body. These take the form of steel reinforcement plates, minimum 3mm thickness. For the main hoop and front, this plate must be 120cm^2 and must be welded to the body. For the backstays, the reinforcement plate only needs to be 60cm^2. The regulations state,

***MSA Yearbook* 2017 (K) Competitors: Safety**
1.3.2 Mounting of the ROPS to the bodyshell
… Each mounting foot must be attached by at least three bolts, minimum M8 150 grade 8.8, on a steel reinforcement plate at least 3mm thick and of at least 120cm^2 area which is welded to the bodyshell … The mounting feet may alternatively be welded direct to the reinforcement plate. This does not apply to the backstays.
1.3.3 Backstays
Their mountings must be reinforced by plates. Each backstay should be secured by bolts having a cumulative section area at least two thirds of that recommended for each roll bar leg mounting in 1.3.2 above, and with identical reinforcement plates of a least 60cm^2 area.

ROLL CAGE CONSTRUCTION

Now that we have outlined a couple of options, we will describe the broad processes and materials used. Anyone contemplating making his or her own cage should have skills way beyond printed DIY instruction, but we will cover the regulations and specifications later in this chapter.

FIA Appendix K details the specification for roll cages in our period use. The same specifications can also be found in the *Yearbook*. The main elements applied to a Mini are the main hoop running behind the front seats within the B-pillars and attached to the floor on each side of the car via support plates. The rear stays join at the top corners of the main hoop and come back to join support plates on the rear arches/bulkhead area. Now mandatory is a diagonal bar to stretch across what was the rear passenger area. Also positioned from the top of the main hoop, running forward along the roof line, within the screen pillars and down to the floor below the A-pillars, again meeting floor support plates, are the front lateral roll-cage tubes. Between these front tubes will be a bar above the windscreen and between the front tubes and the main tubes will be the now mandatory door bars. Optional bars include a dash bar running below the dashboard, additional rear diagonal, roof bar, double door bar and a bar running across the width of the car between the feet of the main hoop. It is probably best to look at Appendix K drawings and what is actually raced at a race meeting to get a proper understanding of the complex structure.

In order to have access to weld the top of a weld-in roll cage, it is necessary to lower the construction through holes in the floor.

With the rear legs through the floor, weld all the way around the top of the cage.

Once the top has been welded, lift the cage into position and insert the footplates between the legs and the floor.

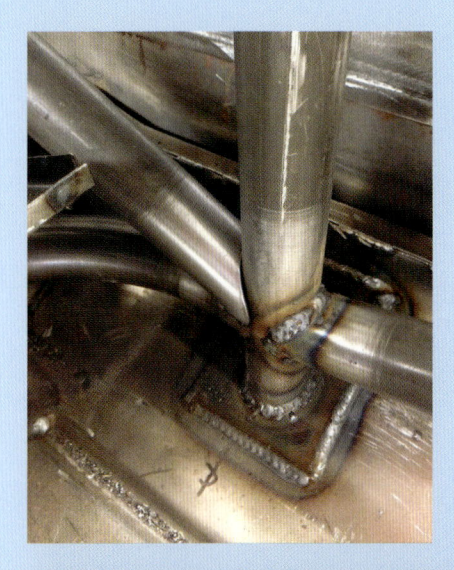

LEFT: Rear leg welded in place.

ABOVE: Rear companion box is cut away for the double door bars.

RIGHT: Roll-cage welding needs to be of a high standard.

ABOVE: Rear companion boxes in position.

Completed roll cage in position with rear diagonals, double door bars, harness bars, diagonal roof bar and B-pillar mounting points.

43

safety first

FIA Appendix K 2017 Appendix VI
1.2.3.3.1 Fixation of the ROPS to the body
… The attachment points of the front and main roll bars to the body must be reinforced with a steel plate of at least 3mm thick and with a surface area of 120cm^2, welded to the body and the attachment points of the backstays to the body must be reinforced with a steel plate of at least 3mm thick and with a surface area of 60cm^2, welded to the body …

At the end of each tube there must be a footplate made from 3mm steel. The footplates must be attached to the reinforcement plates that have been welded to the body. Within these mounts, the FIA specifies at least three ISO 8.8 hexagonal bolts of a minimum 8mm diameter for the main hoop and front legs and at least two bolts of the same specification for the backstays, each fitted with locking washers. Alternatively, the footplates can be welded to the reinforcement plates instead of bolting.

Footplate bolted to the reinforcement plate welded to the body.

Backstays must join the main hoop within 10cm of the top bend with an angle no less than 30 degrees.

safety first

The backstays must join the main hoop as close to the top as possible and within 10cm of the bends. The minimum angle between main hoop and backstays is 30 degrees. For taller drivers, it is possible to move the main hoop further back and still have more than a 30-degree angle with the backstay. At least one rear diagonal is now mandatory. It must be joined to the main hoop behind the driver's head and to the opposite backstay as close to the footplate as possible. The diagonal can be removable if you ever wish to use the rear seat.

Also now mandatory are the door bars. These are a little trickier with the Mk1 Mini. The regulations state that the door bars must not impede the driver's exit and the FIA measures this exit at less than 7sec. The depth of the door pockets on the Mk1 Mini causes a slight issue here as they naturally intrude too far between the main hoop and front legs. Without modification to the door pockets, the door bars of the roll cage must run level above the height of the standard door pocket. Although many cars are prepared this way, it does make entry and exit of the vehicle a little awkward. The ideal orientation for the door bars would be lower at the front, or, in the case of the T45 roll cage we have used, in a cross. This orientation will help entry and exit, but will require modifications to the doors. The simplest solution is to cut the door pockets out and cut the pocket narrower, then weld them back into the door frame.

A dash bar is optional, but highly recommended. In the event of a side impact, it will reduce the risk of the front roll-cage structure deforming around your legs. The location of a dash bar on the Mk1 Mini is limited. It can be positioned just low enough to not obscure the switch panel in the lower dash rail as long as you are using some kind of steering-column drop bracket.

A harness bar mounted to the roll cage is a must-have. It is not demanded by the regulations, but it is the only truly safe mounting point for the harness in a Mini bodyshell. Under no circumstance should you *ever* mount the harness to the parcel shelf of a Mini. In a front-end collision it will pull out, along with the rear bulkhead.

Door pockets are removed and trimmed down to allow clearance for the door bars.

Door pocket removed and trimmed down.

Slimline door pocket welded back in the door frame will now clear the door bars.

safety first

Dash bar positioned in front of the lower dash rail and above the steering column.

A harness bar is the safest place to mount the safety harness.

We have seen it happen and it is not pretty. The easiest place to mount a harness bar is to have it bolt through the footplates where the backstays mount to the rear wheel arch.

This covers most of the key parameters to Mini cage building today. There are a number of optional tubes covered in the FIA/MSA regulations that you may wish to consider. If you go to any race event that period Minis are racing you will see that one can get away with a lot, as a look at winning cars will tell you. This area of body construction and safety is absolutely critical, so make sure you understand not just the ground rules, but also how they are interpreted.

SEAT

For the seat, the first thing to look for is an FIA approval stamp. Seats have to pass stiffer tests these days, including two levels of FIA approval. It is still possible to buy reproductions of the 1960s Restalls and contemporary bucket-style seats that dominated the cockpit furniture of 1960s tin-top racers, but they are not really adequate for racing today. In the UK, under MSA regulations you are not currently required to have an FIA-certified seat, but if you ever plan to race abroad it will be required. There is a wide choice of FIA-approved seating and we can only advise that you try out as many as possible, because they really are an integral key to feeling that you have control, rather than the car. Although the Mini is punitive, there is enough room for most modern racing seats, even those with built-in head protection. The seat we have chosen for our build is the Corbeau Revolution and is of that type. Corbeau is a local East Sussex firm that has been producing seats for motor sport since 1963 (*see* 'Useful Contacts').

Most new race seats have adjustable padding/cushions/bolsters that make a huge difference to security and comfort, benefits you must compromise when sharing with anyone but your identical body twin. The feedback offered by the right seat for you is comparable to the messages you get through the Mini's alert steering. Although not recommended on safety grounds, the regulations do allow for a period seat to be used. If you do happen to use

safety first

Even the Corbeau racing seat with head protection fits in the Mini.

Racing seat side mounts.

a period seat and if it does not have adequate head support, a headrest mounted to the roll cage must be used.

An FIA-certified seat will utilize side mounts. This is by far the best way to mount a racing seat. They are available from most seat manufacturers in either 3mm steel or 5mm aluminium. Like the roll cage, the seat must also be mounted securely to the floor. The regulations ask for four mounting points with 8mm bolts and counter plates of 40cm².

MSA Yearbook **2017 (K) Competitors: Safety Seats, Seat Belts and Headrests**
2.2 Seats
2.2.1 Supports must be attached to the shell/chassis via at least 4 mounting points per seat using bolts with a minimum diameter of 8mm and counterplates, according to drawing No. K32. The minimum area of contact between support, shell/chassis and counterplate is 40 sq cm for each mounting point.

Remember that you may want to share the Mini to defray costs and to contest prestige events, in which case you may consider using runners under the side mounts.

What can you expect to spend? Typical catalogue retail prices from Demon Tweeks showed FIA-approved entry-level steel-frame seats beneath £140 +VAT and top-end carbon-fibre wonderfulness from Recaro topping £2,000 +VAT, that is without supplementary charges for adjustable runners and mounts. We would always recommend composite over steel for entry-level seats. Entry-level GRP seats start from around £200 +VAT. Our carbon-fibre Corbeau seat with FIA approval retails for less than £576 +VAT. Allow at least £30 +VAT for steel side mounts and anywhere from £50 +VAT upwards for aluminium. Demon Tweeks, who stock a huge selection of seats and harnesses in a superstore building with full online facilities, are listed in 'Useful Contacts'. How much to spend is ultimately up to you and the depth of your wallet, but the feeling of total security and command in comfort are the priorities, whatever the brand or materials.

HARNESS

There are a few acronyms and basic phrases that matter in any harness purchase. A fundamental of the twenty-first century is the evolution of the HANS (Head and Neck Support)/Frontal Head Restraint (FHR) device from Formula 1 and single-seat racing to saloon and GT roofed categories. Most top-line brands are sold as HANS/FHR-compatible and although frontal head restraints in the UK are only mandatory in post-1976 vehicles, it is advisable to wear one.

Harnesses are usually sold as four-, five- or six-point mountings, which simply refers to the number of direct links from harness to anchor sites on a car's bodywork, mostly to the floor or harness bar on the roll cage. Incidentally, crutch straps – the single (five-point) or

safety first

Six-point racing harness from Luke.

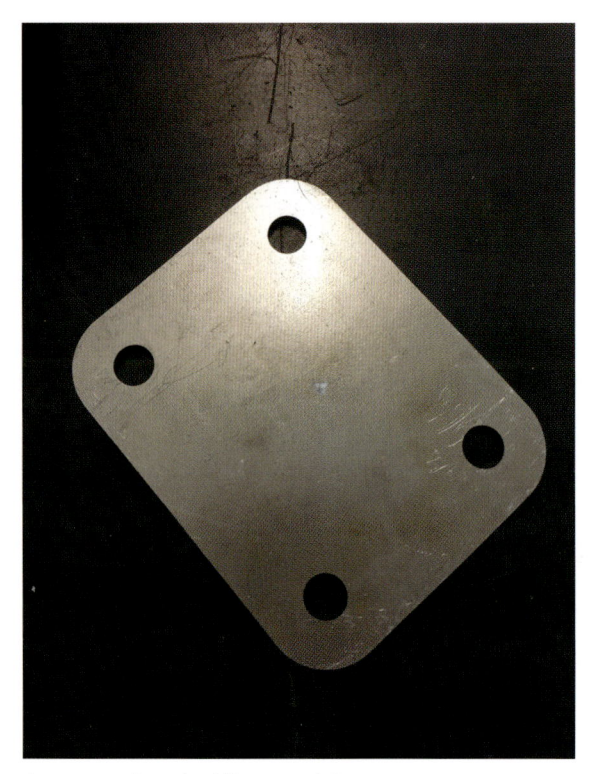

Any counter-plates should have rounded corners.

double (six-point) slimmer webs that link the lower harness release to floor mounts – are not mandatory, although they are strongly recommended. Why? To avoid 'submarining' forward during heavier impacts. Another basic is that the harness should be FIA-approved, a requirement here in the UK. All FIA harnesses are date-stamped and must be replaced after five years. Most FIA harnesses are centrally secured with a twist release, often described as 'aircraft quick release', just like an airline layout.

We mentioned earlier the use of a harness bar for mounting the shoulder straps. The shoulder straps need to be as close to horizontal as possible and no less than 45 degrees from the back of the seat.

MSA Yearbook 2017 (K) Competitors: Safety Seats, Seat Belts and Headrests
2.1.10 The anchorage points to the rear should be positioned so that the strap from the shoulder is as near horizontal as possible. It should not be located on the floor directly behind the driver/co-driver.

Lap and crotch straps should be mounted to the floor symmetrically. Where they mount through the floor, we use a small counter-plate. Wherever a counter-plate is not welded to the floor, it is prudent to round the corners. In an impact, a sharp corner of a 3mm steel plate can easily puncture the thin steel sheet metal of the floor like a tin opener.

The big belt brands are OMP, Schroth, Sabelt, Cobra, TRS and Luke, but we would also recommend Willans, which you may not find in every catalogue. One of us drove a 1.3-litre saloon back in the day with Willans equipment and walked away from at least two inversions without injury. Today, Willans do a nice line in modest black webbing that suits a period feel for a cabin in these hi-tech days.

For the safety harness, allow from £105 +VAT for FIA-stamped four-point equipment and around £110 +VAT for the least expensive six-pointers with FIA backing. Naturally charges vary by brand, but more importantly for the number of mounting points. At top prices, expect to part with over £330 +VAT for an eight-point (the extra mountings are to the roll bar for the HANS device) Schroth harness with HANS provision. For us, the combination of Corbeau seat and Luke belts was a priority, because Luke is also Corbeau-owned and a joint deal looked top value.

Schroth have also made a very impressive effort to understand the needs of longer-distance racers and their

Enduro harness might well be the answer when sharing drives in your Mini. It is a full six-point job with FIA approval and HANS/ FHR compatibility, but what makes it special is the intelligent provision of unique 'ZIP' adjusters integrated into the shoulder and lap belts. Grab-friendly hand loops on the shoulders with bungee loops also assist quick driver changes. Sounds boring and expensive? A bungled driver swap will lose you a lot more time than even an ace can make up in shorter, prestige, two-driver events.

FIRE EXTINGUISHER

Any vehicle competing in FIA-sanctioned motor sports has to comply with its international standards, ratified and observed in Britain by the British Standards Institute (BSI). If you plan to take part only in British club events, you can use a simple hand-held device without FIA approval, but given the type of Mini we prepare, that seems an unlikely cost-cutter. If you plan to race in the big international events, or to race in Europe, you will need a plumbed-in system. You should also consider that it is your life on the line should the worst happen and spending a little extra on a good-quality plumbed-in system could make all the difference.

MSA Yearbook 2017 (K) Competitors: Safety Fire Extinguishers

3 A fire extinguisher/extinguishing system must be carried on all vehicles, the minimum requirement being that the system be charged with one of the permitted extinguishants and be operable by the driver whilst normally seated either by manual operation or by a mechanically/electrically assisted triggering system.

FIA Appendix K 2017
5.7 Extinguishers

5.7.1 All cars competing in circuit races and speed hill climbs must be equipped with at least a hand-operated fire extinguisher complying with current Appendix J, Article 253-7.3.

The FIA's Appendix J specifies that the system be plumbed into the vehicle. The bottle must be mounted within the cockpit and be secured with at least two screw-locked metallic straps. To maintain FIA homologation and approval, you have to follow orders: adding extra nozzles or modifying the system is forbidden.

FIA Appendix J 2012

7.2.3 The driver must be able to trigger all extinguishers manually when seated normally with his safety belts fastened and the steering wheel in place. Furthermore, a means of triggering from the outside must be combined with the circuit-breaker switch. It must be marked with a letter 'E' in red inside a white circle of at least 10cm diameter with a red edge.

We tend to locate a plumbed-in extinguisher bottle in front of the rear seat on the opposite side to the driver. The nozzles will be directed towards the driver's torso and in the engine bay towards the carburettors. There are two predominant modes of operation available, mechanical and electrical. Mechanical systems are operated by pull cables and electric systems by a button. Either system will meet requirements, but the electric systems are more expensive. Whichever system you choose, the driver will need a trigger within reach. This will either be a pull cord or a push button. There also must be a trigger

Plumbed-in extinguisher system from Lifeline.

Extinguisher nozzle aimed at driver's torso.

safety first

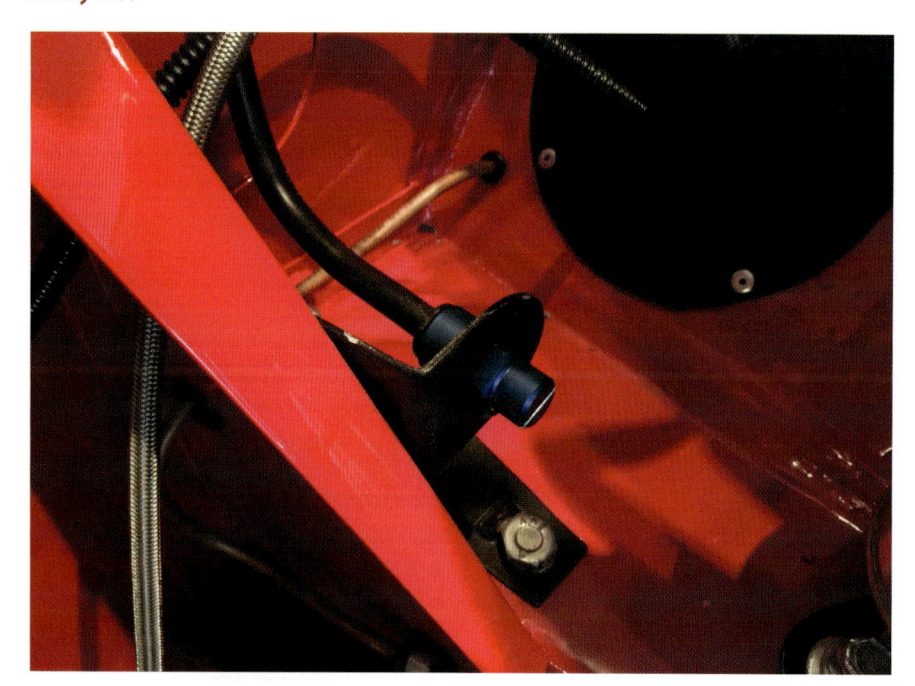

Extinguisher nozzle aimed towards the carburettors.

on the outside of the vehicle so that the system can be triggered by a marshal, but this will be covered in more detail later in the chapter.

The brands of fire extinguisher widely sold in the UK typically include Lifeline, SPA, Willans, Sparco and OMP.

We detail Lifeline here (see 'Useful Contacts') because the British Midlands-based company is a major global supplier at all levels of motor sport and we specify their products for our FIA historic projects. The specific model we like to use is the Zero 360 of 2.25kg capacity. Demon

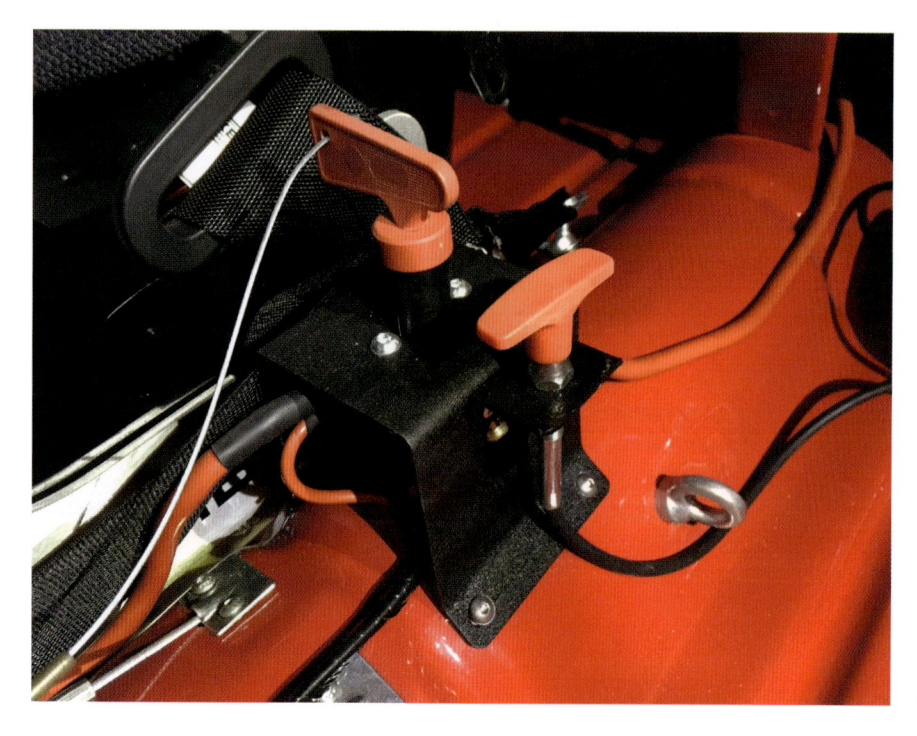

Master switch mounted inside the car.

Emergency pull cables mounted to the front wing.

Tweeks sold the Zero 360 models with 2.25kg capacity from just under £535 and £657 +VAT at press time, depending on the discharge operation via mechanical or electrical.

BATTERY AND CIRCUIT BREAKER

These items will be covered in more detail in Chapter 8 on electrical matters, but we will quickly cover the main points now. Any circuit racing vehicle must be fitted with a circuit breaker, which will not only isolate the battery but will also stop the engine. The circuit breaker or master switch must be able to be operated from the driver's seat, as well as from outside the vehicle.

The battery must be protected from shorting out and unless it is of a dry cell type it must be isolated from the driver either behind a sealed bulkhead or sealed-in battery box. Nobody wants battery acid spilling out in an accident.

TRIGGERS AND PULL CABLES

Both the circuit breaker (master switch) and the extinguisher must be able to be triggered from the driver's seat and from outside of the vehicle. Circuit breakers and extinguishers are both available with electronic triggers in the form of push buttons. Electronic systems are a lot more expensive, but they are a little more discreet. A standard FIA master switch will need to be mounted inside the cockpit within reach of the driver. A pull cable will need to be attached to the master switch and routed to the outside of the vehicle. The same type of pull cable will also be required to trigger the extinguisher.

Polycarbonate windows appear to have a black edge.

MSA Yearbook 2017 (K) Competitors: Safety External Circuit Breaker

8.2 The triggering system for the circuit breaker on saloons should be situated at the lower part of the windscreen mounting, preferably on the driver's side or below the rear window.

Triggers for both the master switch and extinguisher must be located together and be clearly marked with the appropriate symbols. The symbol for the external master-switch pull cable or push button is a red spark in a blue triangle. The symbol for the extinguisher is a red letter 'E' in a white circle. FIA-compliant safety stickers are available from any race supplier such as Demon Tweeks. We tend to use mechanical systems with our pull cables mounted on top of one wing near the base of the windscreen. You can locate your pull cables in the scuttle, but be careful that they do not interfere with the opening of the bonnet.

WINDSCREEN AND GLASS

From our opening chapter you will recall that the 'glass' is a regulated material. The front screen must be of

RACE WEAR

Whatever type of motor sport you plan to compete in, there will be requirements for what you need to wear. One area of competitor safety that has improved enormously over the years is in race wear. Back in the 1960s, there was not much to it. Racing suits were of a simple cotton construction. Fire-resistant Nomex had only just been invented by the Dupont Corporation and it would be some years before it was the standard for racing suits. Helmets are now regarded as the most important item in driver safety, but in the early 1960s they were also very basic, consisting of a simple fibreglass shell with padding for comfort. Nowadays, helmet design is very advanced, with very strict tests for approval.

Today's racing driver is now expected to wear much more than a fire-resistant suit and a helmet. Gloves and boots are mandatory, with many choosing to wear fire-resistant underwear, balaclava and now an FHR/HANS device. FHR are now mandatory when driving vehicles built after 1 January 1977.

Race-wear requirements will depend on the type of racing you do and the type and age of your car. Your national motor-sport governing body will ultimately decide what those requirements will be. In the UK, that is the job of the MSA. For circuit-racing a pre-1966 Mini Cooper S, the MSA regulations that will apply are as follows.

FIA-approved race gloves and boots.

MSA Yearbook 2017 (K) Competitors: Safety
Overalls
9.1 Clean flame-resistant overalls must be worn to cover from ankle to wrist to neck. Acceptable standards:
9.1.1 Racing: FIA 8856-2000
9.1.5 For FIA-standard overalls the homologation label will be stitched into the fabric of the garment or on a sewn-in label. For International use overalls must comply with: FIA 8856-2000.

Crash Helmets
10.1 Crash helmets bearing an MSA approval sticker must be worn at all times during training, practice and competition. The user

FHR and FIA-approved helmet.

must ensure that the helmet is to a standard currently specified (10.3.1), that it fits properly, is secured properly and that it is in a serviceable condition. It is strongly recommended that a flame-resistant balaclava, helmet bib or face mask also be worn.

MSA Yearbook 2017 (Q) Circuit Racing Drivers
10 A driver shall throughout the competition:
10.1 Wear properly fastened and positioned:
(a) A crash helmet to a standard specified in the current regulations and bearing an MSA approval sticker, which fits properly and is in a serviceable condition (see K.10).
(b) Goggles or visor of splinter-proof material (unless in a closed car with a full-size windscreen in use), sufficient to protect his eyes.
(c) Flame-resistant overalls which shall cover arms, legs and the torso up to the neck. The use of flame-resistant balaclava, socks, and underwear is strongly recommended (see K9). Flame-resistant gloves and shoes are mandatory.
(d) For events outside the UK the minimum standards would normally be FIA-specification personal protection equipment.
(e) An FIA-approved FHR device, fitted in accordance with K.10.4, is mandatory for drivers in Circuit Racing. With the exception of Period Defined Vehicles, for which it is recommended.

So, in short, you need a suitable helmet. For a car with a roof and a windscreen you can use an open-face helmet. A current list of the approved standards for helmets can be found in the *MSA Yearbook*. These standards will change over time, so your helmet will not last forever. Typically, you should get ten years from a helmet, as long as it remains in good condition and you do not have an accident. In scrutineering, your helmet will be given an MSA approval sticker. This sticker will cost £2. If a scrutineer finds damage to your helmet he may remove the sticker, which means you will be buying a new helmet.

You also need FIA-approved overalls. The current approval number is FIA 8856-2000, which will be embroidered behind the neck. Like helmets, the standards will change over time and the overalls need to be upgraded. The MSA also requires the wearing of flame-resistant gloves and boots. Flame-resistant socks, underwear and balaclava are not mandatory, but are strongly recommended. All of your race wear needs to be kept in good condition. If it does not pass scrutineering, it may have to be replaced before you are allowed to race.

FIA-approved racing overalls.

safety first

laminated glass and is available from many sources, including Mini Sport at a cost £42 +VAT. The side and rear 'glass' will not be either glass or the formerly ubiquitous Perspex, which can shatter into very sharp-edged shards. Today's racing cars are required to use polycarbonates. If you check an older car for the material used, a simple identification can be made from the fact that Perspex looks blue at the edges, whereas polycarbonates are black. The material used must be a minimum of 4mm thick to satisfy the FIA. The windows in our Appendix K build came from ACW Motorsport Plastics. Their Mk1 window kits start from £105 +VAT, depending on the finish.

FIA Appendix K 2017
7.3.6 … rear windows, door windows and quarter lights must be of safety glass or a rigid transparent material at least 4mm thick (FAA type material, e.g. Lexan 400, is recommended). Vertically opening side-windows may be replaced by horizontally sliding ones.

BONNET AND BOOT LID

Mundane but equally vital, remember to arrange a securing system for the bonnet. Yes, back in the day they really did race on standard centre catches with no back-up security: the rally guys always knew at least that an external leather strap was a good idea. Yet a large Finnish crest and consequent jump, or a hurried mechanic leaving the leather strap loose, could still result in the stubby bonnet flipping up to obscure the windscreen.

FIA Appendix K 2017
5.17 Bonnet (T, CT, GT, GTS, GTP)
5.17.1 Must be adequately fastened. The series production lock must be removed or made inoperative and be replaced by outside safety fastenings.

Bonnet security advice today is to use either bonnet pins (not particularly suited to period or Mini), or the effective leather straps. Terry springs (with rubber covering or

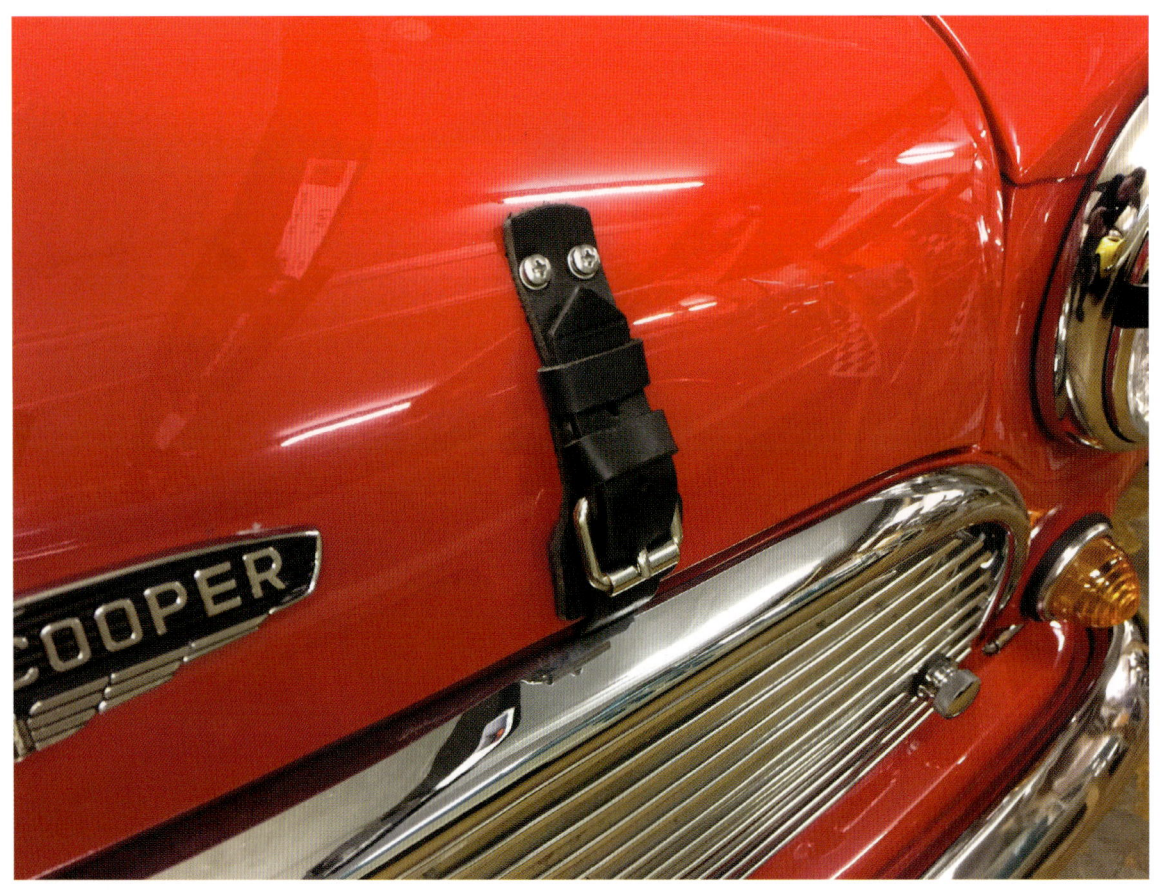

Leather bonnet strap on our Appendix K Mini.

naked according to taste) can also be placed on either corner of the bonnet's leading edge. Whatever your choice, all are catalogued by major suppliers. Expect to pay between £10–30 +VAT per item.

TOWING-EYES

Adequate tow hooks must be fitted so that you can be easily recovered from the gravel trap when you have an off. Regulations state that they must have an internal diameter between 80–100mm and that both are in a contrasting colour to the primary colour scheme of your Mini for fast recognition by the breakdown crew and marshals.

FIA Appendix K 2017
5.18 Towing-eyes
5.18.1 Except single-seat cars, all cars must have towing-eyes at front and rear. Their characteristics are as follows:

- internal diameter between 80mm and 100mm.
- they must be firmly fastened to the front and rear structures of the car.
- they must be located in such a manner that they can be used when a car is stopped in a gravel trap.
- they must be clearly visible and painted yellow, red or orange.

We prefer the use of a tow strap, but either strap or eye will suffice so long as it meets the regulations. Demon Tweeks list FIA-compliant towing-eyes at £25–30 +VAT, with non-adjustable tow straps starting at around £10. Because there are no original manufacturer's pickup points for fixed towing-eyes, Mini racers use high-tensile bolts and single-hole location to the front and rear sub-frames.

OTHER SAFETY PRESCRIPTIONS

You will be required to fit an oil catch tank of at least 2ltr. All engine breather pipes will need to be plumbed into it. The last thing anyone wants is excess oil on the circuit. There are only two places to mount an oil catch tank on a Mini and that is either inside the right-hand front wing, or mounted to the right-hand inner wing inside the engine bay.

You must have working brake lights and a rear-facing red rain light. Details of the rain-light requirements can be found in Chapter 8 on electrical matters.

Maintaining an awareness of what is around you and what is coming up behind should be a serious safety concern for every driver. Regulations stipulate two rear-view mirrors with a combined glass area of 90cm^2. We will usually run a door mirror on each side of the car, as well as a large rear-view mirror, centrally mounted above the windscreen.

Tow straps must be in a contrasting colour.

safety first

All front lamps must be taped or covered. The tape is intended to stop large pieces of glass falling on to the circuit should you get a little too close to the driver ahead and break a glass lens.

The fuel system's safety measures are covered in depth in Chapter 7, but in brief it is required that a roll-over breather valve is installed in the fuel tank(s), along with non-vented fuel filler caps. Throttles should be fitted with an external return spring.

If you are covering the foot pedals with anti-slip tape, or arranging the cockpit controls so that you can reach them with a safety harness on – and retain maximum vision of vital instruments – the details are vital. The consequences of your damp race shoe slipping from bare steel brake pedal are obvious as soon as it happens to you. So learn as much as possible from more experienced competitors; it will avoid drama and leave you more focused on more rewarding racing.

Oil catch tank of 2ltr capacity mounted within the right-hand front wing.

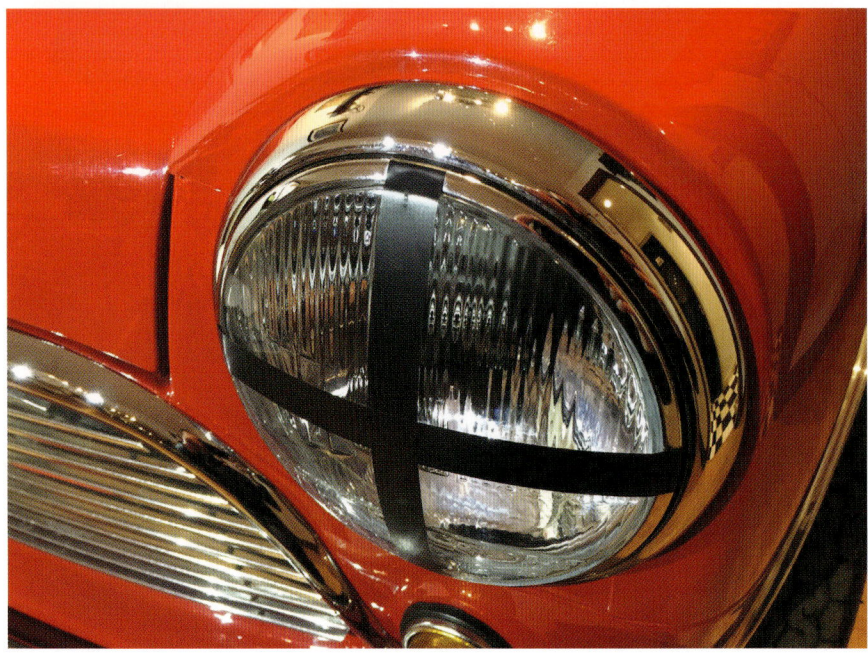

Black vinyl tape to secure the glass in the headlights.

The Mini's transverse-mounted engine and front-wheel drive subframe assembly was revolutionary in 1959.

4
subframes, suspension, steering, brakes, wheels and tyres

GENIUS BY DESIGN – SUBFRAMES AND SUSPENSION

The brilliance behind the design and one of the key aspects to the Mini's tight packaging was in the front and rear subframes – those steel structures at the front and rear of the vehicle that support all of the mechanical components. Maximizing the area available for the passenger compartment whilst maintaining the Mini's diminutive stature required a massive reduction in the space that was usually given for the engine and suspension. What has become commonplace in car design today was totally unheard of in 1959. A transverse-mounted engine driving the front wheels not only allowed for the vehicle to be smaller in size overall, but it also allowed for a relatively large passenger compartment.

The other important element of the Mini's space-saving design was the suspension. The Mini's designer, Sir Alec Issigonis, utilized the Moulton rubber cone in place

subframes, suspension, steering, brakes, wheels and tyres

Alex Moulton's rubber cone suspension.

In 1964, an effort was made to smooth out the Mini's ride by replacing the rubber-cone 'dry' suspension with the fluid-filled Hydrolastic system, commonly referred to as 'wet' suspension. The 'wet' suspension was not a popular choice amongst racers, as it was a little trickier to set up and was also heavier. The Hydrolastic system links the front to the rear via pipework under the body. Under braking, the front compresses and fluid is forced to the rear, which raises it up. Under acceleration, the opposite occurs – the rear compresses, which lifts the front of the car. This situation can make the car unstable, which is not ideal on the circuit. In the late 1960s, when this system had to be used, race teams would sever the link between front and rear to prevent this transfer of fluid from occurring, stiffening the suspension at the same time. Luckily the pre-1966 Appendix K Mini Cooper S was homologated in 1964 with 'dry' suspension, so we don't have to worry about any of this. The dry suspension set-up is a simpler system and hence more popular with racers.

of the traditional coil or leaf springs found on contemporary saloon cars of the time. The rubber cones are incredibly compact and are actuated by what is essentially a pushrod linked to the suspension arms. Anyone who has driven a classic Mini will know how well they handle, but also how the ride is a little bumpy.

The Mini's rear suspension uses a cantilever design with a longer pushrod acting against the rubber cone. The whole system lies horizontally underneath the boot floor, taking up a fraction of the space of a traditional rear-wheel drive, live-axle and leaf-spring arrangement found on most 1950s and 1960s cars. The front suspension is

Hydrolastic suspension introduced in 1965.

subframes, suspension, steering, brakes, wheels and tyres

The rear subframe mounted horizontally under the boot floor takes up very little room.

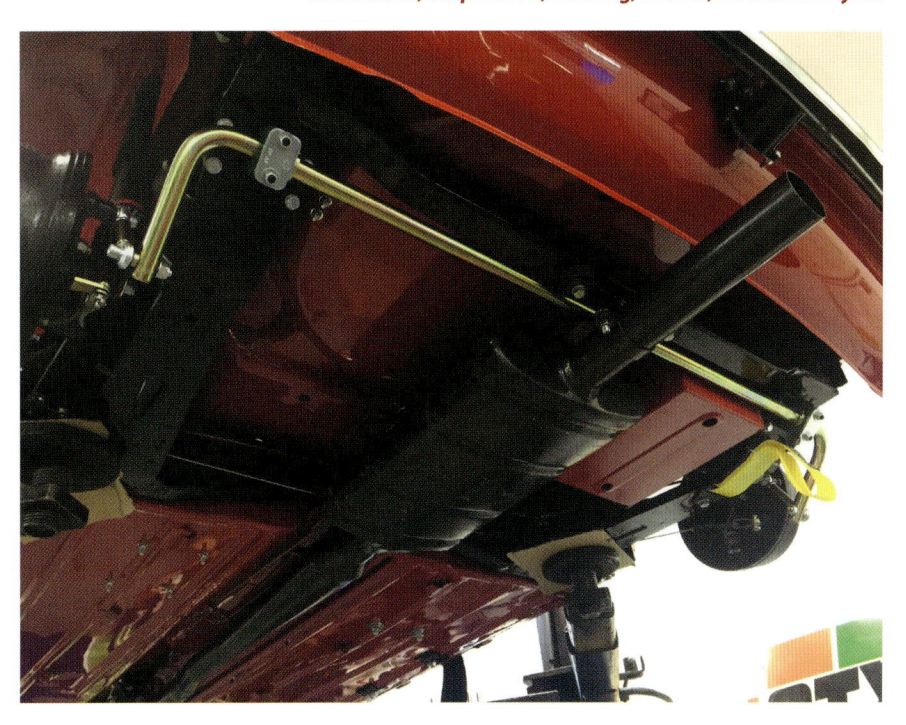

The front subframe supports all of the front suspension, engine and gearbox.

New rear subframe from Mini Sport.

New twin-bolt front subframe from Mini Sport.

59

subframes, suspension, steering, brakes, wheels and tyres

essentially an unequal length double-wishbone design with Moulton's rubber cones contained in two towers either side of the subframe. The engine sits directly on top of the gearbox and the whole unit is cradled in the front subframe.

Both front and rear subframes are well engineered and robust. The rear subframes suffer badly from rust, but good-quality replacements are readily available. You will need a pre-1991 style subframe, which at the time of writing cost around £160 +VAT. Early Minis, including the Mk1, use the twin-bolt front subframes. Twin-bolt subframes attach to the bulkhead cross member using two smaller bolts or studs, whereas the later subframes use a single larger bolt to do this job. Front subframes are made from heavier steel and are less prone to rust. However, if a new subframe is required they are also available for around £375 +VAT.

Bear in mind that Hydrolastic cars have slightly different subframes to the 'dry' suspension vehicles. If you have a 1965–7 car with Hydrolastic subframes, you will need either to replace the 'wet' subframes with suitable 'dry' counterparts, or convert the 'wet' subframes for use with the 'dry' rubber cones. (See the sidebar on how to convert the wet subframes to dry.) Like the body, you may consider seam-welding the subframes for additional rigidity. The Mini's subframes are made from a number of pressed-steel sections spot-welded together. Any point where the pressed-steel sections join can be seam-welded. The FIA states the following:

FIA Appendix K 2017

7.3.7 In addition for Competition Touring, Competition Grand Touring and Special Touring Cars:

…

It is allowed to strengthen the chassis and/or bodywork by adding material. The added material must follow the original structure and must be in contact with it at every point. Other shapes, profiles, gussets or bracings are not permitted unless it is proved they were used and authorized in period.

Most importantly when it comes to suspension in both Appendix K and the HSCC's Historic Touring Car regulations, the suspension pickup points cannot be moved and the wheel base must remain as original and for Appendix K so must the track. The FIA homologation form states that the wheel base must be 203.5cm, with a front track of 124.2 ± 1.1cm and a rear track of 120.7 ± 0.5cm. In the HSCC regulations, article 5.8 refers to suspension. It states that:

HSCC Historic Touring Car Championship Regulations 2017
5.8 Suspension
5.8.1 Permitted modifications
The pickup points and mountings may be strengthened but must remain as original in design and position. The type of suspension joints may be changed i.e. a rose joint may be substituted for a rubber bush but the wheel base must remain as per original specification (a tolerance of ± 1% will be allowed in establishing this measurement).

Front Subframe

The Mini's front subframe is a remarkable piece of engineering. It is responsible for supporting the engine and gearbox, as well as supporting the bodyshell and delivering power and steering to the ground. An original Mk1 subframe is going to be fifty years old now, so we would recommend that you have it media-blasted before a thorough inspection. Check for any damage or cracks and measure the subframe to ensure that it is straight and true. If all is well, you may choose to seam-weld it for added rigidity; other reinforcements such as gussets or lightening the subframe by drilling holes are not allowed for FIA Appendix K or HSCC vehicles.

HSCC Historic Touring Car Championship Regulations 2017
5.6 Bodywork
5.6.2 Modifications Prohibited
Internal panels, subassemblies and chassis members must remain as originally manufactured.

Assembly of the front subframe with new components before being fitted to the car.

Complete front subframe unit lifted into position.

We choose to paint our subframes in black 2-pack paint, although powder coating is also very popular. Once painted, it is time for assembly. It is easier to assemble the subframe before installing it in the car. Most of the suspension components used to build up a subframe are available new. However, there are some popular performance upgrades that are not allowed, so we will aim to outline what can and can't be done, starting with the rubber cones. Any original rubber cones may be as much as fifty years old, so the rubber will be dry, cracked, worn out and unsuitable for racing. These will need to be replaced with something new and better-suited to track use.

FIA Appendix K 2017 Appendix IX
2.4 Suspension springs
2.4.1 These may be replaced with others on condition that their type and number are identical to the period specification ones they replace.
2.4.2 The number of coils/leaves is free.

HSCC Historic Touring Car Championship Regulations 2016
5.8 Suspension
5.8.2 Prohibited Modifications
The original spring system must be retained though the spring rate itself is free.

There are uprated competition suspension cones made from firmer rubber available from Mini Sport for £42 +VAT each. These stiffer rubber cones are designed to keep the mini flat in the corners, but they will wear out in time. The competition cones are also slightly taller than standard, which as well as making the installation a little trickier will need to be compensated for when setting the ride height.

Next in line are the aluminium trumpets. For an FIA Appendix K Mini Cooper S you must use the original aluminium trumpets as opposed to an adjustable ride-height alternative.

FIA Appendix K 2017 Appendix IX
2.3 Spring supports
2.3.1 Adjustable spring platforms and ride height are forbidden …

Adjusta Ride suspension and competition rubber cone.

subframes, suspension, steering, brakes, wheels and tyres

The aluminium trumpets are not always available new, so you will likely need to use your originals. Adjustable ride-height suspension kits have long been available for the Mini and although they are not allowed under FIA homologation they can be utilized successfully during the set-up stage. When testing your completed Mini, you can make the necessary ride-height and corner-weight adjustments before removing the system and transferring the measurements to the aluminium trumpets. The aluminium trumpets must then be cut down to lower the vehicle and achieve the correct ride height. We are using Mini Sport's Adjusta Ride system for this purpose, available for £65 +VAT (part number SUSKIT5).

The top arms are connected to the aluminium cones via knuckle joints. These ought to be replaced as they are prone to wear. Top arms are cast iron and pivot on a shaft with needle roller bearings. The arms themselves are robust, but the bearings and the pivot shaft may need replacing, although the entire top arm assembly is available new. We've fitted new arms and pivot pins from Mini Sport retailing for £35 +VAT and £12.50 +VAT respectively.

Under the FIA's Appendix K regulations moving the suspension points to alter the geometry is strictly not allowed. Also not allowed are adjustable bottom arms. In order to achieve some negative camber you will need the 1.5 degrees fixed negative camber bottom arms available from Mini Sport for £32 +VAT (part number MSLMS0523). These fixed camber arms will allow you negative camber without pushing the front track over the homologated limit of 124.2cm ± 1.1cm.

New knuckle joint in top suspension arm connects to the Adjusta Ride and rubber cone.

1.5-degree negative camber bottom arms should keep the track width within the homologated tolerance.

Top suspension arm mounted in front subframe with pivot pin.

Polyurethane bushes fitted to the tie rod.

subframes, suspension, steering, brakes, wheels and tyres

Likewise, adjustable tie rods are also not allowed for FIA-spec vehicles, although they may be allowed in non-Appendix K race series like the HSCC's Historic Touring Car Championship. Rubber bushes support the bottom arms and the tie rods, although replacement items should be made from polyurethane. Polyurethane bushes have, for a long time, been available in bright colours like red or purple; however, they are now available in black, which may be preferable on a historic vehicle.

The front subframe is mounted to the body at six points. The front two points bolt to the front panel of the bodywork, the rear points mount through the front floor and the top of the subframe towers bolt through the bulkhead cross member. The subframe towers can be fixed with the original type bolts or studs, or alternatively there is a set of high-tensile ARP studs and nuts available for added support.

Rear Subframe

Rear subframes are often replaced due to their propensity for rusting away. If you are not using a brand new subframe, you must make sure that it is up to the job. Check primarily for rust as well as any cracks. Like the front subframe, you can measure it to make sure that it is square and true. You may wish to seam-weld the subframe before painting it, but, like the front, any further reinforcements or lightening are not allowed for FIA Appendix K vehicles.

New competition rubber cones should be used on the rear and, as we did with the front subframe, we have built the rear subframe up using the Mini Sport Adjusta Ride system, which will be used for the set-up of the vehicle before being swapped out for the original aluminium cones. The radius arms are cast iron and pivot around a large pin. The arm is supported by a bronze bush at one end of the pin and a needle roller bearing at the other. Repair kits are available that include new bronze bushes, bearings, pivot pin, seals, washers and nuts. If new bronze bushes are fitted they will require reaming to size. Alternatively, you can purchase complete radius arms ready to fit.

The pivot pin bolts through a fixed point on the inside of the subframe, with the outside point supported originally by a fixed bracket. For FIA Appendix K vehicles the suspension geometry is not allowed to be adjustable. However, as you will see at the circuit most people will use the adjustable camber and toe rear brackets, available from Mini Sport for £45 +VAT (part number MSLMS0510). Once you have tested the vehicle and found a suitable

For Appendix K, adjustable rear camber brackets must be fixed in position once set up.

Cast-iron rear radius arm.

Subframe mounting trunnions with polyurethane bushes.

CONVERTING HYDROLASTIC SUBFRAMES TO RUBBER CONE

REAR SUBFRAME

The easiest way to convert your Mini's rear suspension from Hydrolastic (wet) to rubber cone (dry) is to swap over the complete subframe from a dry suspension car. If, for whatever reason, you choose to convert your existing subframe, you will need a complete donor subframe from a dry car, from which you can scavenge the necessary parts. An otherwise rusty subframe will be fine. From your donor subframe, you will need to salvage the radius arms and handbrake quadrants unless fitting new, the aluminium trumpets and, most importantly, the domed locating plate from behind the rubber cone.

The radius arms on a dry subframe are virtually the same, but have a stud for the shock absorber on the back and use a different handbrake quadrant. The most important part in converting the rear subframe is the domed locating plate. Unlike on the front subframe, the rear subframe's rubber-cone locator is a dynamic part of the suspension. It incorporates a metal dome that protrudes into the open space behind the rubber cone, preventing the cone from collapsing. The rear suspension arms have a ratio of 5:1 and without the metal dome behind the cone the car's suspension would bottom out as the rubber cone compressed completely.

To change these plates over, first remove the domed plates from the dry subframe by drilling the spot-welds out, or by cutting the material around them. On the Hydrolastic subframe, each of the Hydrolastic displacer locating rings will need to be removed, replacing them with the rubber-cone locators from the dry subframe. These will need welding into place.

FRONT SUBFRAME

The front subframe is a little more straightforward, although a lack of access makes the job a bit trickier than it needs to be. The Hydrolastic displacer unit is located in the tower by a locating ring just like the rubber cone, only the displacer sits outside the locating ring and the rubber cone is seated around the inside. The locating ring for the displacer has four lugs bending inwards. In order to fit a rubber cone, it is necessary to remove these lugs with a die grinder. The rubber cone will then sit inside the ring. The last thing will be to drill the necessary holes for the dry subframe-type bump stops.

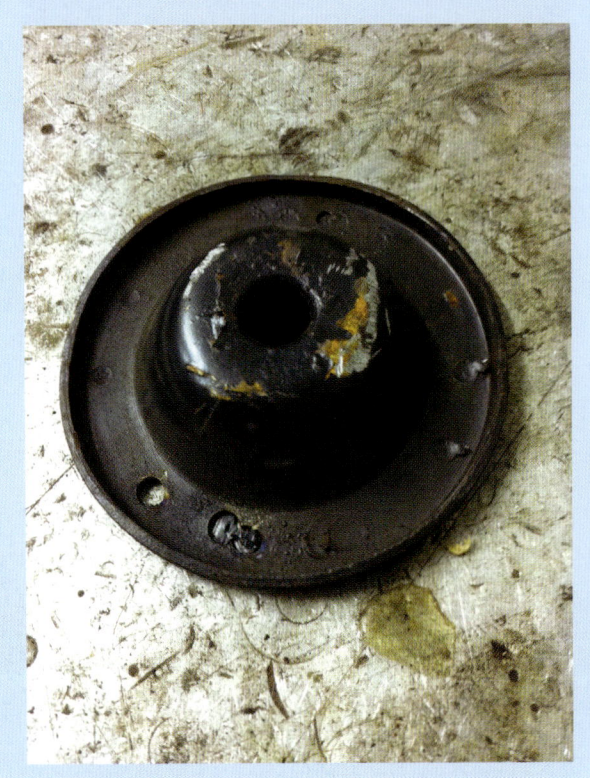

This domed plate prevents the rubber cones collapsing in the rear subframe.

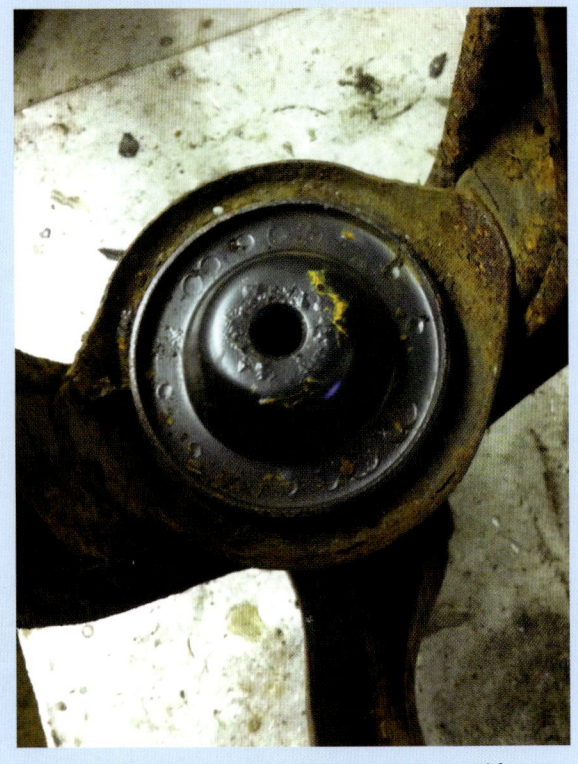

A domed plate needs to be utilized when converting a wet subframe.

subframes, suspension, steering, brakes, wheels and tyres

setup, the adjustable brackets can be fixed in place either by tack-welding or drilling and pinning with a bolt.

The rear subframe is mounted to the body in four locations by rubber-bushed trunnions. The Mk1 rear subframe utilizes four small trunnions rather than the two large and two small found on later models. Again, polyurethane bushes are a popular choice, but solid nylon bushes are also available and may offer a slight advantage. New billet steel trunnions are available CNC-machined in-house by Mini Sport and retail for £20 each (part number 2A5819).

SHOCK ABSORBERS

Shock absorbers can, and should be, adjustable and suitable for competition use. If you are building to FIA spec, they must be a steel-bodied twin-tube type. Remote reservoir-type shock absorbers are strictly forbidden and you will also get a slap on the wrist if you try to use an aluminium-bodied shock absorber. We have used AVO almost exclusively for some years now. We find AVO shocks provide great performance and good value and they are made right here in the UK. As we have already seen, suspension and shock-absorber pickup points must remain in their original locations.

FIA Appendix K 2017 Appendix IX
2.2 Shock absorbers
Adjustable shock absorbers of the same type as the period specification ones are permitted.

FIA Appendix K 2017 Appendix VIII
2 Suspension
2.1.3 The spring supports and suspension mounting points may not be changed in any way.

For other race series such as the HSCC's Historic Touring Cars things are a little more relaxed. In this particular series, anything goes.

HSCC Historic Touring Car Championship Regulations 2016
5.8 Suspension
5.8.1 The type, make and number of dampers is free.

The FIA homologation forms also allow for a rear anti-roll bar that you will definitely want to fit. The benefits of this will greatly reduce body roll, helping to reduce understeer by keeping all four wheels firmly planted on the track. It needs to be mounted to the rear subframe and, strictly speaking, should be non-adjustable and of a one-piece construction, although we would take a peek under the competition to see what is commonly used. There has been a lot of discussion about the need to have a one piece anti-roll bar, but up until recently there were none on the market. However, Kent Auto Developments (KAD) have recently stepped up to the plate and now produce a ¾in one-piece anti-roll bar for Appendix K Minis. It is

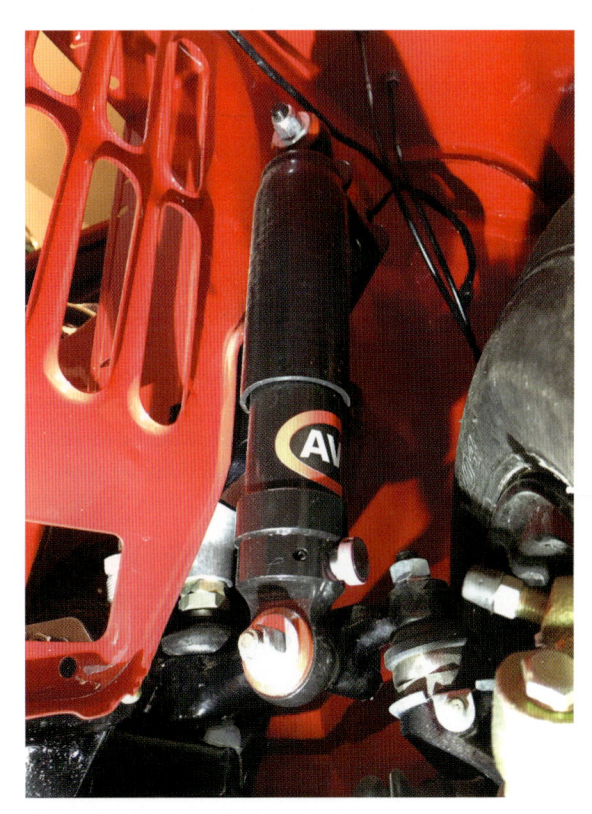

AVO steel-bodied adjustable shock absorbers on our racer.

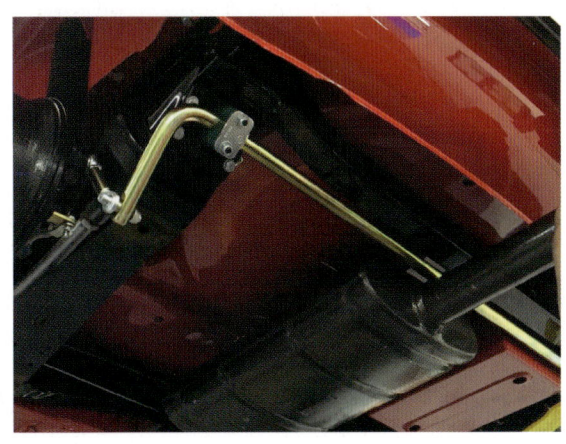

KAD's one-piece non-adjustable anti-roll bar for Appendix K Minis.

subframes, suspension, steering, brakes, wheels and tyres

available directly from KAD at £200 +VAT. It is a tight fit under the rear subframe, but there are a number of suitable products available from most major suppliers. The regulations state:

FIA Appendix K 2017 Appendix IX
2.1 Anti-roll bar
2.1.1 Fitting authorized, on condition that it does not constitute an additional wheel location device.
2.1.2 The anti-roll bar must not be adjustable and must be of one-piece construction from a solid bar.

CHANGING DIRECTION – STEERING

The challenge for all front-wheel-drive cars is applying power to the ground and steering through the same pair of wheels. The fitment of a limited-slip differential will improve a Mini's ability to power through corners, but controlling that turn will come down to a few simple components. Starting at the front, there will be a pair of steering arms bolted to the front hubs. Mk1 steering arms are specific to the Mk1 and need to be matched to a Mk1-type steering rack. However, you will likely be fitting a

Our new steering rack installed before the front subframe was fitted.

Longer track rod ends are needed when using negative camber bottom arms.

new steering rack, so will also need to replace the steering arms to those fitted from the Mk2 onwards. Changes were made to improve the turning circle and the two types are not compatible.

If, like us, you are building your car from a basic 850cc drum-braked model when you buy a complete 7.5in Cooper S disc brake package it will come with the Mk2-type steering arms, identifiable by two small 'ears' where the track rod end bolts through, and will match the new steering racks. It is worth mentioning that the steering rack should be fitted before the front subframe.

Since we are using the negative camber lower suspension arms we also need to use the extra-long track rod ends. Standard track rod ends do not have enough thread to use with the longer negative camber arms.

The Mk1 steering column must be retained. Original items can be rebuilt. The use of a drop bracket to lower

Steering arms mounted to front hubs.

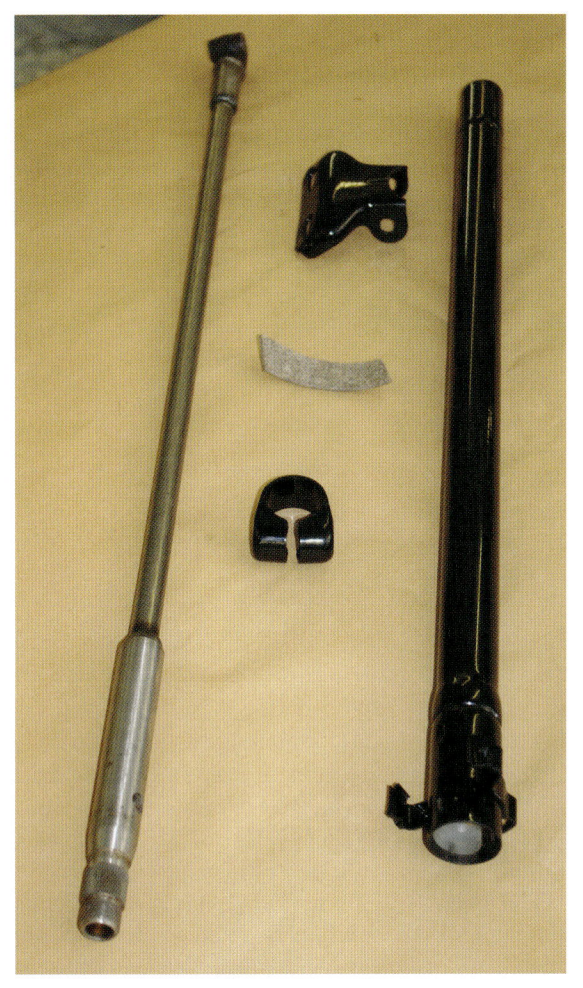

subframes, suspension, steering, brakes, wheels and tyres

The original steering column can be rebuilt.

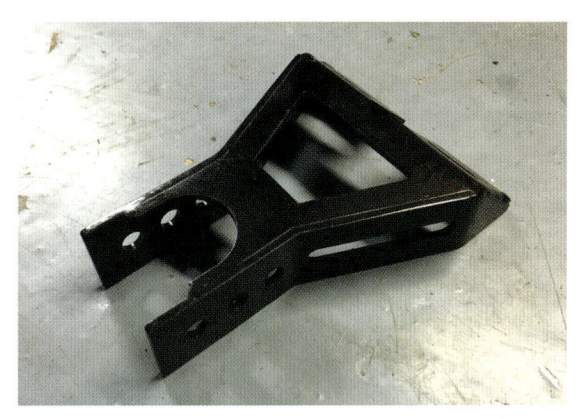

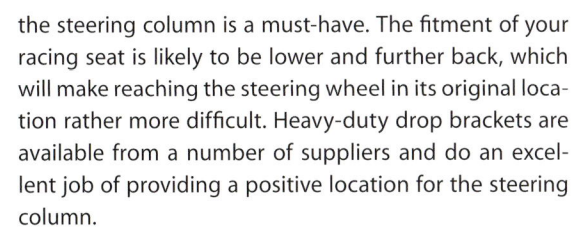

Drop brackets such as this one are used to lower the steering column.

Custom suede-trimmed Moto-Lita steering wheel.

the steering column is a must-have. The fitment of your racing seat is likely to be lower and further back, which will make reaching the steering wheel in its original location rather more difficult. Heavy-duty drop brackets are available from a number of suppliers and do an excellent job of providing a positive location for the steering column.

You may also find that the steering wheel is not close enough. Swiftune produce their own steering wheel boss, which brings the steering wheel 10cm closer. These are available in both a Moto-Lita nine-hole version and a six-hole version for Momo, Sparco, OMP-type steering wheels. The type of steering wheel and its size is up to you, but 13in seems to be the most common size in many historic racing Minis, with Moto-Lita providing the classic look. A lot of people like the feel of suede, which can be found on most new racing wheels. However, suede trim can also be custom-ordered on any Moto-Lita steering wheel if you want to retain a classic look.

STOPPING POWER – BRAKES

When the first Minis rolled off the production line in 1959 they had drum brakes fitted all round. With the Mini's diminutive weight and little 848cc engine, the drum brakes performed adequately, but as the interest in competition increased and with the introduction of the first 997cc Cooper models an upgrade to discs was necessary. The 997cc Mini Coopers came with a 7in disc brake set-up and although this was an improvement over the drums, it has gained a reputation for being rather less than adequate. The shortcomings of the 7in discs were, however, rectified in 1963, when the Mini Cooper S was released with a new 7.5in disc brake set-up. The 7.5in disc

subframes, suspension, steering, brakes, wheels and tyres

brakes perform admirably and if you are building to FIA specification the stock set-up is all you are allowed. The disc brakes on the front of the Mini have a wider track, so when the first Cooper S models came out, the 3.5in wide wheels had a deeper offset to compensate. In order to bring the rear track in line with the front, a spacer was incorporated into the brake drum. From 1959 to 2000, the rear brakes on all Minis are the same dimensionally and aside from the spacer in the Cooper S drums, the only variation among models is in the bore size of the wheel cylinders.

Those who were there will remember the charismatic driving style of John Rhodes smoking the tyres through the corners. He was famous for a driving style that used a lot of tyre and not a lot of braking. The brakes on a historic Mini are adequate, but where they may be lacking this is compensated for by the Mini's light weight and excellent handling characteristics. You can carry more speed through the corners than the larger, more powerful cars and it is this advantage that creates the David and Goliath battles we so enjoy. And in the wet with front-wheel drive that advantage is further exaggerated.

The hydraulic system on our early Mk1 Minis is also rather basic. The master cylinder is mounted vertically in the engine bay on the bulkhead cross member. A hydraulic line from the master cylinder joins a three-way T-piece that splits the braking between the front and the rear.

The rear brake line, originally running underneath the car, runs to a pressure-regulating valve mounted to the rear subframe and on to the rear wheel cylinders.

We are building a race car and like everything else the regulations must be applied, so let us look at what you are allowed to do with your brakes and what you are not. It is worth mentioning at this point that your brakes are also your primary safety measure. Under no circumstance must you ever use old or second-hand brake equipment on a racing car. You not only put your own life in danger, but all of those around you on the circuit. Master cylinders, wheel cylinders and calipers are all available new. All brake lines, hoses and unions should also be new when fitted.

Front Brakes

Like most other areas of the car, if you are building to Appendix K then you are stuck with what was homologated by the factory back in 1964. That means 7.5in Cooper S discs with standard cast-iron calipers.

FIA Appendix K 2017 Appendix IX
12 Brakes
The braking system must be entirely to period specification:
…
12.3 Brake discs must not be modified.

Cooper S 7.5in disc and iron brake caliper.

subframes, suspension, steering, brakes, wheels and tyres

The disc itself must be exactly as it was when these cars were delivered in the 1960s. So no vented, drilled or grooved discs are allowed – just plain solid discs. It is worth mentioning that solid discs with a high carbon content will be more stable at high temperatures with less risk of distorting. Mini Sport sell these for £30 +VAT each.

The only area that does allow some freedom is in the choice of friction material. Here you are free to choose whatever you like:

FIA Appendix K 2017 Appendix IX
12.4 The friction material and method of attachment are free but the dimensions of the friction surfaces must conform to the homologation form.

There are many, many brake pads to choose from on the market and much of your choice will come down to experience and personal preference. Typically, a set of racing brake pads will cost anywhere between £100–150 +VAT. We've used Mintex F2 and F4 compounds for many years on many different race cars. It is not a cheap compound, but it does perform well on circuit with good bite and stability. If you are on a slightly tighter budget, the Mintex 1166 pads are a good place to start. There are many other compounds available, all with slightly different characteristics. A popular choice for many racers has been the carbon metallics, which are made using a sintering process that fuses iron and carbon particles. They have very good bite and no fade, but disc wear is excessive. All of our brake pads are supplied by Questmead (*see* 'Useful Contacts').

If you plan to race your Mini in a less restrictive formula such as the HSCC, you will likely have more freedom.

HSCC Historic Touring Car Championship Regulations 2017
5.11 Brakes
5.11.1 Permitted modifications.
The braking system is free, together with modifications to the chassis/bodyshell necessary for the fitment of a pedal box. Brake cooling ducts and hoses are permitted, but they must not pass through the external bodywork or protrude forward of the bodywork.

The diameter of the discs will still be limited by your 10in wheels, but you will be allowed to fit discs that are vented, drilled and grooved, as well as four-pot alloy calipers. Depending on what type of wheels you run, it is possible to fit 10in wheels over 7.9in discs, instead of the standard 7.5in. Technically speaking, the rear brakes are also free; however, with the limited grip available from historic tyres and with such little weight over the rear wheels, there is really no need for rear discs on a Mini. There are many brake upgrade packages on the market that include the four-pot alloy calipers, for example Mini Sports 7.5in and 7.9in kits start at around £600 +VAT.

Rear Brakes

The rear brakes on all Minis are essentially the same, with the exception of the wheel cylinders. Over the years there were five different bore sizes of wheel cylinders fitted to the Mini. It is important to remember that the larger the rear wheel cylinder, the more braking force there will be at the rear and conversely the smaller the wheel cylinder, the less braking force. If you have any experience driving classic Minis, you may be aware of how it is often very easy to lock up the rear brakes before the front due to the back of the car being very light, especially in the wet or on a loose surface. Having the rear brakes lock up before the fronts is dangerous, as it encourages the rear of the car to overtake the front. Not ideal. You could experiment with smaller rear cylinders until you found a good balance, but this would be time-consuming and rather pointless, as the brake balance might change if it happened to be precipitating. Fortunately for us there is a better way. Our Mk1s were fitted with a pressure regulator as standard to reduce the braking force at the rear of the car. The FIA regulations state that it can be made adjustable:

FIA Appendix K 2017 Appendix IX
12.2 Pressure-limiting devices must not be fitted to the hydraulic braking system unless a period specification. Any device allowing the balancing of braking effort between front and rear wheels must not be operable by the driver whilst seated in the driving seat.

The standard pressure regulator valves are set to a fixed pressure limit by way of a spring. However, to keep the rear of the car firmly in control the pressure-limiting device needs to be adjustable. It is fairly straightforward to modify the original pressure regulators to be adjustable, or alternatively you can purchase one that has already been done. Part number MS72 uses the standard cast-body found on all Mk1s with a T-handle on the back for adjusting how much brake pressure is sent to the rear brakes. Having this adjustment makes the choice of rear wheel cylinder easy as you can

subframes, suspension, steering, brakes, wheels and tyres

simply adjust the regulator until a suitable front-to-rear balance is found. The only stipulation in the FIA regulations is that it must 'not be operable by the driver whilst seated'.

We've mounted ours in the original location on the rear subframe with a access hole drilled through the subframe mounting panel. To make adjustments, the T-handle is accessible from inside the car under the rear seat pan. As for the wheel cylinders, you can use the most common ¾in cylinders as the balance can now be adjusted until the rears no longer lock up. Depending on grip level, this balance may vary. If it is wet, you will want to reduce rear

Adjustable brake bias valve mounted to our rear subframe.

Iron rear brake drums with built-in spacer are required for Appendix K.

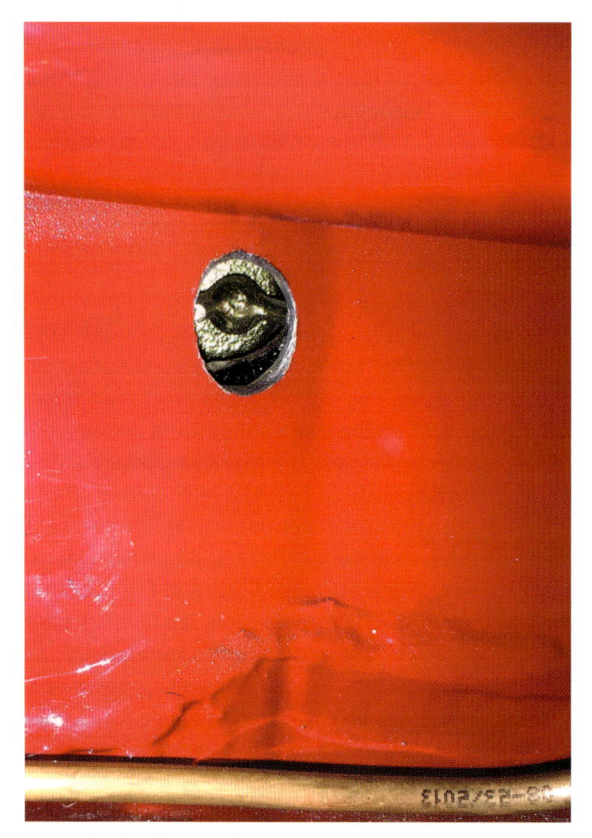

The rear brake adjustment is accessed under the rear seat pan.

Original tin master cylinders.

subframes, suspension, steering, brakes, wheels and tyres

Braided stainless-steel brake lines.

braking. If traction is high, you may want a little more so as to not overheat the front brakes.

Rear drums will need to be the type with the built-in spacers if you are to satisfy the FIA inspector. Aluminium 'Minifin' or 'Superfin' brake drums may be good for keeping the rear cool, but are definitely not allowed under Appendix K. As with the front brakes, alternative series regulations may be more lenient.

The master cylinder is the original type fitted and in the original location. It is worth mentioning again that the brakes are your number one safety item, so fit a brand-new master cylinder. It is not worth the risk of using an old or unknown item. The Mk1 Cooper S type master cylinders have a larger tin reservoir than those used on the 850cc drum brake models. This is to allow for the larger volume of fluid needed to displace the pistons in the disc brake calipers. They are available new from most suppliers. Mini Sport stock this item for less than £65 +VAT (part number GMC172OE).

Flexible brake lines should be made from stainless-steel braided hose. A braided hose kit can be picked up inexpensively from all major suppliers. Mini Sport stock Goodridge kits for around £35, which includes the front and rear hoses. The rest of the brake lines can be made up from $^3/_{16}$in copper tubing. Like the fuel line and battery cable, the front-to-rear brake line should run inside the vehicle for safety reasons. We ran our line through the front bulkhead, along the inner sill and back out through the subframe mounting panel.

The fluid we use in all of our race cars has always been ATE Racing Blue, as we have never found anything better. Racing Blue has recently been superseded by ATE Type 200, since the blue dye has been prohibited. The fluid is exactly the same, only without the blue dye.

WHEELS AND TYRES

Wheels

A Mini is a very small saloon car with a very small wheel – 10in in diameter was the original fitment from 1959 up until the 1970s. 10in × 3.5J steel wheels were fitted to all 850cc Minis, as well as the original 997cc and 998cc Mini Coopers. When the Mini Cooper S arrived with the 7.5in disc brakes, a deeper offset wheel was required. The Cooper S was fitted with 3.5J wheels with a deeper offset, with a 4.5J wheel available as an option. The wider wheels were the obvious choice for any sporting activity. Many early Cooper S racers can be seen sporting the 4.5J steel wheels up until the Cooper Car Company began producing the famous 'Rosepetal' wheel. The eight-spoke wheels were 4.5J wide and available in either magnesium or aluminium alloy. By 1965, nearly all racing Minis in the British Saloon Car Championship (BSCC) were running Rosepetals and the modern recreations remain the most popular choice in historic motor sport today. For any pre-1966 historic racing Mini, we will be limited to a 10in wheel, so let's look at what the regulations say and what options we have.

FIA Appendix K 2017
6.12 Wheels
6.12.1 All wheels must be period specification and of the original diameter used during the car's international life.
6.12.2 Rim widths must not be increased but may be decreased in order to accommodate available tyres.

FIA Appendix K 2017 Appendix IX
11.1 Wheels
Must be of a type homologated or to a specification available in the period.
11.1.1 The wheels may be reinforced, which may entail a modification of the attachment system provided such an attachment system was used in period for that model.
11.1.2 Competition Touring Cars and Competition Grand Touring Cars of Periods F and G1 may be equipped with 'Minilite' style alloy wheels to the original wheel dimensions, on condition that no alternative period specification lightweight wheel is available. The maximum allowed track widths must be respected.

Accepting these regulations would technically limit us to 10in × 4.5J steel wheels or Rosepetals only. Minilite wheels are specifically not allowed in period F if an alternative lightweight wheel is available; however, in reality you are unlikely to be reprimanded if you use them. The most popular wheel fitted is the reproduction Rosepetal. These modern reproduction wheels are 4.75in wide and have been designed to keep the track width

Reproduction Rosepetal wheels.

Reproduction of the Cooper S steel wheel in alloy.

within homologated tolerances. The wheels are supplied with a small spacer to allow clearance of the brake calipers on non-FIA vehicles, but for FIA cars you have to run these wheels without the spacers and grind a little off the calipers for clearance. Mini Sport keep these in stock with a price tag of £76 +VAT per wheel.

As an alternative to the Rosepetal, you could fit the 4.5J steel wheels. Under no circumstance would we recommend fitting fifty-year old originals and fortunately a modern reproduction is available. They look just like the originals and are available from Mini Sport from around £42 +VAT. Also available from Mini Sport is a very smart alloy reproduction of the steel wheel, which are perfect if you want that early factory look, but with a lighter, stronger wheel. These retail for £46 +VAT.

Alternative race series that run to their own regulations, such as the HSCC's Historic Touring Cars, do have a more relaxed outlook on wheel choice, although you will still be somewhat limited.

HSCC Historic Touring Car Championship Regulations 2017
5.12 Wheels/Steering
5.12.1 Permitted options
Wheel widths are free.
5.12.2 Prohibited options

subframes, suspension, steering, brakes, wheels and tyres

The diameter of the road wheels must conform to the original showroom diameter plus or minus 1 inch, or the diameter homologated within the cut-off date.

All four wheels must be of the same diameter during practice and during the race.

Wheels and the tyres fitted to them must be housed within the original bodywork. This is interpreted as the tread must be covered as seen from above though sidewall bulge may be uncovered.

Split-rimmed wheels are prohibited. It is recommended that all road wheels used are of period appearance. e.g. Weller Historic, Minilite or original steel.

The regulations allow you to go up 1in on wheel diameter but there are of course no 11in wheels and tyres available. Wheel widths may be free but the tyre must be housed within the original bodywork which will realistically limit you to 5in width at the very most. The HSCC also permits you to fit Minilite style wheels.

Tyres

To think of tyres and racing a Mini Cooper S it is impossible not to picture John Rhodes shredding Dunlops in a cloud of smoke. For all FIA Minis in our chosen period F there is no tyre choice. The FIA has it all wrapped up and Dunlop is the only tyre available to you.

FIA Appendix K 2017
8.2.3 Period F cars must use Dunlop Vintage, 'L' or 'M' section racing tyres in tread pattern CR65 or earlier and 204 compound or alternatively may use 404 compound if the race is declared wet.

The regulation tyres are Dunlop CR65 5.00 L 10, available in the UK from HP Tyres for £126.25 +VAT each at the time of writing. Depending on your driving style and how many races you do, it will probably be necessary to buy a couple of sets or more each season. Those at the

John Rhodes in a cloud of smoke.

subframes, suspension, steering, brakes, wheels and tyres

top or those who can afford to will fit fresh tyres more often. The HSCC's Historic Touring Car Championship also uses the Dunlop tyre, although the Classic Sports Car Club's (CSCC) 'Swinging 60s' series also allows the use of E-marked Yokohama tyres, as well as the Dunlops. Knowing what series you want to run with will determine what tyres you have to use.

Many of the top racers claim to improve lap times and longevity by buffing or shaving their tyres. Buffing tyres basically involves shaving off some of the tread. Doing this achieves a few things – the now shallower tread block moves a lot less than the original tall tread block and thus generates less heat. Overheated tyres will lose grip and wear out more quickly. Reducing the temperature of your Dunlop tyres helps to improve grip and also helps the tyre to last longer. The other benefit of buffing your tyres is to true them. Some people feel that the current Dunlop historic tyres are not always completely round.

Dunlop CR65 tyres are required for Appendix K Minis.

Non-buffed Dunlop CR65.

Buffed Dunlop CR65.

5

gearbox, differential and drivetrain

POWER TO THE GROUND

We have seen how Issigonis applied his engineering genius to the subframes and the cunning suspension arrangement, but another significant space-saving design was to be found in the relationship between the engine and the gearbox. Placing a transversely mounted engine directly above the gearbox and allowing both units to share the same oil was revolutionary in 1959 and made for an enormous saving of space. Not only could the front of the car be of greatly reduced proportions, but the given area for the passenger compartment could be further maximized. Without a gearbox and prop shaft running under the car and with the two isolated subframes at the front and the rear, the floor of the car could be lower, allowing those on board to have considerably more room. The overall proportions of the Mini could be minimized without compromising passenger comfort. The transverse engine, front-wheel drive concept has been one of the most influential in the history of car design and continues to be the standard layout for most small and medium-sized saloons.

Mounting the engine on top of the gearbox was never going to be easy. What would have been a linear transmission of power in a conventional longitudinal layout now had to exit the engine stage right, drop down half a foot and head back through a gearbox in the opposite direction. Being front-wheel drive, the gearbox also had to accommodate the final drive and differential, with an output to each of the front wheels. There was also the small problem that the gearbox was no longer positioned between the front seats, with the gear lever within easy reach of the driver. On the earliest Minis this gear-lever problem was solved by an extra-long lever protruding from the bottom of the front bulkhead, colloquially referred to as a 'magic wand' or 'pudding stirrer'.

There is a great deal of functionality contained within an extremely small area. This tightly packaged drivetrain is responsible for getting all of the power to the ground and it does so remarkably well. A design, intended to create a cheap and efficient family saloon, just happened also to produce a car with exceptional handling and performance potential and created one of the most entertaining vehicles in motor-sport history for both driver and spectator. In the hands of John Rhodes, those ravenous front wheels erupt clouds of smoke as the rest of the car was dragged around behind. Front-wheel drive may be seen as compromised when it comes to performance, but the Mini could hold its own against more powerful rear-wheel drive machines in dry conditions and when it rained it was in a class of its own. The Mini's drivetrain may be compact and it may be powering the front wheels rather than the rear, but it is perfectly adept at getting the power to the ground effectively, which makes an enormous difference to lap times. It does not matter how

The 'magic wand' gear lever was standard for 850cc Mk1 Minis.

75

gearbox, differential and drivetrain

John Rhodes' smoking tyres lead the way.

much power your engine may produce, as you will only be able to use as much as your drivetrain can deliver to the ground.

Cars from 1959–67 only had synchromesh on second, third and fourth, with selection made by the 'magic wand' gear lever. This long gear lever came directly out of the back of the gearbox, providing a gear change that was slow and a little vague at best. The introduction of the Mini Cooper in 1961 brought with it the development of the 'remote' gearbox. An aluminium casing mounted directly to the back of the gearbox and running under the car brought the gear lever back towards the driver. The gear lever was connected directly to the gearbox via a metal selector rod, making for a much quicker and more accurate shifting experience. Thanks to BMC's Special Tuning Department, the availability of close-ratio gear sets and alternate final-drive ratios added significant performance gains for the Cooper and Cooper S. The Mini's drivetrain utilizes unequal-length driveshafts to deliver the power to the wheels.

To allow for the suspension's travel, most of the original Mk1 vehicles utilized a flexible rubber coupling to connect the driveshaft with the gearbox's output. With the Mini Cooper S, and also fitted to automatic gearbox vehicles, came the famous Hardy Spicer universal joints. Not only were the Hardy Spicer joints stronger, but they used a flange to mount to the gearbox outputs, which meant that the driveshafts were easily separated for quicker engine changes in a competition environment. Eventually, synchromesh would become available on all four gears and from 1973 the 'remote-change' gearbox was replaced with what is commonly referred to as the 'rod-change' gearbox. This gearbox did away with the long aluminium housing and instead utilized exposed linkage rods to connect the gear lever with the gearbox casing. In the context of this book we will only be concerned with the earlier 'remote-change' gearbox, but there are a few different types and there will be some modifications required.

For a pre-1966 Appendix K Mini Cooper or Cooper S, the gearbox itself must be of the remote type. The original Cooper S gearbox was of the three-synchro type. The casings with casting numbers of 22G190 and 22G333 are quite rare and highly desirable for the purists' restorations. The availability of straight-cut gear sets for the three-synchro remote gearboxes is limited, so they are not often utilized in race cars. Most people will use the four-synchro remote gearboxes as they are far more common. Although any remote gearbox casing will satisfy the FIA, the gearbox casing that most people will want to use is the four-synchro 22G1128. If you are building to HSCC regulations it will still be necessary to start with a remote-change casing. Now that you have got your gearbox, let's look at what goes inside.

Straight-Cut Close Ratio

You will want to use a close-ratio gear set in your racing Mini. A race engine with a race camshaft will deliver its

gearbox, differential and drivetrain

Four-synchro remote gearbox casing with casting number 22G1128.

Four-synchro remote gearbox with straight-cut close-ratio gears.

Steel competition baulk rings from a synchromesh gearbox.

Dog teeth of dog-engagement gear set.

power high up in the rpm range and the power band will tend to be somewhat narrower. For example, a full race camshaft profile will start producing power from 3,000–4,000 rpm, with peak power above 6,000 or 7,000rpm, whereas a standard road camshaft will start making power virtually from idle. The narrow power band of the race camshaft requires closer gear ratios to help keep the engine in that narrow power band. By having the ratios closer together, the engine will remain closer to peak power and be prevented from dropping 'off cam' when changing up gears.

Except for the original, and very rare, 1275GT gear set, all new close-ratio gear sets available today will also have straight-cut teeth rather than the helical-cut teeth of a standard gear set. Straight-cut teeth are not inherently stronger. They will only be stronger if they are made from a stronger material. The purpose of straight-cut teeth is to reduce the contact area between the teeth, reducing friction and thrust loading and ultimately reducing power loss through the transmission.

The three-synchro and four-synchro gearboxes have different internals and are not interchangeable. If you have a three-synchro gearbox there is really only one option for a straight-cut gear set to Special Tunings close ratios. There are far more people manufacturing close-ratio gear sets for the four-synchro box and with a wider range of ratios. When considering which gear set to choose, the first option will be between synchromesh and dog engagement. This decision will likely be made by budget or regulations. For those who are not familiar with the difference, a brief explanation follows.

A synchromesh gearbox uses bronze collars known as baulk rings. When shifting gears the gear selector will act on the baulk ring, which will in turn apply pressure to the gear being selected. The baulk ring, or synchro, uses friction to bring the gear up to speed to synchronize,

77

gearbox, differential and drivetrain

allowing for a smooth gear change. Gear changes with synchromesh can be a little slower and always require the use of a clutch.

The baulk rings, or synchro, also wear out and will need to be replaced from time to time. With a dog-engagement gearbox the gears are engaged by way of large square teeth, or dogs, without the use of baulk rings to synchronize speed. Fast and precise gear changes are required, but it is also possible to change up without the clutch. If you pre-load the gear lever, a quick lift of the throttle will release the engine load from the gears, allowing the change to be made.

A dog-engagement gear set will offer greater performance, but it can cost two or three times more than a synchromesh set. Strictly speaking, if you are building to FIA regulations the 'dog box' is prohibited, although many do get away with using them. The regulations state:

FIA Appendix K 2017 Appendix VIII
8 Transmission/Clutch/Gearbox and Final drive
8.2 Gearboxes in which gear selection is made with dog clutches are not permitted.

FIA Appendix K 2017 Appendix IX
10 Transmission
10.1 Gearbox
Only a gearbox (manual or automatic) and the ratios therein which are in the period specification may be used. Helical-cut pinions may be replaced with straight-cut ones.

The FIA states quite clearly that a dog-engagement gearbox is not allowed, but it is unlikely anyone will ever take a look inside. Likewise, a five-speed gear set is not allowed, as the Mini was never homologated with one. If you are building a car to race with the HSCC then things are a little different.

HSCC Historic Touring Car Championship Regulations 2017
5.9 Transmission
5.9.1 The internal parts of the gearbox are free.

For our race-car build, we are using a 22G1128 gearbox casing with a synchromesh gear set, as stipulated by Appendix K. There are a number of synchromesh gear sets with various ratios available from all of the major suppliers. When we look at the FIA Homologation form 1300 for the 1275 Mini Cooper S we can see that BMC had a lot of ratios homologated. Strictly speaking for an Appendix K Mini, you will need to use the ratios from this form. However, when looking at what good-quality kits are available, each has slight differences in ratio and many will be slightly different to what is homologated, but is quite unlikely that anyone will ever check. At the time of writing, synchromesh close-ratio gear kits start from around £270 +VAT, going up to almost £600. You will also need competition baulk rings at around £25 each and a competition layshaft spindle at around £30. It is relatively simple to use the later style rod-change A+ gear sets along with the thicker, three-step, layshaft spindle. A slight modification needs to be made to the casing to allow the three-step layshaft spindle to fit. Dog-engagement gear kits are considerably more expensive, costing around £1,600 +VAT.

One other important component that will be required is a central oil pickup. Although it is part of the oil system, this has to be fitted whilst building the gearbox. As the gearbox casing is also the engine's sump, the engine's oil system is fed from the bottom of the gearbox through a pipe. Standard gearboxes have a pipe that draws oil from the right-hand side of the gearbox. In right-hand bends, the oil will be drawn away from the pickup pipe, leading to oil surge and starving the engine of oil. This can be remedied easily by fitting a central oil pickup pipe, which will draw oil from the centre of the gearbox.

DIFFERENTIAL

Now that you have selected a gear kit it is time to look at the differential and the final drive. This is arguably the most critical component in getting power to the ground. The differential splits the power and sends it out to each

A central oil pickup pipe must be installed when building the gearbox.

gearbox, differential and drivetrain

Limited-slip differential with Hardy Spicer output flanges.

of the front wheels. Most production road cars, the Mini included, are delivered with an open differential. This device allows for the outside wheel to rotate faster than the inside wheel when cornering. When a vehicle is cornering, the weight of the vehicle is transferred to the outside of the turn. Without any weight over the inside wheel, an open differential will allow that wheel to spin up. With most of an engine's power lost into spinning-up the inside wheel and the resultant loss of traction, the front of the car will push wide and its corner speed will be compromised. We need to maintain traction in order to maintain corner speed. To solve this problem, a limited-slip differential (LSD) is used.

There have been many types of LSD produced for the Mini over the years, but the most common is the clutch-plate type, often referred to as a 'Salisbury', or plate-type differential. At the centre of an LSD is the same differential gear mechanism found in an open differential, but the outputs have to go through a series of clutch plates. The clutch plates provide friction, which slows down whichever wheel wants to spin up, thereby allowing less power to be wasted and more power to be transferred to the ground. The clutch plates are engaged by angled slopes or ramps. The angle of the ramps will determine how aggressively the LSD is engaged. The more power that is applied, the more pressure is applied to the clutches.

Different ramp angles are used for a road car, rally car or circuit racer. It is often said that driving a Mini with an LSD requires strong arms to hold it in a corner. Due to the front wheels having to do the steering and put the power down, the result of the resistance produced by an LSD in a corner will cause the steering to want to centre.

An alternative to the traditional plate-type LSD is the Automatic Torque Biasing (ATB) differential from Quaife Engineering. The ATB does not limit the slip through clutch plates or other means, but instead distributes torque to the wheel, with the most grip through a clever set of gears. The ATB does not pull on the steering wheel like a plate differential, which can make it much easier on the road. The downside of the ATB is that without a mechanism to limit slip physically, it can allow the inside wheel to spin if it does not have contact with the ground. For our build, we will be using a plate-type limited-slip differential. Whichever type you choose, a good-quality differential will cost in the region of £500–£600 +VAT.

FIA Appendix K 2017 Appendix IX
10.2 Final Drive
Only the ratios which are in the period specification may be used.
10.3 Differential
A limited-slip differential of a type conforming to a period specification for that model may be used.

HSCC Historic Touring Car Championship Regulations 2017
5.9.1 Final drive gears, differentials, shafts and bearings are free, subject to 5.(9).2.

For an Appendix K Mini this would technically exclude Quaife's ATB, although it would be a less likely choice for a serious competition car. Under HSCC regulations any differential would be allowed.

It must be noted that in order to fit most limited-slip differentials the gearbox casing does need a small amount of modification. To clear the LSD's casing, the inside edge of the differential bearing seat on the gearbox casing needs to be relieved. To allow clearance for the LSD's crown wheel bolts, the ribs on the inside of the differential cover also need to be removed. This can be done quite easily with a die grinder.

FINAL DRIVE

Next in the drivetrain is the crown wheel and pinion, or final drive. Selecting the correct final-drive ratio will make

gearbox, differential and drivetrain

A bevel is added to the inside edge of the bearing seat to clear the LSD.

The inside of the differential casing is relieved to clear the crown wheel bolts.

The other deciding factor that will affect your choice of final-drive ratio is at what rpm your car's power is and what its red line is. You might be running an all-steel bottom end with a full race or sprint camshaft that you are happy to rev to 8,000rpm, or you may have a slightly more conservative set-up with a more tractable camshaft that comes on at 3,000rpm but stops at 7,000rpm. Selecting the right ratio is all about drivability and there may be a certain amount of compromise – you want to be able to get down the straights without running out of revs, as well as getting through the corners without dropping off cam. You will probably find that most historic racing Minis in the UK will be using 3.9:1 and 4.1:1 ratios at all UK circuits.

Like the other ratios, there were a large number of final-drive ratios homologated with the FIA back in 1964, from 3.765:1 up to 4.786:1, but again like the gear sets you will find that what is currently available may vary slightly. For example, a 4.26:1 ratio with a tooth count of 15/64 was originally homologated. The equivalent from Mini Sport today is a 4.23:1 with a tooth count of 13/55. Today's 3.9:1 has a tooth count of 14/55 compared to the homologated 3.938:1 with a tooth count of 16/63.

For a long time, crown wheel and pinions have been available with straight-cut teeth. However, due to excessive wear most crown wheel and pinions now have teeth cut with a slight angle, referred to as semi-helical. It is worth mentioning at this point that standard crown wheels will not work with most LSDs. Due to the larger size of the limited-slip units compared to the original open-differential casing, the LSD crown wheels have a hollow centre like a ring gear. All of the major parts suppliers can supply you with any of the popular ratios. Mini Sport cut their own gears in their machine shop and offer good-quality LSD final drives for around £161 +VAT.

a massive difference to the ultimate performance of your Mini and will depend greatly on the type of racing you are doing and at what motor circuit. Selecting the correct ratio is all about keeping the engine in the power band and this will depend on how fast the circuit is. For example, for sprints and hill climbs where there are rarely any long straights, top speed will require acceleration through tight corners and short straights. A very short ratio like 4.9:1 will therefore be needed. This will keep your engine at a higher rpm and in the power band at relatively low speeds. For a large, fast circuit like Goodwood or Silverstone, a taller ratio like 3.9:1 would be more suitable, as this would keep the engine in the power band through large, fast corners and down the long straights. At a smaller circuit like Brands Hatch, where the corners are slower and the straights are shorter, a slightly shorter ratio like 4.1:1 would be more suitable.

A semi-helical 3.9:1 final drive from Mini Sport.

gearbox, differential and drivetrain

DROP GEARS

The first set of components in the Mini's transmission are the transfer gears, commonly known as the drop gears. The drop gears are a set of three gears that quite simply make the drop from the crankshaft down to the gearbox input shaft. There are a number of options available when it comes to choosing a drop gear set. Originally the drop gears had helical-cut teeth, but for racing purposes you will most likely want a set of straight-cut drop gears. The main advantage of straight-cut gears is a reduction in friction between the mating teeth, which in turn reduces the loss of power through the transmission. The teeth on a conventional helical gear are cut at an angle and therefore have a much larger surface area. The larger surface area and the angle of the cut mean that there is more metal in constant mesh and for longer. The result is a much quieter gearbox, but one that generates more friction and therefore more transmission loss.

The first of these gears is the primary gear. It rides on the crankshaft's tail and is directly connected to the clutch-driven plate by a large splined boss. The primary gear rides on a pair of bronze bushes, which have in the past been subject to failure due to excessive heat transfer from the clutch. When the bronze bush overheats it can pick up on the tail shaft and spin within the primary gear. The latest solution to this problem is the use of a floating front bush in the primary gear. It is also crucial that the primary gear end float is set up correctly in order to maintain reliable running and longevity for the bronze bushes. The correct tolerance is stated as 0.003–0.006in, but with the excess heat generated by racing it is prudent to err on the larger side. A wide range of thrust washers of various thicknesses is available to achieve correct tolerance.

The second transfer gear in line is the idler gear. Supported by bearings in the gearbox and transfer gear casings, the purpose of this gear is to reverse the rotation for the third and final gear. Most racing straight-cut drop-gear sets sold today can utilize an idler gear with its own internal roller bearing instead of using the needle roller bearings held in the gearbox and transfer-gear casings. This bearing arrangement reduces the risk of damage due to bearing wear. If you do use a standard type of idler gear, be sure to replace the needle roller bearings in the cases with every rebuild. Like the primary gear, care also needs to be taken to set up the end float properly on the idler gear. Thrust washers are available in a range of thicknesses to achieve the correct tolerance of 0.003–0.006in. Measuring the clearance of the idler gear with a feeler blade needs to be done with the clutch case trial-fitted before the engine is mated to the gearbox.

The third in the set is the input gear and it is connected directly to the gearbox input/first motion shaft. There is not a lot that is special about this gear as long as it is matched to your drop-gear set. Most straight-cut drop-gear sets are not interchangeable. The original pre-A+ gear sets used twenty-four-tooth primary and input gears, whilst later gearboxes used twenty-nine-tooth versions.

With some straight-cut drop-gear sets, it is possible to make fine adjustments to the gearing by altering the ratio of the drop gears. A standard set of drop gears will have a ratio of 1:1, with the primary gear and the input gear both having the same number of teeth. By changing the number of teeth on the primary gear or the input gear, the ratio can be altered, making the overall gearing taller or shorter. For example, a twenty-four-tooth primary gear and a twenty-five-tooth input gear will give a ratio of 1.0416:1. If using a 3.9:1 final-drive ratio and 1:1 drop gears at 7,500rpm in fourth, you would be travelling at 108mph. By using a 1.0416:1 drop-gear ratio with a 3.9:1 final drive, you would have a speed of 104mph at

Mini Sport straight-cut drop-gear set.

gearbox, differential and drivetrain

7,500rpm. If you used a final drive ratio of 4.1:1 with 1:1 drop gears, your speed at 7,500rpm would be 103mph. For our build, we will be using a set of 1:1 ratio straight-cut drop gears from Mini Sport (part number MS2048).

DRIVETRAIN

Limited-slip differentials require different output shafts from the standard open differential and you will need to select which type of differential output according to what type of universal joint you intend to use. Any serious competitor will use Hardy Spicer universal joints due to their strength and easy serviceability. Also, being flange-mounted makes for easier engine removal without the need to separate the driveshafts. The original Hardy Spicer output flanges had a larger diameter shaft than standard outputs. This meant that the differential side covers had to have a larger hole. The part number for these side covers is 22G419 for the original Cooper S part and 22G240 for the later replacement. Swiftune Engineering now make LSD output flanges with the smaller diameter shaft, so that you can use your original differential side covers.

Driveshafts are fairly straightforward. Competition driveshafts are again available from all the major suppliers. This is one area where you can apply the FIA's metallic freedoms.

Hardy Spicer output flanges.

FIA Appendix K 2017
3.7.4 Thus, for example, «aluminium» is metallurgically aluminium but may be of a different grade and contain elements not present in the original component …

So it is well within the rules to use higher-grade steel such as EN24. Mini Sport make just the pair for Hardy Spicer joints or rubber couplings priced at £180 +VAT (part number MS3341H/S). It is worth noting that although you will find many people who use original standard driveshafts with no issues, they have been known to shear.

Hardy Spicer universal joints connect the driveshafts to the gearbox.

gearbox, differential and drivetrain

Good-quality outer CV joints will cost you around £25 +VAT. You will need disc-brake type CV joints that are suitable for both the 7.5in Cooper S disc brakes, as well as the later 8.4in disc brake set-up. It is not worth trusting poor-quality or cheaper alternatives, as they will fail.

Remote Gear Linkage

The only thing left to consider now is the gear linkage. The remote housing is a simple casting and rarely sees any wear or damage. Most of the wear will be seen in the two bushes that support the vertical linkage rod that travels through the differential housing. These should be replaced (Mini

Mini Sport's competition half-shafts are made from EN24 steel.

Good-quality CV joint being installed in our race car.

83

gearbox, differential and drivetrain

Sport's part number is 105143). There were a few different gear levers originally fitted. The early Cooper S had a solid gear lever with a slight kink in it. Later gear levers had a rubber isolation bush at the base to help reduce vibrations transmitted from the engine. If well built, the remote gear linkage should provide a positive and slick gear change.

There are short-shift gear levers available if you wish, but it is not strictly necessary. When using a short-shift lever with a synchro gearbox, the faster shift can cause greater wear on the synchro rings. Most racers using a dog box also use a short-shift gear lever.

Remote gear lever housing for the four-synchro 22G1128 gearbox.

Short-shift gear lever in our race car.

The bronze gear linkage rod bushes in the differential housing should be replaced.

1293cc FIA race engine.

6. engine specification and guide to assembly

POWER POTENTIAL

The BMC-created A-Series engine dates back to 1956 and the debut of a 948cc unit for Morris Minor 1000 and A35 saloons, itself redeveloped from an earlier Morris Minor motor of 803cc. BMC employed it as a then conventional rear-drive power unit and the tough 4-cylinder with overhead valves (ohv), siamese-port cylinder head and a single SU carburettor delivered an economy-biased 37bhp. When the 1959 Mini used the A-Series as a front-drive revolution in 1959, it started life at 34bhp from just 848cc located transversely across the engine bay, atop the integral four-speed gearbox. The 998cc Cooper engines in race trim were capable of 90–95bhp. Our latest expectation with the larger 1293cc race unit would be around 120–125bhp.

In Britain today, and back in the late 1960s and early 1970s, the 1-litre Hillman Imp engine with its Coventry Climax ancestry, with major components in aluminium and a single overhead camshaft, simply generated more power (circa 100bhp+) than BMC's 998cc Cooper unit and in a lighter package than the Mini's ancient iron four.

engine specification and guide to assembly

The other factor, rarely mentioned, is that for all of the Mini's outstanding handling, the integral gearbox saps the amount of power transmitted to the road – plus the Imp's rear-engine layout with separated gearbox allows both superior traction and fewer frictional losses in the gear sets.

All is not lost, because at 1293cc Imp advantages disappear, as the motor is very tricky to push over 1150cc and was never mass-produced – or FIA homologated – for international motor sports. Thus the 1275 Mini Cooper S stays the choice for FIA/prestige events. Most (not all) Mini competitors in FIA formula tend to migrate to the bigger Mini motor.

The basic 998 Cooper is not a weak engine – far from it, but you just cannot get the power out of it that is needed now. A 970S may deliver a bit more power, but the cost and effort in locating a 970S block that will take a +20thou overbore to meet the capacity limit of 999cc or machining down the deck of a 1275 block and sourcing a 970 crankshaft and connecting rods is not cost/time attractive to the majority of historic category Mini racers. It would likely cost more to build a smaller capacity 970 or 1071 engine than it would to build the 1275, so not many people do it. The only real advantage is that the 1071 is homologated at 588kg (1,296lb), 32kg (70lb) less than the 1275.

Thus the 1275cc Cooper units stretched by +20thou to 1293cc, not the 998, 970 or 1071 smaller brothers, are our primary subject. The desired horsepower from this 1.3-litre A-Series would be the magic 125bhp, nearly 100 horsepower per litre. While there are normally aspirated road cars exceeding 100bhp a litre now, we are dealing with a strict set of regulations monitoring an economic motor design some sixty years of age.

The A-series has always been a popular target for the tuning and motor-sport community. Considering that its assembled features are now ancient in today's turbocharged 16-valve universe, why has it remained such an enduring competition and classic engine a decade after the demise of the last tangible Rover-MG link with the BMC era? A couple of contrasting A-words underline that continuing appeal: affordability and abuse.

Although the most successful specialists charged £20,000 or more for a drop-in race motor and gearbox in 2017, there are many cases of individuals preparing excellent A-series engines at more affordable rates. This has particularly applied in tightly regulated series, where DIY labour and detailing on a scale uneconomic for professionals working to a deadline help privateers to offset some of that pro-expertise. Some of them – notably David Vizard and Clive Trickey – wrote extensively in books and magazines on the A-series subject, now-deceased Trickey underlining the worth of his advice by driving and winning in his own Mini 850 within the tightly regulated Mini 7 Championship. Vizard has been a consultant on many power unit projects and the results of his work can still be bought today, notably in a road and rally exhaust system for Minis that is still retailed by Mini Sport.

Abuse? There has probably never been a production-racing engine that has suffered so much for so long at the hands of those with a discipline deficit alongside a lack of talent, yet the plucky old-timer comes back for more. That is assuming it has been properly screwed together initially and that excess enthusiasm has not led to really extreme exploration beyond designated rev limits.

All motor sports are demanding for preparation and race personnel and the Mini has lived longer than most rivals, so it makes sense when searching for specialized parts or modifications to note the names of those with hard-won experience behind them. If a Mini specialist started back in the heyday and is still supplying race skills/components that are used on the successful racers

Clive Trickey's famous 850cc race car on the cover of his book.

today, there is a good reason for such success survival. Your compulsory race weekends to check out the opposition will tell you who they are and at least put them on your shortlist for further investigation. Their prices may be higher, but be sure that they learned something worthwhile, the hard way!

There are a number of sources that earned their way into the present day over fifty years and there are plenty of younger outfits that do an equally effective job, but in engine building and motor component supply, there is more inaccurate talk than in any other aspect of race preparation. The A-series engine is an established legend with power, torque and durability parameters well established. Ignore the hot air, go and observe performance today to buy accordingly.

RACE ENGINE BASICS

We will deal with the major engine build components sequentially, but before we do, two repeated guidelines. Never forget, cleanliness is the only way to make a top race engine. Cleanliness in every aspect must be your priority – any dirt in a hand-built motor intended to live at 7,500–8,000rpm and 120bhp, instead of its old 1275 S production peak of 76bhp at 5,800rpm, could literally wreck it and your race. Secondly, lubrication is not just for the finished article, but also at every stage where new components are in trial-fit or final assembly. When in doubt, lubricate.

First consideration, as with any area of race-car construction, is the regulations. For any pre-1966 Mini race car regardless of which race series you choose to compete in the general principles of engine building will be much the same. Non-FIA race series may let you run a larger capacity or different carburettors, but apart from some material differences the engine itself will be much the same. For an FIA engine build you will need to consult Appendix VIII and IX of the FIA's Appendix K document. In the 2017 issue they start on pages 79 and 84 respectively. The first rules governing your Mini engine build will be found on page 68 in Appendix VII – 'Specific to Certain Cars'.

FIA Appendix K 2017 Appendix VII
BMC Cylinder heads bearing the casting number 12G940 are accepted as an alternative only on the 970cm^3, 1070cm^3 and 1275cm^3 Cooper S engines.
Following the remanufacturing of «Swiftune» 12G940 cylinder head, it is possible to use this replacement cylinder head for the 970, 1070 and 1275S, 1275 Sprite/Midget and the BL Marina. These cylinder heads must be marked visibly with the word «Swiftune» on their casting.
Cylinder block for the BMC Mini Cooper S – The following block (foundry No. 12G1279 as used in the Austin 1300 – Homologation No. 5335) is authorized as a replacement for the original block of the BMC Mini Cooper S.

In brief, this little excerpt tells us that we are not confined to using an original Cooper S engine block or the famous AEG163 Cooper S cylinder head. This is good news, because these items are rather scarce and more valuable to the restoration purist than the historic racer. Alternatively, the FIA has granted the use of later pre-A+ 1275 engine blocks from the 1275GT and Austin/Morris/MG 1300s. What you are most certainly not allowed to use are the far more plentiful A+ engine blocks from the Austin Metro.

At present, there is no supply of new engine blocks, but with early 1275 engine blocks becoming ever more scarce, this situation may soon change. A few variations of the 1275 block have been produced, but our preference is what is known as a 'thick flange' block. The 'thick flange' refers to the bottom of the engine, which bolts to the gearbox. The thick flange makes for a more rigid engine block.

The 12G940 cylinder heads are relatively bountiful and can be found on most 1275 A-Series or A+ engines, including MG Midgets and Austin Metros. Be careful to inspect for cracks. All of these heads have been used and abused for a number of years, so it is best to make sure

Pre-A+ 1275 engine blocks can be identified by their lack of external webs in the casting and the non-Cooper S 1275 engine block has no tappet chest covers on the back.

engine specification and guide to assembly

that you have a good one before spending out on the porting. If you can afford it, Swiftune's new cylinder head castings have been approved by the FIA for use in historic racing Minis.

MAJOR COMPONENTS

Let's take a look at what makes up a historic racing A-series Mini engine and what the FIA's regulations have to say about what we are and are not allowed to do. First of all, remember the material regulations set out in Appendix K.

FIA Appendix K 2017
3.3.5 Unless otherwise specifically authorized by these regulations, any component of a car must have identical dimensions and material type must be the same to the original part. Evidence of this must be provided by the applicant.
3.7.3 The term «material type» indicates the same material, but not necessarily to the same specification.

For an Appendix K engine build the material used for a component must remain the same, although the specification of that material can be changed. For example, the original valve spring caps are made from steel. Therefore you will not be allowed to use titanium valve spring caps, but you can use spring caps made from EN24 billet steel. This applies to all components, so no aluminium pushrods or rocker arms either. Let's move on to further engine stipulations.

FIA Appendix K 2017 Appendix IX
5. Engine
5.1 Reboring
Allowed to a maximum oversize of 1.2mm of the original bore, provided that the increase does not change the period capacity class of the car.
5.2 Cylinder head and block
The compression ratio may be modified by machining the face of the block or cylinder head and/or by omitting the gasket or using a gasket of different thickness.
Only homologated rocker arm assemblies may be used.
5.3 Pistons, camshafts and valve springs
They may be altered, or alternative pistons, camshafts and valve springs of different specification or manufacture may be used, provided that the number employed does not exceed that of the homologated engine.

Block

Our engine build commences with the biggest single casting, the cylinder block. We are starting with a thick flange pre-A+ engine block. The regulations allow for a maximum overbore of 1.2mm, or approximately 50thou. However, the capacity class of our 1275 Mini Cooper S is up to 1300cc. The maximum overbore without exceeding 1300cc is +20thou, giving us a total displacement of 1293cc.

Our first step for any engine block is a strict visual inspection and measurement. We want everything straight and true with no visible damage: the top of the block will be checked individually, as it should conform to the correct deck height before any skimming that may be necessary for absolute true height versus the chosen pistons, along with the likely compression ratio. The cylinder bores need close inspection, as we would ideally like to avoid using liners. Cylinder liners can be used quite successfully if they are installed correctly, but if there is any chance of the liner moving it can wreck the whole engine, so finding a block at standard bore with minimal wear is most desirable.

Next step is the overbore. Just 20thou oversize will move it from production 1275cc to 1293cc, the upper limit within a 1300cc class. Any good machine shop should be able to bore and hone your block from around £100 +VAT. When you take your block to be bored, you will also need to take the piston you intend to use and specify that this will be a race engine. A racing A-series will run a slightly greater tolerance between the piston and the bore than an engine destined for road use. By having the piston you intend to race with, the machine shop can set this tolerance more accurately.

12G940 cylinder head casting.

engine specification and guide to assembly

ARP main cap studs will hold the crank securely.

It is worth mentioning at this point that a cast-iron engine block will have a certain amount of flex at high rpms. Excessive flex of the block and crank will cause undue wear of the main bearings, so improving rigidity is worth considering. However, there are pros and cons involved with any treatment of the main caps and different engine builders will have different opinions on what is best. There are many race-engine builders who will simply use the original cast main caps without experiencing any issues. Most issues will likely occur through over-revs and aggressive downshifts causing the crank to whip. A good driver with smooth control of the engine should not experience these issues. If you do use the original main caps, using a high-quality washer is recommended, such as those available from ARP, or better yet a set of ARP main studs.

The next most basic attempt to stiffen the block is with a centre main strap. This is quite simply a machined block of steel that is strapped to the top of the centre main cap with longer bolts to hold it all together. The top of the centre main cap needs to be machined flat and to do the job properly the centre journal line must be honed with the strap in place, as the addition of the strap can distort the journal ever so slightly.

The next step up from the strap is to use a steel centre main cap. This is a complete main bearing cap machined from a steel billet. It will be an improvement in rigidity over the strap, but it does mean that the block will need to be line-bored. This means that the journal for the crankshaft must be machined round, in line and to the correct tolerance. The accuracy of this job is critical and the machining can therefore be expensive. Most of the cost of line-boring is in the set-up, so ultimately the cost-saving of fitting one steel main cap over all three may be negligible in the end. The centre cap on its own will cost around £80–100, whereas a complete set of three will cost around £220 +VAT. The machining to line-bore the caps will likely cost another £200, whether you are replacing just the centre cap or all three.

Mini Sport's centre main strap.

engine specification and guide to assembly

Another popular trick to improve the rigidity of the bottom end is to enlarge the size of the bolts used to attached the gearbox from ¼in to 5/16in. This is a relatively simple job that requires drilling and tapping the larger holes in the block and drilling out the holes in the gearbox.

11 STUDS

An important step in block preparation is to drill the block and the head for 11 studs, if they are not already of the 11 stud type. The Cooper S was the first to employ 11 cylinder head studs over the original 9. This process should be left to a professional engineer. Any machine shop familiar with the A-series engine should be able to carry out this task for you.

Cylinder Head

The next major iron casting is the cylinder head. As a major source of bonus power when modified, more rubbish is talked about this Mini motor part than is decent. Headwork comes in the 'hideously filthy' job category and finding horsepower is really a bit of a black art, requiring as much creativity as it does science. Currently there are veterans of the Mini race-tuning trade who have records to prove their effective workmanship. You can buy ready-to-run heads from outfits like Mini Sport, but you may want to research some of the established engineering specialists to see what they can deliver – Janspeed and Longman still have guys on their workbenches with painfully earned A-series cylinder-head pedigree. We are lucky enough to have a close association with a true artist with a long list of high-profile successes in the world's most renowned historic motor-sport events.

Our fully ported cylinder head.

The FIA specifies many cylinder-head details through application of the 1964–5 homologation details, so inlet and exhaust valve diameters are specified at 35.58–37.71mm inlet and 30.84–30.96mm exhaust tolerances. Even though a large 37.7mm valve is specified, it is considered to be something of an anomaly, as the valve of choice is the 35.6mm. A 37.7mm valve offers no real benefit and would require the exhaust valves to be offset

Gearbox to block bolts are enlarged from ¼in to 5/16in to improve rigidity.

35.6mm inlet and 31mm exhaust valves from Paul Ivey's Race Engine Components Ltd.

engine specification and guide to assembly

in order for it to even fit. All our valves come from Paul Ivey at Race Engine Components (REC). Paul Ivey has been supplying valves for decades and has an expert knowledge not found anywhere else. Paul Ivey, like many other old-school engineers, has a true legacy that is at risk of being lost in time. We have included REC in the 'Useful Contacts' section, but there is a possibility that REC may not be around as you read this book.

The inlet valve we use (part number REC105) has a head diameter of 35.6mm. The exhaust valve (part number REC107) has a head diameter of 31mm. Both use a single groove collet. These valves have a slightly longer stem for use in the 12G940 cylinder head. It is unlikely that you will be using an original Cooper S cylinder head AEG163, but if you do, it will require the shorter-stemmed valves that are also available from REC.

We use bronze valve guides for racing applications, as they produce less friction. We prefer the slightly shorter guides available from Mini Sport for £22 +VAT (part number C-AJJ4037).

Blended and polished ports made their way on to the ancient and original FIA homologation papers, with specified 33.22–33.73mm port diameters at the port seat on the inlets and the exhaust recorded at 28.47–28.98mm. However, this really is not an area that ever gets inspected. A good cylinder head will have ports modified to increase efficiency, as well as increasing the total volume of air they are capable of shifting. The shape of the combustion chamber will also be modified. The trick with the combustion chamber is to improve combustion efficiency, to achieve as close to a full burn of all the fuel as possible and to improve the flow of air into and out of the cylinder. Achieving those last few bhps can only come through years of experience, so choose who modifies your cylinder head carefully. The final consideration when getting your head done is the combustion chamber volume. This will depend on your desired compression ratio, which we will look at next.

Compression Ratio

For 2014, the MSA brought in a regulation requiring all vehicles to run on pump fuel with a maximum octane of 102. Higher octane fuels are still available at the circuits, including 105, but for our purposes Sunoco's R5SR+ is a high-quality 101 octane fuel that will reliably meet the demands of our racing A-series engines. How much compression you choose to run will depend on the octane of your fuel and how reliable you want your engine to be. We see no need to run more than 12:1–12.5:1. You can achieve proper power and still maintain reliability without going to 13:1 or beyond. To achieve a ratio of 12:1 for your 1293cc race engine, the 12G940 cylinder head will need a combustion chamber volume of 21cc if it is running Omega pistons with a 5.8cc dish.

Rockers and Springs

The final line of this part of the regulations tells us quite clearly that only the homologated rocker arms must be used. For the Mk1 Cooper S this means the 1.3:1 ratio forged rocker arms, available new from Mini Sport for less than £10 +VAT each (part number 12G1221). No high-lift 1.5:1 ratio rockers are allowed and no aluminium roller rockers are allowed. This the scrutineers will check for by simply removing the oil filler cap on the rocker cover and having a peek inside. We would recommend a hardened rocker shaft, as well as replacing the rocker shaft spacer springs with solid spacers. We produce a set of these from billet aluminium for £25 +VAT. For other race disciplines, such as HSCC's Historic Touring Cars, the rules are a little more relaxed. A set of 1.5:1 ratio rockers may provide a useful gain in bhp.

Bronze valve guides from Mini Sport.

engine specification and guide to assembly

Cooper S-type forged rocker arms.

Piper competition valve springs.

While we are still looking at the cylinder head, the choice of valve springs is important. You will need double valve springs with a rating of around 280–300lb. Camshaft profiles are sometimes suited to a certain weight spring, so if in doubt ask your camshaft supplier which springs they would recommend. We have used Piper Cams race valve springs and spring caps for years and never had a problem. The springs retail for £94 +VAT and the steel spring caps at £51 +VAT.

Camshaft

There are many camshafts on the market and many differences in opinion as to what works best. While you should always do your homework, it is difficult really to understand the performance characteristics of any camshaft without trying it out. Talk to other racers in the paddock and see what they are running whilst looking at the top finishing Minis, noting who built their engines. The camshaft you choose needs to complement and promote those high (by A-series standards) revs, like the legendary 649 profile of BMC factory era. Today, you will not be grinding your own profiles, as the professionals have that well covered after some fifty years' experience. The current breed of racing camshafts generally have around 300 degrees' duration with around 420in valve lift from the mandatory 1.3:1 ratio Cooper S forged rockers. For FIA Appendix K and most historic race series the camshaft profile is free.

The choice for our build is Pipers 649+, an updated version of the original Special Tuning 649 profile with a power band between 3,000–7500rpm. If you are an experienced racer and accustomed to driving a 'cammy' engine, the 649+, with 300 degrees' inlet duration and 312 degrees' exhaust duration, will perform admirably.

There are many full race cams available and most will have a power band beginning above 3,000rpm. There are some camshaft profiles that rely on more lift with a little less duration for a better torque curve, but any high-revving race cam will need to be kept in its power band in order to perform. Below the power band they will have very little performance at all.

If you are not an experienced racer, you may get on more easily with something a little less aggressive. For novice racers, a profile with less duration and a power band between 2,000–7,000rpm might be more suitable. This type of camshaft will produce a little less peak power but will have a wider power band, which will make the engine more tractable and easier to drive. We would stress that if this is your first racing car, you should consider the choice of camshaft very carefully. If you have an opportunity to test-drive a car with full race camshaft this will allow you to experience it before making a commitment. It is always tempting to want the most bhp or the same engine as the top drivers, but when you are learning your race craft it can be less than helpful and could even put you off altogether. A more tractable engine will be more forgiving while you are learning the ropes. You can always fit a more aggressive camshaft for your second season's racing. Developing the car as you develop as a driver is an important consideration that is often overlooked. Whichever camshaft profile you choose, it should be on a new billet and will likely set you back around £170 +VAT.

A good-quality cam follower should be used in conjunction with your new camshaft. The bottom of a good-quality follower will be ground with a slight radius. This allows the follower to rotate when in motion, ensuring even wear of the camshaft and follower. A good set of followers will set you back around £40–50. It is worth noting

engine specification and guide to assembly

Piper 649+ is a modern development of the original BMC 649 profile.

Vernier timing gear set allows for accurate timing of the camshaft.

Good-quality cam followers will be ground with a slight radius on the bottom.

Omega forged pistons are the best for any race application.

new cam followers should always be fitted along with a new camshaft. Any good camshaft supplier will be able to supply a suitable set of competition followers to match your camshaft.

To time a camshaft correctly, you will need an adjustable timing gear, otherwise known as vernier timing gear or offset keys. Vernier timing gears are most often supplied as a duplex chain arrangement and from most good suppliers will cost in the region of £80–140 +VAT.

Pistons and Connecting Rods

Pistons are pretty straightforward as there is not a great deal of choice when it comes to racing. You should buy the best pistons you can afford, with a dish in the top of approximately 6cc. Omega Forged pistons are our preference as they are the best, although there are other adequate pistons out there. Ensure, as with every aspect of the build, that you put nothing in or on the motor that does not have an established reputation. Do not use budget pistons. A good-quality piston will be made of a high-quality aluminium alloy; it will be stronger, lighter and each piston in the set will be the same weight. A set of forged Omega pistons will cost around £416 +VAT.

With connecting rods, there are two main choices – standard 1275 rods or machined steel 'H' or 'I' beam rods. The choice will largely depend on budget. Standard rods are adequate and can be modified to improve strength and reduce weight. The original Cooper S and 1275 Midget/Sprite con rods are very good, but they have a smaller big end than the later A+ type, so it will depend on which crankshaft you are using. If you do use standard rods, you must upgrade the rod bolts to ARP. Most con-rod failures are caused by failure of the rod bolt. Never fit used

engine specification and guide to assembly

rod bolts in a new engine and if you are rebuilding an engine, it is always prudent to replace the rod bolts as they will have stretched. There are still people out there that will modify standard rods; turning down the big ends reduces weight considerably and the removal of any sharp edges will eliminate stress points. These methods have been covered at some length in publications by David Vizard and others. It is a really horrible job, dirty and time-consuming, but can be worthwhile. Those that know and perform these modifications are rather a dying breed, as machined steel rods have become more widely available.

Steel 'H' or 'I' beam con rods are what we use in our own race engines. Steel rods are lighter, stronger and, being CNC-machined, will come perfectly balanced. The uniform machined surface has been designed to eliminate any stress points and they come shot-peened to relieve surface tension. The high-grade steel is less prone to stretching (yes, con rods can stretch in an over-rev, far enough to touch the valves). Arrow Precision in the UK make superb-quality rods, but the most famous name in connecting rods is of course Carrillo. They can be expensive, so expect to pay upwards of £800 for a good-quality set.

Crankshaft

Next on your list is the largest component in your engine and the heart of its rotation – the crankshaft. Like the connecting rods, your budget will decide what options you have, ranging from a standard factory crank, a modified factory crank to an aftermarket steel crank. The difference among these cranks is not just about strength, as the standard cranks are plenty strong. It will be down to revving ability. The standard Mini crankshaft is poorly balanced. The big ends are too heavy and there is not enough counterweight, which will ultimately limit the engine's ability to rev beyond around 7,500rpm. Modifications to standard cranks will improve this dramatically. Modified cranks and steel cranks will allow an engine to rev beyond 8,200rpm. It is worth mentioning that although the original Mini Cooper S crankshafts were made from strong EN40B steel, they are pushing fifty years old now and even if they are crack-free they will be fatigued, so are not worth considering for a race engine. Don't forget that the crankshaft and gearbox are sharing the same space, so any failure of the bottom end can take out your gearbox as well as everything else.

Over the years, many variations of the standard 1275 crankshafts have been made. Some are better than others. The latest production A+ crankshafts were still available new in 2017 and carried the casting number CAM6232. These cranks were fitted to the Austin/MG Metros, including the Metro Turbo. They feature the fillet-radius journals and the larger 1.75in big ends. This is by far the best standard crank to use as it is very strong, brand new and will have no fatigue. It will also be at standard grind, rather than having been ground undersize. If you are on a budget, this is a great crank to start with, although it will only produce around 7,500rpm. Competitive engines are now running to 8,200rpm regularly. If you want to improve a standard crank to keep up, there are many modifications that can be carried out, in order to make it lighter and improve its balance and its strength. These methods have been discussed many times over the years, but we will touch on them briefly here.

The first and most important of these modifications is to wedge the crankshaft. Wedging the crank involves

We are using billet steel con rods in our race engine.

We are using a standard crankshaft for this engine build.

engine specification and guide to assembly

Modified standard crankshaft – the webs are machined to resemble a wedge.

milling the edges of the crank webs at an angle, making them narrower at the big-end journal, the result of which resembles a wedge shape. This process reduces the weight at the big end, improving the crank's balance dramatically as well as bringing the overall weight down. If you only do one modification, then wedging is the one to do. A lighter crank will accelerate more quickly and the improved balance will open up the engine's maximum rpm.

Further reduction of weight at the big end can be achieved by 'back drilling' a hole into the web on either side of the big-end journals. Or alternatively a large amount of material in the same area either side of the big-end journals can be removed. Getting as much weight off the big end as possible will allow it to rev more. Next on the list of mods is to round off all the edges and corners. This will reduce the air and oil drag as the crank rotates, as well as relieving potential stress points. A sharp edge or a corner can be a point of stress and form the starting point of a crack.

Blading or knife-edging the counterweight has questionable benefits. Some say it reduces drag, but removing material from the counterweight will affect its balance. Cross-drilling the big-end journal oil galleries involves plugging the original oil galleries and redrilling them at 90 degrees to the originals. A standard crank is drilled so that the oil will exit at the crank's outer radius. The flow of oil to the big-end bearing is thus encouraged by the centrifugal force of the spinning crank. This all sounds very good, but the fact is that in a high-rpm A-series engine the standard drillings provide the big ends with more oil than necessary, leaving the main journals with not enough. The cross-drilling of the crank's big-end oilways reduces the oil to the big end, returning a better distribution of oil to the mains.

The final process for a modified crank would be heat treatment. Heat-treating will improve the strength of the crankshaft, but it will inevitably bend the crank by a few thousandths of an inch. To straighten the crank, the journals can be reground by 0.010in. There are few machine shops that carry out such modifications today, so you may have to do some searching.

The most popular choice for today's racing engines is a steel crankshaft, although it will likely be the most expensive item on your shopping list. The official line on crankshafts from the FIA is:

FIA Appendix K 2017 Appendix VIII
5.8 Crankshaft
May be replaced by a component manufactured from a ferrous material, provided that it is identical in design and in all of its dimensions to the original component. The original main bearing caps, or reproduction caps manufactured to the same pattern and from the same material as the originals, must be retained.

The regulations allow for an alternative component as long as it is identical in design and dimensions. This detail is somewhat overlooked, as most steel cranks on the market are of an improved design. Between £1,500–£2,000 will buy a high-quality steel crankshaft. As well as being stronger and lighter, a steel crank will have less flex, which will improve the life and reliability of the bottom end and its ability to rev. A well-designed steel crank will be better balanced, incorporating improvements over the original BMC design that will allow it to rev better. A lighter crankshaft with a better natural balance will rev more quickly and freely, even up to 8,500rpm. The higher rpm not only means the potential for more power, but will also let you hold on to each gear for longer. Like the steel con rods, a uniform machined surface will eliminate stress points. A steel crank is a luxury that has distinct advantages, but it is by no means a must-have item. Many historic racers have built competitive engines around a standard crankshaft.

Crankshaft Damper and Flywheel

There are two more components in your rotating assembly that require some consideration – the flywheel and the front pulley. A lightweight steel flywheel is a no-brainer. There are a number on the market from around £130 that fall between 3.8–4kg (8.4–8.8lb). Reducing the

95

engine specification and guide to assembly

Mini Sport's lightweight steel flywheel weighs just 3.9kg (8.6lb).

Mini Cooper S type crankshaft damper.

weight of your engine's internal components and especially the flywheel increases the engine's rate of acceleration. The lighter the components, the less energy it takes to move them. This has a real-life benefit in improving your car's overall acceleration. There are even lighter flywheels available right down to 2.5kg (5.5lb), but the price of these increases to around £300.

The A-series engine suffers from a harmonic imbalance. At the factory the fitment of a rubber and steel crank damper in the front pulley went some way to resolving the issue. However, the front pulley that came with your donor engine can go straight in the bin. The rubber part will have deteriorated completely, making it useless as a damper and impossible to balance. There are a number of refined front pulley designs that will improve the reliability of your engine and the life of your bearing shells, and reduce the risk of breaking a crankshaft. It is worth noting that crankshaft life and bearing wear can be improved dramatically with good driving behaviour and smooth gear changes. Harsh use of the clutch and shifting gear without heel and toe will put a lot of stress through the crank. A harsh and rapid change in rpm causes crank whip, which can lead to a broken crank. The standard Cooper S-style dampers are available, but for an improved design expect to pay from around £150 for a rubber and steel version, or £250 for a viscous damper.

Balancing

The rotating assembly of any race engine should be balanced. A balanced engine will run more smoothly and improve bearing life. Dynamic balancing of the bottom end will see that each component is added one at a time and balanced as an assembly. A professional will start by balancing the crankshaft on its own, then add the flywheel and balance the two items together, followed by the clutch pressure plate and diaphragm. Finally, the front pulley will be balanced on its own. All items will be marked so that they can go back together in the same position in which they were balanced. The current cost of balancing a complete assembly is around £140 +VAT. It is worth mentioning here that the flywheel must be lapped on to the end of the crankshaft prior to balancing.

Steel rods are usually made to very exacting standards and a set will normally come very well balanced. Each rod in the set will be nearly identical to the next. However, if you are using standard con rods, they will be far from it. Each of the four rods will not only need to be the same weight, but should also be end-to-end balanced. This means that all the big ends and all the small ends will be the same weight. The current rate for this process is around £65 +VAT.

A high-quality set of pistons such as Omega or JE will all be of equal weight. Cheaper pistons may not be so well balanced, but a good balancer will offer this service.

Oil and Water Pumps

Until recently, there has not been a lot of choice when it comes to pumping oil and water around your engine. The best-quality standard items have, for the most part, done the job adequately. For oil pressure, you want to see 60psi. You don't need more than that. A good-quality OE spec item will set you back around £25, but always buy from a reputable dealer. We are using an oil pump from Mini Sport (part number AHU1048). For £80–100, you can buy a competition item CNC-machined from a billet in the UK. These are said to be built to more exacting standards and will maintain greater oil flow at high rpm.

With water pumps, again buy from a reputable supplier. There are not really any options and you have to

engine specification and guide to assembly

Slot-drive oil pump supplied by Mini Sport.

Water pump without bypass hose.

Maniflow's large bore stage 2 LCB exhaust manifold.

run a standard item. We are fitting the high-capacity water pump from Mini Sport (part number GWP187). Ideally, you would run without the bypass hose. If your cylinder head has a bypass on it, then simply remove it, tap the hole and fit a blanking plug with PTFE tape. The bypass blanking plugs are available from Mini Sport (part number 88G619).

Exhaust System

To our benefit in the 1960s BMC homologated a tubular steel exhaust manifold. The dimensions of the original are not of great benefit, but over the years there have been many variations on this theme, some better than others. The FIA regulations state that:

7. Exhaust systems
7.1 The exhaust manifold must remain identical to the original but the silencer and exhaust pipe are free.

Strictly speaking, we should be limited to a manifold identical to that which was homologated, but in the real world that is not the case. Any tubular manifold seems to be accepted. Over the past decades, many exhaust manifold ideas have been tested extensively by David Vizard, the best of which have since been developed even further. The leaders in Mini exhaust systems have for a long time been Maniflow, a British company started by ex-Downton Engineering employee David Dorrington in 1971.

The ever-popular long centre branch, or LCB, has for many years been the standard for Mini performance. The LCB features a centre primary tube that is twice as long as the primaries from the first and third exhaust ports. The stage 2 variation of the LCB uses a larger bore centre primary and it is this type of manifold that is currently

engine specification and guide to assembly

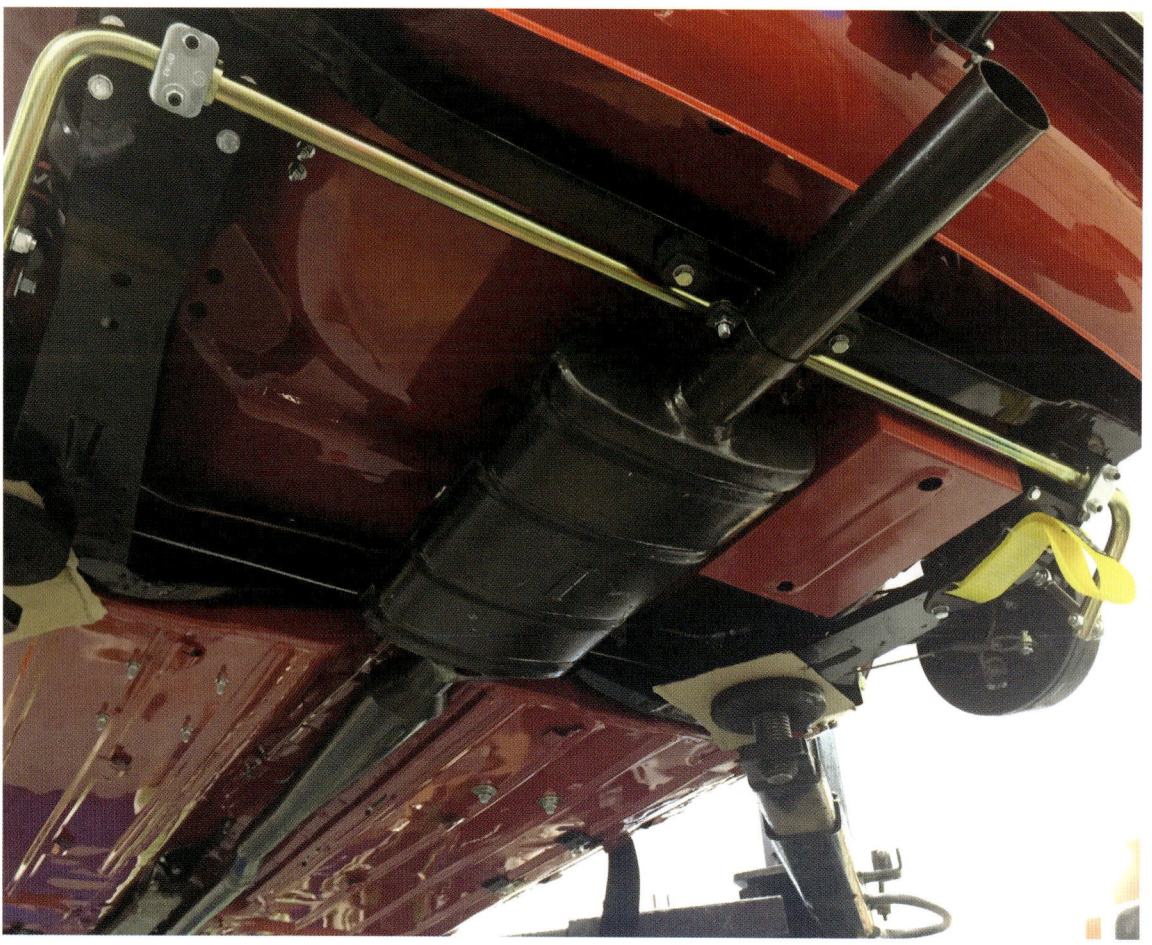

Maniflow's 2in reverse-cone exhaust system.

the go-to manifold for all racing Minis. Along with most historic racing Minis, we are using this same manifold with the 2in bore reverse megaphone centre exit system behind it.

There are not many well-known alternatives on the market, so most stick with Maniflow. Our exhaust system has been provided courtesy of local Mini specialist Nick Paddy at Play Mini Ltd. Play Mini specialize in the international export of, most notably, classic Mini components. Nick currently competes in his own historic racing Mini, which he shares with Mini racing legend Bill Sollis.

ENGINE ASSEMBLY

Now you have spent your money wisely and amassed a large collection of shiny bits it is time to assemble them into a reliable race engine. Many of you will employ a professional engine builder but for those who wish to do the job themselves we will briefly outline the important steps.

Block

Preparation of the engine block usually comes first. Subject your engine block to a compressed air and soapy water pressure test; the head face and water pump orifices need to be sealed with Plexiglass. We look for any evidence of cracking or leakage, but this should be unlikely in any decent block – you are much more likely to find a crack in the cylinder head. If the block passes this test, the next step is to acid-dip it. Remove all core plugs and gallery plugs so that the acid can get to every part of the casting. Most machine shops will have an acid tank and offer acid cleaning as a service. The acid will remove all paint, enamel, carbon and any other sludge that might be found in the deep orifices of the block. The importance of

engine specification and guide to assembly

a clean block cannot be stressed enough. There are many small galleries in the block that are responsible for distributing oil to all the moving components. A small amount of debris in one of these galleries could easily block the oil supply to the main bearings, causing a premature failure. Make sure that all galleries are clear by blowing them through with compressed air.

After the acid dip, we will wash the block in paraffin before treating the water jacket for rust. We immerse the block in a concentrated solution that dissolves the rust. Leaving this to soak overnight will see that every trace of rust inside the block is dissolved and washed away. Now we overbore the block, which in this instance is +20thou. Any swarf created from the machining process will need to be washed out carefully. We use a paraffin wash tank and a brush. It is also recommended that at this stage the holes for the gearbox fixing bolts are enlarged from ¼in to ⁵⁄₁₆in. This helps to improve the rigidity of the whole unit.

The next step is to check the piston's clearance to the top of the block. Our advice here is to take the piston and rod, minus rings, and slide them into the cylinder bores. Assemble the crankshaft and main bearing caps, without torquing them to final settings. The big end and main bearing cap should be lubricated and the assembly turned over until it reaches TDC (Top Dead Centre). Check the top of the block deck to the piston crown for clearance above the block. We like to have a 5thou clearance at the top of piston travel to arrive just short of the cylinder block deck. It is our safety margin. Yes, there is the additional thickness of the head gasket, but at 7,000 rpm plus, there is inevitably some stretch in the rod, which it is best to guard against. The crank assembly will need to be removed and the top of the block decked on the mill to achieve the desired 5thou clearance and to clean up the block face.

Looking at the freshly prepared bare block, the easiest way of working is either on a rotating engine stand or with it head face down on a (very) clean work surface. The first step is to paint the block. For a Mk1 Cooper S the factory BMC green enamel will be applied with a brush. We also like to paint the inside of engine blocks with red oxide. It looks good, but also has the added benefit of helping the oil run back to the sump. Plus if there are any small flakes of rust it will prevent them from ending up in the oil. We have never experienced the red oxide paint coming off the inside of the block.

Now it is time to move on to core plugs and gallery plugs. New core plugs can be fitted with thread lock. If further security of the core plug is desired, a simple solu-

Gallery plugs and core plugs have been removed so that the inside of the block can be cleaned adequately.

Core plugs are held in place with an M4 cap head screw and aluminium retainers.

Oil galleries are taped for ¼in NPT threaded plugs.

99

engine specification and guide to assembly

tion is to drill and tap a hole on either side of the plug and use a small M4 cap head screw with a washer or home-made retainer to prevent the core plug from ever escaping. Instead of replacing the gallery plugs, all galleries should be taped for ¼in NPT threaded plugs. These should be fitted with PTFE tape to prevent any leaks.

We suggest trial-fitting the camshaft with new camshaft bearings. Inserting the camshaft bearings accurately demands a special tool and the key check is to ensure that the cam is rotating cleanly within them. Our priorities, when the cam is withdrawn from the block, are that no high spots can be observed. A good machine shop or engine builder will be able to do this job for you.

Back on the table, it is time for a trial-fit of the crankshaft, main and big-end bearing shells, all liberally covered in oil, looking out for high spots or frictional resistance. Usually any problems will be associated with stray dirt under a bearing. Fit the main bearing into the block with plenty of oil. Oil the main journals and lay the crankshaft in the block. Now fit the centre main bearing cap with bearing and thrust washers, again apply oil liberally.

Measure the end float on the crankshaft: you should

Camshaft bearings ready for installation.

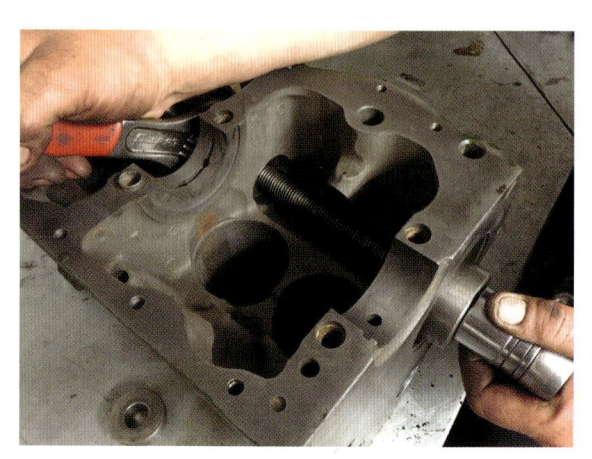

The camshaft bearing tool pulls the bearings into their journals.

Camshaft trial-fitted in the block should rotate freely.

engine specification and guide to assembly

Main bearings in the block. Oil liberally before fitting.

With plenty of oil to lubricate, lay the crankshaft in the block.

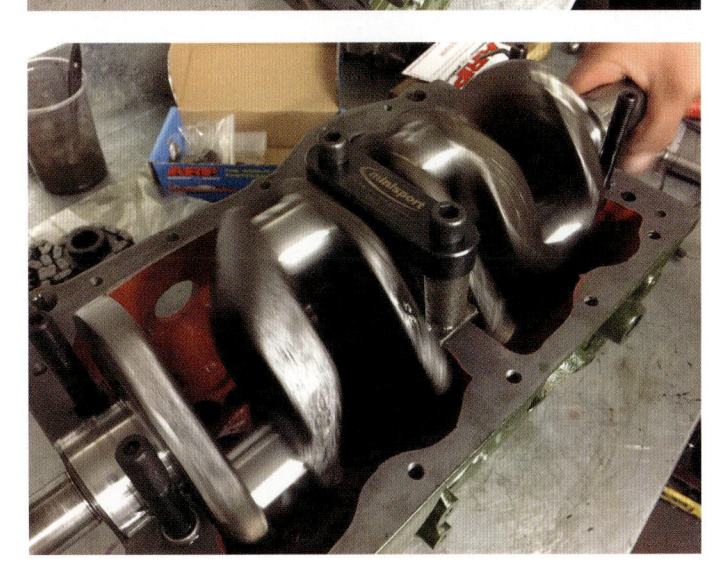

With the centre main cap fitted, nip the bolts and check that the crank spins freely.

engine specification and guide to assembly

look for a tolerance of no more than 6–8thou, using different thrust washers to adjust within those parameters. Tighten the centre main cap to nip rather than full-torqued levels. Spin the crank; it should move fluidly, requiring no more than finger and thumb effort. Take it all apart and inspect for high spots, even if you have felt no frictional tightness. If all is well, repeat for the front and rear cap assemblies.

If all is well at this point, you can now torque up to recommended tightness, beginning with the centre bearing assembly, then the front, followed by the rear. Ensure that the crankshaft still spins freely, as it must for any racing application.

Now turn to the piston and connecting rod assemblies. Piston rings need to be in place and pistons fitted to the rods. Most piston rings will come pre-gapped. If you need to gap the rings, a ring gap grinder will be required. You can measure the ring gap with a feeler gauge by sliding the ring into the cylinder bore. Depending on your combination of components, you may have either press-fit, where the gudgeon pin has an interference fit with the rod and requires the use of a hydraulic press or heat to instal, or floating, where the gudgeon pin floats in the rod and is located in the piston with the use of two circlips.

With the big-end assembly split, coat the cylinder walls with lubricant and insert the piston and con-rod assemblies slowly. Please note that it is essential to use piston ring compressors very carefully in order to compress the rings on the pistons, prior to installing the pistons in their respective cylinder bores. Make quite sure that each lubricated piston/ring assembly slides seamlessly from the piston ring compressor 'tube' and into its cylinder. If the rings are permitted to catch on the top of the cylinder block as they go into the bore, they could fracture, so great care must be taken. Tap the pistons into position within the cylinders; use a wood hammer as a tap, if necessary. Add the lower half of the big-end assem-

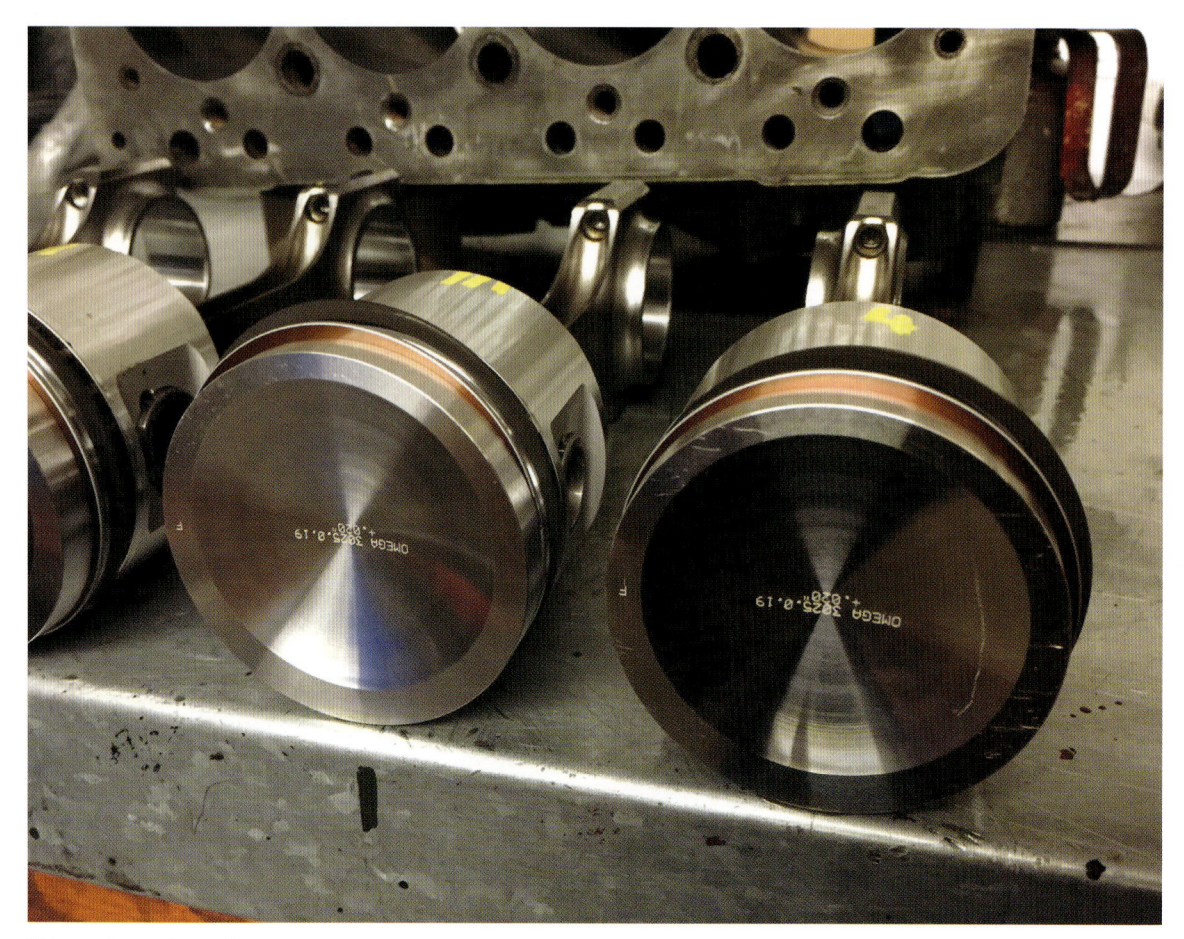

Piston and con-rod assembly.

bly and nip up the rod bolts, rather than torque them into fully tightened location. Check that the assemblies spin freely. Torque up the big-end bolts properly. Again, we suggest only using ARP bolts in your con rods.

We have dealt with trial-fitting the camshaft; now it is time for the real thing to the accompaniment of heavier-grade oil, especially to those peaky camshaft lobes. Most camshaft manufacturers will supply a sachet of cam lube. Slide the cam carefully into the cylinder block, being particularly careful not to knock into the bearings.

Time to secure the front engine plate with gasket sealer and torqued bolts – the gasket employed is just a quality service item, not a race special. The plate that retains the camshaft is bolted on and torqued exactly to the recommended poundage.

Now it is time to get the main block and the assemblies within into a new position. From the upside-down location that was easiest to deal with all the previous work, we now want the main motor components and block turned the right way up.

Turn the crank until you reach TDC, or as close to this as is practical. The crankshaft sprocket from the vernier timing gear set is now a slide fit. Ensure that the crank sprocket is running in line; if not, shims are needed underneath the crank sprocket to correct alignment. Remove sprockets and refit with the timing chain, ensuring that the cam-timing dot lines up for the TDC location. You will need a protractor and dial gauge with magnetic base in order to set up the motor timing accurately. The camshaft timing data will have been supplied with the camshaft, but is usually between 100–110 degrees. Follow the camshaft timing guidelines in the sidebar.

We need to attach the oil pump to the back of the motor, using a conventional gasket and gasket sealant.

The timing chain cover will need a new oil seal and gasket to refit; the front pulley is a slide fit into its oil seal. Next, torque up the bolts, ensuring that the cover is central to that pulley. It is essential to lubricate (with engine oil) the oil seal that fits within the timing case and which seals against the crankshaft nose. Otherwise, when the engine starts up for the first time after its rebuild, the localized heat generated by friction here could destroy the seal's lip.

Before installing the gearbox, fit the distributor drive with all the associated parts lining up TDC at approximately the 20 to 2 (clock face) reading. Do not try to fit the distributor drive and associated components after gearbox installation, as you will only have to remove the Mini box again.

Once you have assembled the short motor, you can mount it to the gearbox. Be sure that you have a good seal where the main oil gallery in the block meets that of the gearbox. A failure here can lead to a total loss of oil pressure. Once the gearbox is fitted, you can fit the transfer case with the appropriate gaskets, the drop gears and the flywheel and clutch assembly.

TOP END ASSEMBLY

Most will purchase a complete cylinder head with valves and springs already fitted and ready to fit to the block. If you've modified your own cylinder head or sent your 12G940 casting off to a reputable cylinder head expert, then you will need to assemble your head. Relatively speaking it is a simple task. We use a special set cylinder head stands to hold the head off of the bench. The first thing we do is to lap the valves; this ensures that a perfect seal is achieved when the valves are seated. We pop the spring caps on the valve springs and set the double valve springs assemblies in their places on the head, with the head on the stand and the combustion chamber face down. We insert the valve from underneath with a little assembly lube on the stem. The valve spring compressor is clamped down around the springs and the single groove cotters are installed. A little grease on the cotters makes sure they stay put when the tension is released from the valve spring compressor. Check that the cotter and spring cap have seated properly, and move onto the next.

One thing you must consider when assembling your head is the fitted length of the springs. Your chosen race specification valve springs will specify a recommended fitted length – this might be 1.4in, for example. When your cylinder head was modified the valve seats may have been cut deeper: this allows the valve to sit deeper, which increases the fitted length of the spring. You need to measure between a fitted valve spring cap and the valve spring seat in the top of the head. If this gap is larger than the required length, then you will need to shim the valve springs. Valve spring shims are readily available from most suppliers. This is a 'must-do' task to achieve appropriate valve seat pressure.

Now back to the block. If you are using the later 1300 GT block without tappet chests, rather than the Cooper S block, then you'll have to insert the cam followers from the top. Ensure they are well lubricated with assembly lube. We then fit the ARP head studs to the top of the block and slide the head gasket into place. There are two types of head gaskets that we use and trust: the Cometic multi-layer shim (MLS) (around £75 +VAT in 2017) and the

engine specification and guide to assembly

Installing the piston and con-rod assembly in the block.

Put plenty of oil on the big ends and check that everything spins freely before torquing down the bolts.

Instal the camshaft carefully with plenty of cam lube.

Engine front plate installed with gasket and sealer.

CAMSHAFT TIMING

To carry out camshaft timing, first you need to fix a pointer to the front plate and a protractor to the front of the crank. Set up your dial gauge on number one piston and find TDC. Rotate the protractor so that 0 degrees lines up with the pointer.

Now instal a cam follower and pushrod into number 1 inlet (second pushrod hole back from the front) and set up the dial gauge on top of the pushrod. Rotate the crank clockwise to find maximum camshaft lift. When you have found maximum camshaft lift, 'zero' your dial gauge.

Rotate the crankshaft until the dial gauge drops by 0.025in, then rotate back until it is 0.05in below maximum lift. Make a note of the protractor reading; it might be 122 degrees, for example. Then repeat this measurement in the opposite direction. Rotate the crankshaft anti-clockwise to 0.025in below maximum lift, then back to 0.05in. Make a note of the protractor reading; it may read 92 degrees.

Add the two numbers together and divide by two. In this example, we get 107 degrees. Our Piper 649+ needs to be timed in at 100 degrees. We will need to adjust the vernier by 7 degrees. Make the adjustment and repeat the measurements to verify.

Take measurements 0.05in either side of maximum lift.

Set up dial gauge on number 1 inlet and find maximum lift.

Adjust vernier to achieve the correct camshaft timing.

engine specification and guide to assembly

Oil pump installed in the block.

Make sure that there is a good seal between the engine and gearbox oil gallery.

cheaper but still perfectly reliable Payen BK450 composite gasket (around £18+VAT). The cylinder head can then be slid into place, followed by the push rods and then the rocker assembly. Four of the cylinder head studs also serve to retain the rocker posts so these must be in place. Make sure the rockers line up with the top of the valve stems before you tighten the nuts on the studs: as with all cylinder heads there is a sequence for tightening and torquing the nuts. With the head now in place you can set your tappet clearances to what is specified for your particular camshaft. For our engine that is 0.014in inlet and 0.016in exhaust.

ENGINE BAY AND INSTALLATION

Installing your freshly built engine and gearbox is a relatively straightforward process, but there are a few things that are worth mentioning. If you are dropping the engine assembly into the engine bay from above, a cradle that allows you to angle the engine will make your life easier. The engine sits on two rubber engine mounts on either side. We have used standard items from Mini Sport with captive nuts. The original engine mounts without captive nuts created much difficulty. The Mini Sport part number for these is SPD0012.

The top of the engine is supported by an engine steady bar, which links the cylinder head to the front bulkhead cross member. The original item uses rubber bushes, but is not really up to the job, as it allows more engine movement. It is recommended that you at least use polyurethane bushes here. Make sure to use a good earth strap and ensure that all of your oil and fuel unions are tight before starting the engine. A high-quality competition engine oil must be used, with a recommended weight of 20W50. We use a semi-synthetic competition 20W50 from Driven Racing Oils. Filling up the oil cooler will help to reduce the time it takes to raise oil pressure when first starting your new engine. The starting procedure will be covered in Chapter 9.

KEEPING COOL

Keeping a racing Mini engine cool is difficult at the best of times. The transverse engine layout and the tight packaging meant the radiator had to be squeezed into the left-hand inner wing. A simple fan attached to the front of the engine helped to push the hot under-bonnet air out through the radiator. This works fine on a road car, but the layout is somewhat restrictive when on the track and within the rules of historic motor sport the radiator must remain in its original location.

In addition to keeping the engine cool, its oil will also need to be kept cool. A simple thirteen-row oil cooler is as much as can be fitted into the engine bay. It is a tight squeeze between the grille, distributor, starter motor and alternator, but will do the job adequately. The oil cooler can only really be mounted to the bottom of the grille opening as there is not really anywhere else it will fit. You will have to find just the right spot that will ensure it will not foul the above mentioned ancillaries. Nick Paddy and Play Mini kindly provided the oil cooler hoses, which were made to measure by Think Automotive. When your engine is in and you have positioned the oil cooler, you can determine the length of hoses you need and Think Automotive will make them to suit.

For the coolant system, you will need to run a suitable radiator and the original heater matrix under the dash-

engine specification and guide to assembly

Finding the best spot to mount the oil cooler.

Oil cooler mounted behind the grille.

engine specification and guide to assembly

board. There is not much room for a larger radiator and for FIA purposes an aluminium radiator cannot be used. The larger four-core radiators are popular, but require the removal of the inner cowling on the inner wing. The FIA says this:

FIA Appendix K 2017 Appendix VIII
6. Cooling system
6.1 Radiator
6.1.1 Any radiator provided by the manufacturer for the model concerned is authorized but its attachment system must not be modified in any way and its position must not be changed.
6.1.2 The addition of a radiator screen whether fixed or mobile, regardless of its system of control, is authorized.
6.1.3 Heater matrices for liquid-cooled engines and heat exchangers for air-cooled engines can be removed but their location cannot be changed.

6.1.4 The location of water pipes is free.

6.2 Fan
6.2.1 Freedom regarding the number and the dimensions of the blades.
6.2.3 It is permitted to replace the original fan with an electrical one.

We have opted for a two-core super-cool competition radiator from Mini Sport at a cost of £103 +VAT (part number C-ARA4442). Standard radiator hoses can work fine, but the bottom hose has been known to go soft and close up at the bend, reducing the flow of coolant. We are using Swiftune's Kevlar historic radiator hose set. These

Mini Sport two-core competition radiator.

engine specification and guide to assembly

Swiftune's Kevlar radiator hose set.

Original Mk1 Mini heater mounted under the dashboard.

engine specification and guide to assembly

hoses are reinforced in the corners with a hard plastic to prevent them closing up; they retail for £78 +VAT. The fan most people use is the eleven-blade plastic fan, available from Mini Sport for around £12 +VAT (part number 12G2129/Y).

The original Mk1 heater box and matrix are retained under the dashboard and plumbed in accordingly, although the heater tap is replaced with a simple 90-degree union. Keeping these racing Minis cool is tricky and it may prove necessary to run the heater at all times – and yes, it will get hot in there for the driver. We ran a fresh air supply from the grille though the bulkhead to the heater box under the dashboard as would have been originally fitted from the factory. We also replaced the original Lucas heater fan, which was fifty years old, with a new in-line blower.

On the subject of heat, something that is sensitive to heat is the ignition coil. It is always worth locating the coil where it can be kept cool, either by distancing it from the engine and/or by cool air flowing in through the grille. It is also worth considering the heat that the carburettors are subjected to, being situated directly above the exhaust manifold. A suitable shield should be used to isolate the heat of the exhaust from the carburettors. We will discuss carburettors and the rest of the fuel system in the next chapter.

Cold air supply for the heater matrix and ignition coil mounted on the inner wing.

Standard production left-hand fuel tank.

The right-hand fuel tank became optional on the Cooper models.

fuel system and carburettors

7

FUELLING THE FIRE

When the Mini entered production in 1959 it had a single 5.5gal (25ltr) fuel tank on the left-hand side of the boot. This was of course perfectly adequate for running an 850cc family saloon down to the shops, but as engine size and performance increased and as the racing and rallying potential of the Mini was realized, so was the need to carry a little more fuel. When the Mini Cooper arrived, a second fuel tank mounted on the right-hand side of the boot became available as an option. This extra fuel tank doubled the fuel capacity, which was especially important as engine capacity increased to 997cc and ultimately to 1275cc in the Cooper S.

The BMC-prepared rally cars were often fitted with a special long-range 13gal (60ltr) fuel tank made from aluminium and fitted in the right-hand position. The two tanks were linked with a pipe before sending the fuel underneath the car to the carburettors in the engine bay. Fuel supply was handled by the old SU fuel pump mounted to the rear subframe underneath the boot floor. Many will remember the days of sticky SU fuel pumps and crawling under the car to give it a knock with a hammer to get it pumping again.

In the engine bay the fuel was supplied to the engine via one or two SU carburettors. The 850cc Minis utilized a single HS2 SU carburettor with a 1.25in bore on a one-piece cast-iron inlet and exhaust manifold. The Cooper and Cooper S models used two HS2 carburettors with a cast-aluminium inlet manifold now separate from the exhaust manifold. This arrangement was adequate for impressive street performance, but was not enough to

111

fuel systems and carburettors

Original Cooper and S models used two HS2 carburettors.

Development of 8-port cylinder head and fuel injection.

supply the volume of air required by a full race engine. For the Cooper and Cooper S models two H4 SU carburettors with 1.5in bore were homologated.

Up until 1965, the British and European Saloon Car Championships were running to FIA Group 2, which limited competitors to the standard 5-port head and the homologated carburettors. In 1966, a change to Group 5 meant that the cylinder heads and induction were both free. Initially, most teams adopted the Weber DCOE, but as 1967 approached, cross-flow 8-port cylinder heads and mechanical fuel-injection systems were quickly being developed. These radical machines were powerful, fast and expensive, but as we are building a car to the FIA's period F it is the H4 carburettors we will require. Other non-FIA series may allow the use of the later HS4 SU carburettors or even Weber DCOEs.

When building any historic racing car it is likely that the original fuel system will be inadequate for two reasons: safety and the volumes of fuel and air required by a race engine. So let us assume you will be starting from a blank canvas and we will work our way from the fuel tank at the back to the carburettors at the front.

fuel systems and carburettors

FUEL TANKS

There are a few things to consider when choosing which fuel tanks to use, whether you choose to use original tanks, or an aftermarket aluminium fuel cell. First is how much fuel you will need to carry. The volume of fuel required will depend on the length of the races you wish to enter. For sprints and hill climbs, you will only ever be running for a few minutes at most, so you can save a little weight by installing a very small fuel tank. If, on the other hand, you wish to compete in a six-hour race at Spa-Francorchamps, you will need to carry as much fuel as is allowed. With the 1275 Mini Cooper S that will be 85ltr. Added to the optional equipment list on the homologation form was the long-range 60ltr fuel tank with a BMC part number of 21A1469. This fuel tank took the place of the original right-hand tank and was originally homologated for use in the rally cars, as they had to cover long distances. Most Historic Touring Car races today are between fifteen minutes and one hour in length, so you need to carry enough fuel to last for the length of race you intend to compete in. For longer races, you need 45ltr or more. If you are only going to be doing fifteen- or thirty-minute races, then a 30ltr tank may suffice.

Original fuel tanks will be fifty years old and may well be full of rust. If this is the case, it would probably be better to replace them. You may choose to use an aluminium tank or new reproductions of the original left- and right-hand tanks. Both options are fine, but other than capacity your chief concern is in satisfying the safety regulations set out by the MSA and FIA. Which fuel tanks you choose to use is up to you, but they must be properly vented with secure filler caps and adequate spill protection if they become inverted. The following regulations tell us what is required.

MSA Yearbook 2017 (K) Competitor Safety Tank Fillers, Vents and Caps

6 …The [filler] caps must have an efficient locking action to reduce the risk of opening during an accident and to ensure closing after refuelling (14.1.2). Air vents must be at least 25cm to the rear of the cockpit and must be designed to prevent the escape of fuel should the vehicle be inverted. It is recommended that a non return valve is incorporated in the vent system. …

There are two major considerations here – security of the filler caps and ventilation of the tank, with roll-over protection. We will first take a look at the filler caps and what is required by the regulations and what is expected by the

Monza filler cap on standard Mini fuel tank.

scrutineers. The last thing anyone wants is to have a filler cap come open or get knocked off during a race; likewise, every effort should be made to ensure that the fuel caps remain secure in the event of an accident and will not leak if inverted. It may sound obvious, but consideration for the security of fuel caps is a paramount safety concern and is treated as such by scrutineers. This will mostly apply to anyone who is planning to use the original Mini fuel tanks with the filler necks protruding through the rear quarters, as any aftermarket aluminium fuel tank that has been designed for the purpose of racing should have a suitable cap already fitted. If you choose to use the original type of fuel tank you must change the original bayonet filler cap for something more secure. The aluminium Monza or Aston style of filler cap are good alternatives and can be easily fitted to the original filler necks. A 2.5in Monza or Aston filler cap will use a threaded collar and will fit over the 2.25in filler neck on the original fuel

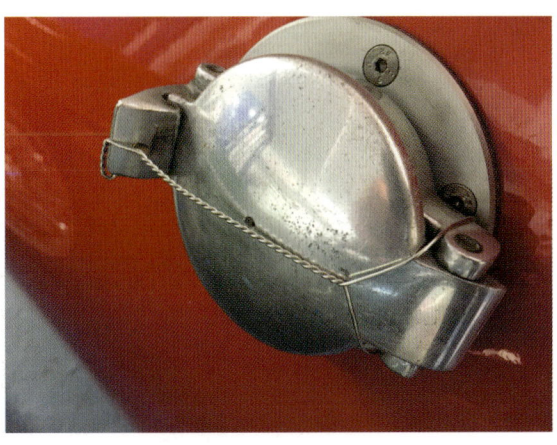

Filler caps are lock-wired shut once the tank is filled.

113

fuel systems and carburettors

tanks. You will need to braze or bond the threaded collar to the filler neck, so that the Monza or Aston filler cap can be threaded on securely.

Whichever filler cap you choose, you must make sure it is not vented. If you happen to have a vented filler cap, it may be possible to solder up the vent hole and thus convert it to non-vented – otherwise, if the car becomes inverted, fuel will be able to escape from the vent hole. The other advantage to the Monza and Aston filler caps is that they can easily be lock-wired shut once the tank is filled. Although to do this you will need a lock-wire tool and a roll of lock wire, this method of securing filler caps before a race is popular amongst scrutineers.

As an alternative to the original fuel tanks, many racers choose to fit a specially built aluminium fuel tank in the boot. Usually, these will have their own threaded filler neck and cap within the boot, which will adequately satisfy the regulations and also reduce the risk of a filler neck or cap being damaged in an accident.

The second point one must consider is tank breathing or ventilation and the associated roll-over or non-return valve required by the regulations. Fuel tank breathing is a necessity. Without it, a vacuum would be created within the tank as the pump extracts the fuel, which would reduce the fuel flow and starve the engine. As the tank is emptied of fuel, air needs to flow in to fill the void. Many fuel caps incorporate vents within them and although

Fuel tank roll-over breather valve.

these vents will allow the tank to breathe, they will also allow fuel to leak out should the car roll over. As mentioned above, whichever filler caps you choose, they need to be non-vented, as the ventilation must come directly from the tank. Whether you choose to use original-type fuel tanks or an aluminium racing fuel tank, they must have a designated breather pipe with a roll-over valve.

The original Mk1 Mini used non-vented filler caps with a small breather pipe brazed to the top of the fuel tank. From the breather pipe was a rubber hose that exited through the boot floor. If this fuel tank were to become

Aluminium racing fuel tank mounted in the boot of our racer.

fuel systems and carburettors

Cooper Car Company Minis ran fuel tank breathers around the rear screen.

Fuel tank foam to help suppress explosions and reduce surge.

inverted, fuel would be able to flow out through this breather. If you are going to use the original fuel tank, you either need to instal an in-line roll-over valve in the breather pipe or ideally this breather needs to be removed and a roll-over valve installed in the top of the fuel tank in its place. It is recommended that roll-over valves are mounted upright, as they will shut off if they are upside down. Most of them use a ball bearing, which will allow air to pass, but will block the flow of fuel with any pressure behind it. Many aftermarket aluminium racing fuel tanks will come with a suitable roll-over valve already fitted.

You cannot have fuel tanks breathing into the confines of the vehicle, so a length of hose must be fitted to the roll-over valve outlet to exit the vehicle into fresh air. This should ideally be through the boot floor, or, like the original Cooper Car Company's racing Minis, through an aluminium pipe that exits through the top of the boot lid opening and up the C-pillar around the outside of the rear windscreen.

If you are planning to race abroad in FIA-sanctioned events, your fuel tank may need to be foam-filled, or even have an FIA-approved fuel cell. Fuel tank foam is designed to suppress explosions by helping to fill the large empty space that would otherwise by occupied by fuel vapour and air. Fuel tank foam can be purchased from any good race preparation retailer and fitted to almost any tank. Fuel tank foam also has the added benefit of baffling the fuel, which will help to reduce fuel surge in long corners. FIA-approved fuel cells are lined with a bag that prevents fuel spilling, should the fuel tank be damaged in an accident. They come with a certificate and are good for five years. Following an inspection, the five years may be extended by a further two years, but after seven years the fuel cell must be replaced. For racing in the UK, you will not be required to run an FIA-approved fuel tank.

FUEL LINES

From the fuel tank, the fuel will travel via fuel lines to the front of the car. There are essentially two options when choosing fuel lines. Both are adequate to satisfy the scrutineers, but one is more expensive and ultimately more secure in a collision. The MSA Yearbook states the following:

fuel systems and carburettors

Solid copper fuel line running inside the vehicle.

MSA Yearbook 2017 (J) Competitors: Vehicle Fuel Systems

5.13.1 Have any fuel lines passing through the driver/passenger compartment protected and, if non-metallic, to be internally or externally metal braided hydraulic pressure hose or fuel lines complying with FIA specifications.

5.13.2 They may only be joined by screwed sealing joints or vehicle manufacturer's approved joint.

The original fuel system would have used rubber hoses from the fuel tank outlet to the fuel pump and from the fuel pump to a metal fuel line that travelled the length of the car to the engine bay. Originally, this fuel line travelled along the underneath of the car, but for safety reasons we run it inside the car. In the engine bay the metal fuel line would again meet rubber hoses that take the fuel to the carburettors. This system relies on push-on hose fittings with hose clips. For those on a tighter budget, this type of system will be cheaper and provided that it is maintained in good condition will happily satisfy the scrutineers. One consideration when using a solid metal fuel line is the potential for the line to get kinked and split in an impact, so perhaps choose a route closer to the centre of the vehicle.

An alternative method, although considerably more expensive, is to use braided hose with reusable aluminium fittings (Aeroquip). The size of hose needed for this type of system will depend on the fuel demands of the application. To fulfil the fuel demands of the BMC A-series engine, -6JIC hose with the equivalent fittings will suffice.

If you choose to use braided hose, you will need the appropriate -6JIC fittings on the fuel tank, fuel pump, fuel regulator, filter and carburettors. These fittings are available in a number of different angles to suit almost any application. Like the metal fuel line, it would still be preferable to run the line inside the car, but with braided hose you have the option of using bulkhead fittings that seal against the bulkhead and allow for a hose to be attached on either side. Bulkhead fittings allow the bulkheads to

Stainless-steel braided -6 hose is excellent, but expensive.

fuel systems and carburettors

PUMPS AND REGULATORS

A single fuel pump will suffice and the most convenient location for this is in the boot. We use the Red Top Works fuel pump from Facet. In many years of racing we have always found these pumps to be most trustworthy. The Facet Red Top pump provides ample flow at a pressure of 6.5–7.25psi. This is a little more pressure than needed, so we would incorporate a pressure regulator in the system. This will be mounted after the fuel pump in the boot or in the engine bay on the front bulkhead and would be in line before the carburettors.

The most popular choice of pressure regulator is the Malpassi Filter King. Available from all good race preparation retailers, this fuel-pressure regulator has a built-in filter and will keep the pressure below 5psi. Too much fuel pressure at the carburettors can cause the float bowls to overflow, which will flood the carburettors and bog down the engine, or, worse, cause a fire. If there is not enough fuel flowing to the carburettors, on a long straight the float chamber will empty more quickly than it can be refilled, leaving the engine running very weakly. A very weak mixture will do a great deal of damage to an engine and is best avoided.

Use of rubber grommets will suffice.

remain completely sealed without the need for a grommet. Alternatively, you can simply run a fuel line through a hole in the bulkhead with a suitable grommet to seal the hole and prevent the fuel line chafing against the edge of the hole and wearing through. Any fuel line running through the cockpit of the vehicle must be secured. We use P-clips to do this job.

Facet Red Top Works fuel pump located in the boot next to the fuel tank.

Malpassi Filter King regulating the fuel pressure.

fuel systems and carburettors

CARBURETTORS

In the 1960s, the Mini Cooper S was delivered from the factory with twin HS2 SU carburettors with a bore of only 1.25in. However, for competition our Mini Cooper S was homologated with twin H4 SU carburettors with a larger bore of 1.5in. It is the H4 carburettors that must be used if you are building an FIA Appendix K Mini Cooper S.

If you are not restricted to running to the FIA specification, you may have other options. If you choose to race with the HSCC, for example, you may wish to use a Weber carburettor or the more common HS4 SU carburettors. Appendix K says that:

FIA Appendix K 2017 Appendix VIII
5.7 Carburettor(s)
Only the jets and chokes may be changed; the make and type homologated and the manufacturer's specification must be retained.

FIA Minis are required to run the H4 SU carburettors.

30-degree float chambers are required so that the carburettors clear the Mini's bulkhead.

fuel systems and carburettors

In order to satisfy the homologation requirements for an Appendix K Mini you will have to use twin H4 SU carburettors. Reconditioned pairs are available from around £800 +VAT, or you can locate an old pair yourself and rebuild them. H4 carburettors were factory fitment to a number of vehicles in the 1950s including the Triumph TR2, MGA, Ford Consul, Zephyr and Austin-Healey 100/4, although on most of these applications the carburettors were mounted horizontally, or nearly. Due to the restricted space available in a Mini's engine bay, the SU carburettors had to be mounted at a steeper angle of 30 degrees. This angle allows them to clear the front bulkhead cross member, but it means that the float chambers also need to adopt a steeper angle.

If you find a pair of H4 carburettors from an alternative source, the float chambers will need to be replaced with the correct type. For this application they will need to be at 30 degrees, with part numbers AUC 4814 for the right-hand float chamber and AUC 4815 for the left. A popular modification amongst Mini racers is to fit float bowl extensions to the top. This modification raises the float chamber top, increasing the volume of fuel available to the carburettors. Care should be taken when using these,

One side of the throttle spindle is cut away and the butterfly is thinned and knife-edged.

Float chamber extensions increase the volume of fuel in the chamber.

because if the fuel level in the float chamber is higher than the jet in the bottom of the carburettor, it can cause flooding.

In order to get the very most out of your H4 carburettors, you may choose to modify them. There are various modifications to increase flow that have been established over many years. The first of these modifications is to cut one side away from the butterfly spindle and to thin down and radius the other side. Make sure you keep the side with the threads, as you will still need these to retain the butterfly. The butterflies themselves can be thinned and knife-edged.

Another popular modification is to fill the area directly in front of and behind the bridge with epoxy. Be sure to drill a couple of holes into the carburettor's body for the epoxy to grip into. The last thing you need is a chunk of epoxy getting pulled into the engine. For the last few cubic feet per minute of airflow, you can smooth any hard edges within the carburettor body behind the piston and file off the bottom leading edge of the piston where it hangs down into the airflow at full lift.

fuel systems and carburettors

For Appendix K, you must use an original-type cast-aluminium twin SU inlet manifold. These are known to have very poor flow characteristics due to the way the balance pipe intersects with the inlet ports. A great deal of turbulence is created at this point, which greatly reduces the potential airflow. A little work smoothing all the internal edges and rounding off any corners can help to improve things dramatically. Technically speaking, you should be using the earlier Cooper S manifolds with the small vertical carburettor mounting flange; however, in practice the later 1275GT manifold with its larger square mounting flanges are also accepted.

You will find that non-FIA Appendix K race series, including the HSCC's Historic Touring Cars, may allow alternative carburettors and inlet manifolds to those that were originally homologated. The HSCC regulations are as follows:

HSCC Historic Touring Car Championship Regulations 2017

5.7.8 Fuel delivery systems
Carburettors, inlet manifolds, fuel pumps and hoses are free subject to the prohibitions of 5(5) and 5(6)2.

The area in front of and behind the bridge is filled in with epoxy.

The standard Cooper S manifold must be used in Appendix K.

fuel systems and carburettors

Essentially, the HSCC allows any carburettors or manifolds, as long as you do not modify the bodywork. If you wish to stick to SU carburettors, you may look at the HS4. A cheaper alternative to the H4 SU carburettors, the HS4 can be found on many 1960s cars, including the MGB. The HS4 carburettors will still perform as well as the H4s, but are far more common and consequently easier to get hold of and cheaper. Again, if sourcing a pair of carburettors from an MGB, or other source, the float chamber angle will need to be altered. On the HS4 carburettors, the angle is set by small metal or plastic blocks between the carburettor body and the float chamber. These can be changed easily to alter the angle.

Within the HSCC's Historic Touring Cars, Weber DCOE and Dellorto DHLA side-draft carburettors can be utilized, as long as the bulkhead remains unmodified. While an unmodified bulkhead will limit the benefits of using a side-draft carburettor, it may still be advantageous. The limited space allocated to the carburettors makes the fitment of a single side draft difficult. There will always be a compromise. The inlet manifold will have to be shorter than optimal and the front of the carburettor will be very

A cheaper alternative, the HS4 is allowed in most non-FIA club racing.

Weber carburettor on an HSCC Mini.

fuel systems and carburettors

close to the bulkhead, which can affect the free flow of air to the inlet. Strictly speaking, no modifications are allowed to the bulkhead, but the clearance to it can be improved with the subtle use of a hammer and a piece of wood.

There are many Weber manifolds on the market, but without the use of an air box cut into the bulkhead you will be limited to the shorter ones. According to David Vizard's extensive research for his book *Tuning BL's A-Series Engine*, the optimum manifold lengths when using a single side-draft carburettor are over 5in. (D. Vizard, *Tuning BL's A-Series Engine*, p. 152, Fig. 8.14, 'Intake manifold length'.) Without bulkhead modifications, these long manifolds are not an option. The longest usable manifold is probably 3.5in and with that the front of the carburettor will be right up to the bulkhead.

Given that we are building a race car, we can rule out the use of the swan-neck manifold. Although this provides a great deal of clearance to the bulkhead, its poor flow performance makes it entirely unsuitable for racing. (D. Vizard, *Tuning BL's A-Series Engine*, p.148, Fig. 8.13, 'Comparative dynamometer test of three types of side-draft Weber manifold and a reference single 1.5in SU induction system'.) If space wasn't tight enough already, one cannot overlook the benefit of using a full-radius ram pipe. You are only going to have room for a very short ram pipe, if any, but by not using one at all the airflow into the carburettor will be greatly reduced. Vizard showed us that the benefits of using a ram pipe with a full radius at the leading edge are huge. (D. Vizard, *Tuning BL's A-Series Engine*, p.57, Fig. 6.4, 'Ram pipe cross-sections'.) Even if the ram pipe is very short, the benefits are a big improvement over no ram pipe at all. So there is a balance to be found and it is ultimately a compromise regarding the length of the inlet manifold versus ram-pipe length and clearance to the bulkhead. These compromises may make the advantage of running a single side-draft carburettor negligible. It will ultimately come down to drivability, personal preference and how much time you spend fine-tuning

Split Weber carburettor set-up.

fuel systems and carburettors

on a dyno. You may find it to be a useful advantage, or it may prove not to be worth the bother. With other non-FIA race series such as the CSCC's 'Swinging 60s', you may be allowed to box out the bulkhead and use a longer 6in manifold to maximize the potential performance.

Another variation on the Weber theme would be a pair of split Weber DCOE carburettors. A split Weber carburettor is where two side-draft Weber carburettors are used side by side, but only one half of each carburettor is used. This use of Weber carburettors can be utilized on engines with Siamese-inlet ports, such as BMC's A-series and B-series engines. These engines only have two inlet ports, so only two carburettor barrels can be utilized. The initial benefit of split Weber carburettors is that each carburettor barrel can be positioned directly in line with the inlet port. With a single side-draft carburettor, the inlet manifold has to curve in a shallow 'S' bend between the carburettor and the inlet port. This bend in the inlet manifold adds a small amount of restriction to the airflow. By making the inlet manifold straight, that restriction is reduced and airflow is improved.

The other benefit of this set-up on a Mini is the clearance issue to the bulkhead. Having a straight intake path rather than curved goes some way to make up for the lack of available manifold length. If you choose to use side-draft carburettors on anything over 1000cc, you will benefit from the use of a 45 DCOE/DHLA carburettor over a 40mm unit. Under 1000cc, a 40 DCOE/DHLA will be best.

Whichever carburettors you choose, they will need to be properly set up on an engine dyno or rolling road. Correct fuelling is critical, not only for maximum performance but also for the health and reliability of your engine. A lean or rich mixture will cause internal damage. With access to a dyno or rolling road you can also explore the potential of every component. Making tiny adjustments, changes and modifications can help to find the very best performance. We will look further at tuning and set-up in Chapter 9.

Our rolling road is used to achieve the very best performance.

Auxiliary panel from a period rally car.

8 wiring loom, instruments and switch gear, safety, engine electrics

BRIGHT SPARK

When the Mini first hit the forecourts it was fitted with the bare essentials and little more. Having a heater was optional in 1959 and features such as reverse and fog lights had yet to be a requirement. A speedometer and a fuel gauge were present, as were the basic red, blue and green warning lights to indicate the ignition system, high beam and low oil pressure. There were two courtesy lights either side of the speedometer pod and an interior light above one's head. The headlight dip switch was on the floor accessible to your left foot.

The starter button was also famously on the floor, with the ignition switch, headlight and wiper switches in the central panel on the lower dash rail. The steering column had a simple indicator stalk with a novelty green warning light on the end. Charge was provided by a 22amp Lucas dynamo with current regulated by a simple control box. Current was distributed by the wiring loom, which had only two fuses.

As production continued through the 1960s, a few changes were made. When the Mini Cooper was introduced in 1961, a water-temperature gauge and an oil-pressure gauge were added to a larger central speedometer housing and by 1965 the floor starter button had been deleted, with the start function incorporated into the ignition key switch and a separate starter solenoid added.

wiring loom, instruments and switch gear, safety, engine electrics

All Minis were 12V from the start, with the early examples being positive earth. Because of the tiny size of the engine bay, the battery was located in a small box in the boot floor. Although this was done out of necessity, it had the added benefit of improving the weight balance. The original battery cable travelled the length of the car underneath the floor via the floor-mounted push button and on to the starter motor. The ignition system utilized a Lucas 23D4 distributor with points, condenser and coil.

Competition vehicles in period would have had many modifications to the electrical system. There would have been the addition of a Smiths electric tachometer at least and if it were a rally car it would have received an awful lot more. This would have included fog and spot lights to the front of the car and the roof, reverse light, map-reading lights, cigar lighter socket and even heated front and rear screens. Auxiliary dash panels were added to the left and right of the speedometer to house the extra gauges, switches and timing clocks.

The electrical system in any old car is one of the most crucial systems when it comes to maintaining reliability. A system that is fifty years old may not only be unreliable, it may also be dangerous with the potential to cause a fire. A system that was adequate by the standards of the day may not meet the expectations we have today. A well-maintained stock electrical system may be adequate for a road car, but for a race car there are a few areas that could lead to unreliability. A very simple electrical problem can

Switch panel in the lower dash rail.

Three-gauge instrument binnacle introduced with the Cooper.

Dip switch located at the top of the toe board.

125

wiring loom, instruments and switch gear, safety, engine electrics

end your race immediately, wasting not only your entry fee but the time and money you put into the whole race weekend. Maintaining a reliable electrical system that is designed to suit the needs of a race car is critical and there are several things you can do to make life easier. In this chapter, we will look at the wiring loom, the ergonomics of the controls, electrical systems for racing, gauges, safety measures, engine electrics and the ignition system.

FRUIT OF THE LOOM

The wiring loom is where we have to start. It connects every electrical component in the vehicle and any failure in the loom cannot only end your race, it may also be a massive fire risk. Under no circumstance would we build a car using an original wiring loom, as this would be fifty years old and unsafe. The insulation will be dry and cracked, the copper will be brittle and it will have been cut, modified and repaired dozens of times in the past. It will be unreliable at best and at worst it could set fire to your freshly built race car.

Step one is to place your original wiring loom carefully in the bin. Following that, you have two options. First is to buy an off-the-shelf replacement wiring loom and the

New standard wiring loom from Mini Sport. This one is wrapped in PVC rather than the original braid.

second is to make a bespoke one. There are pros and cons to each method and there are things to consider when you make your choice.

Let us first take a look at a standard factory-style wiring loom. They are available off the shelf and are relatively inexpensive from around £150 +VAT. They should be relatively easy to instal and you can even get them to accommodate an alternator instead of the original dynamo and control box. All of these things are great, but there are a few downsides that you may want to consider. When a racing seat is used in a Mini and you are tightly strapped in with your racing harness, it may become almost impossible to reach the original switch panel in the centre of the lower dash rail. This means that all the switches will need to be moved to an auxiliary switch panel within easy reach of the driver.

When using an off-the-shelf wiring loom you will need to add an extension to the loom to go from the original switch location to the auxiliary switch panel. There will be some electrical controls that will need to be moved and some you may want to remove altogether, such as the overhead interior light and door switches. With a factory-style loom, some modifications may be necessary

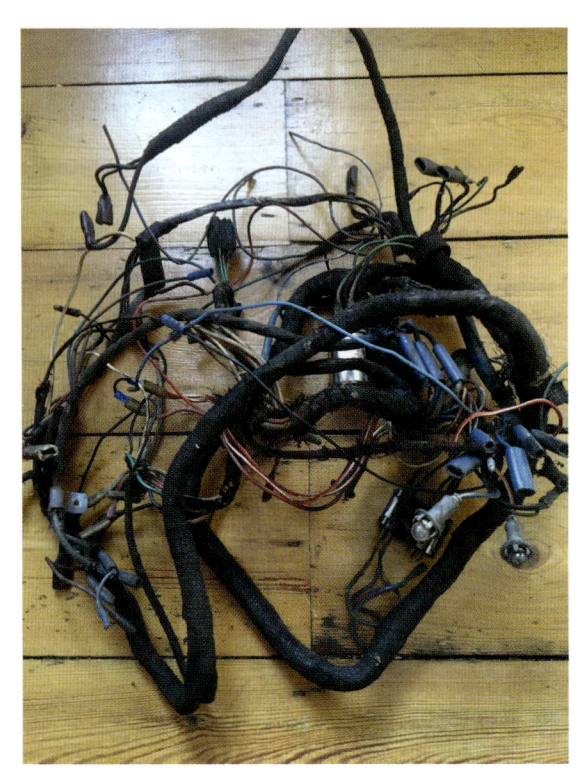

Original wiring loom that is fifty years old and in poor condition.

wiring loom, instruments and switch gear, safety, engine electrics

in one place close to the driver, avoiding the need for modifications or extensions. Any system you may want to add to a race car can be built into the loom, instead of needing to be added to an existing loom. The wiring for a tachometer, warning lights, fuel pump switch, a large fuse box and relays for the lights can all be incorporated into the loom. This will make for a more reliable loom and one that will weigh less.

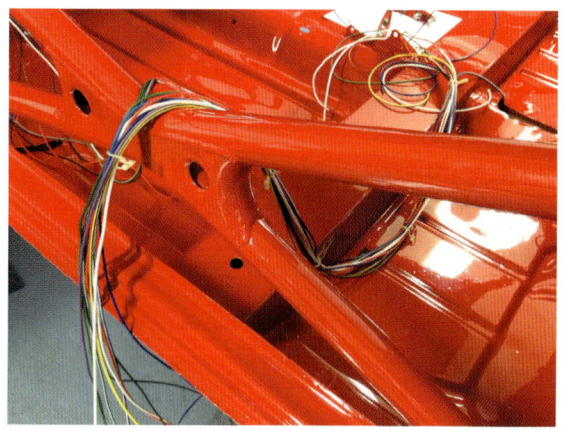

Auxiliary switch panel in easy reach of the driver.

Our race-car build has a bespoke wiring loom.

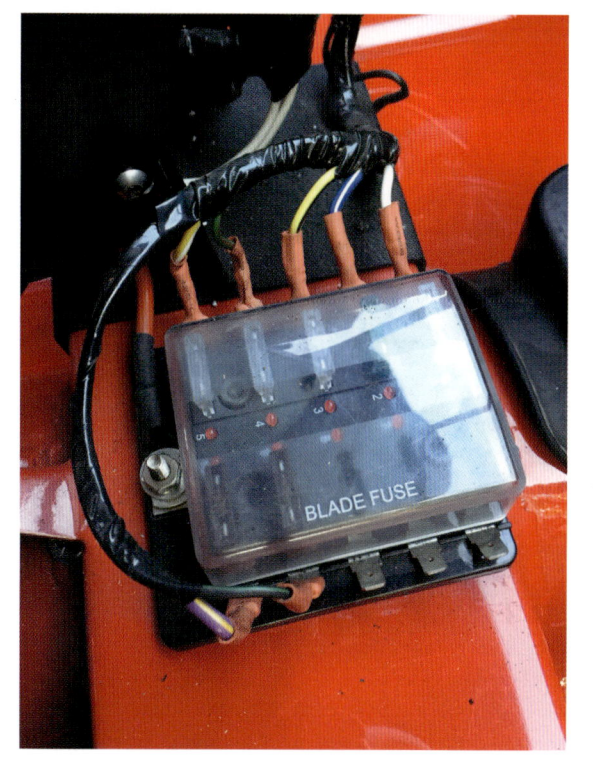

and there may be some leftover wires. While not a great consideration, extra wiring is extra weight and modifying the loom creates potential for less reliability if a connection is broken. In the case of the Mk1 Mini a factory-style loom will be made to incorporate the two-fuse fuse box so will again need to be modified if you wish to add more fuses. If you have limited electrical knowledge or a tighter budget, this option may be more appealing. The alternative is either to make your own bespoke wiring loom, or have a professional make one for you.

The bespoke wiring loom also has its pros and cons. The major downsides are that a custom-made loom from a professional vehicle electrician will inevitably leave a rather large hole in your pocket, while doing it yourself will not only take a lot of time, but will also require a knowledge of vehicle electrics if it is to work reliably and safely. On the plus side, there are many advantages to a bespoke wiring loom that an off-the-shelf item cannot offer. The bespoke loom will be made to accommodate the systems you need to run in your race car and nothing else. That means no extra wires and no extra weight.

A 1960s Mini did not have a lot of electrical systems to begin with, so you cannot gain too much in simplicity, but you can design it so that all of your switches are

Competition fuse box in our Appendix K racer.

127

wiring loom, instruments and switch gear, safety, engine electrics

Our dash panel has all instruments and warning lights placed in front of the driver.

ERGONOMICS AND RACING ADDITIONS

The ignition switch, headlight and wiper switches were originally located in the lower dash rail, which is too far to reach when tightly strapped into your racing seat. You will need to relocate these controls, as well as add some additional features, when building your race car. You will probably find that you will require two auxiliary panels.

The first will be a dash panel ahead of the driver. On the dash panel you will, at the very least, need to mount your tachometer and oil-pressure warning light. We would also recommend that you fit an oil-pressure gauge and water-temperature gauge in this panel, so that they are close to the driver's line of sight. Additionally, you may like to relocate the ignition warning light and also the shift light, if you use one. The most important items on this panel are the tachometer, oil-pressure gauge and oil-pressure warning light. These should be fitted as close to the driver's line of sight as possible. These need to be visible with only the slightest glance.

If you cannot reach the dash panel whilst strapped into your racing seat, you will need a second auxiliary panel that is within reach. All your switches and controls need to be within easy reach when seated. For a basic electrical system, a race car will need the following controls: ignition switch and starter button; fuel pump switch; headlights on/off; headlights dip/main beam; wipers on/off; and rain light on/off. You may also choose to fit an electric screen-wash pump, in which case a momentary on/off switch will be needed. If you lose the function of the horn push in the middle of the steering wheel due to the fitment of an aftermarket steering wheel and boss, but the car requires an MOT test, a horn button will need to be added. Indicators will also be required for road use. It is worth noting that you will also need to reach the master switch whilst seated. If you have no plans for a passenger seat, the master switch and auxiliary switch panel can be mounted to the cross member on the floor. In this location, they can easily be angled to face the driver and also be in close proximity to the gear lever for quick access. If you want to maintain the ability to have a passenger seat fitted, another location will need to be found.

SWITCHES, GAUGES AND WARNING LIGHTS

If you have chosen a bespoke wiring loom, these auxiliary panels can be wired directly into the loom. If you have chosen to use a standard factory-style loom, you will need to extend the loom to accommodate the auxiliary panels and additional functions. For period-correct looks, you can purchase new switches in the old Lucas style. Alternatively, a simple metal toggle switch will not look out of place. If you want the ultimate in functionality, LED-tipped toggle switches are excellent, as they make it very easy to see at a glance that everything is on that should be on. If you should accidentally switch off your

wiring loom, instruments and switch gear, safety, engine electrics

fuel pump during a race, you would be able to tell why the engine died with a glance at the switch. It happens.

The old key barrel ignition switch can be utilized, but as well as being hard to reach, these switches can also prove to be unreliable. It may be preferable to instal a toggle-type ignition switch with a starter button. The ignition toggle switch should be installed in the auxiliary panel so that it can be reached easily.

The only indication you will have of your engine's condition during a race is through the gauges and warning lights. A reliable gauge or warning light is far cheaper than a new engine. The first gauge you need is a tachometer. Good tachometers can be purchased for around £200. We like to use the Stack ST200, as it has proven to be very reliable, accurate and it has a tell-tale. For a racing A-series engine you will want a gauge that goes to 10,000rpm. You don't ever want to see 10,000rpm, but having that range and a tell-tale will help to explain what happened when your engine went bang and lost all power. For those that like to retain a period look but want the accuracy and reliability of a modern digital tachometer, Stack do have a range of classic gauges.

For keeping the engine's rpms within safe limits it may be helpful to instal a shift light. Most digital tachometers will already be equipped to run a shift light, so all you have to do is connect one up, or alternatively you can buy a standalone module that can be wired in separately. Likewise, standalone rev limiters can be installed in non-FIA Appendix K vehicles, although we do not like to use them as they have the potential to cause ignition issues. Also, the rev limiter will only stop an over-rev on the way up, whereas nothing can prevent an over-rev during the downshift and this is when the most damage is done.

Your auxiliary gauges come next and we must stress again that good-quality, accurate gauges are far cheaper than building a new engine. For most applications we find that the installation of an oil-pressure gauge and water-temperature gauge is sufficient. Both gauges should be capillary-type gauges, rather than electrical. Electric gauges are cheaper, but they can be affected if your car experiences an electrical issue, whereas a capillary gauge will always give you a reading. We would install the oil-pressure gauge close to the rev counter and as close to the driver's line of sight as possible, with the water-temperature gauge below it or beside it. An oil-pressure warning light should also be installed as close to the driver's line of sight as possible. Some people like to instal a very large and bright warning light so that there is no chance of missing it.

Switches in our Mini race car.

Stack rev counters have proven to be effective and reliable.

Oil-pressure gauge, warning light and temperature gauge close to the driver's line of sight.

The oil-pressure warning light will have a pressure switch that is usually fitted to a T-piece along with the capillary feed for the oil-pressure gauge. We use a switch that will illuminate the warning light when the oil pressure drops below 20psi. Although you have this warning light, it does not mean that you can ignore the gauges. If you see the oil-pressure gauge dropping during a race, you can be reasonably confident that you have a problem and might save a little more of your engine if you switch it off before the light comes on. If you do see the oil warning light come on during a race, shut down the engine immediately if you want to have any chance of salvaging your crankshaft and con rods. For the A-series engine, you need an oil-pressure gauge with a range of 0–100psi (0–7bar) and a water-temperature gauge with a range of 0–120°C (0–250°F).

SAFETY MEASURES

There are, of course, a number of safety regulations that must be incorporated into your Mini's electrical system if you are to satisfy the scrutineers. Let us start by looking at the battery. The MSA says:

MSA Yearbook **2017 (J) Competitors: Vehicle Electrical Systems**
5.14.1 Have any wet batteries in driver/passenger compartment enclosed in a securely located leak-proof container.

If located in the Driver/Passenger compartment, where a Passenger/Co-Driver is present the battery must be situated behind the base of the Driver's or Passenger/Co-Driver's seat.
5.14.2 Have batteries duly protected to exclude leakage of acid and to protect terminals from short circuiting and producing sparks.
5.14.5 Have the battery earth lead, if not readily distinguishable, identified by a yellow marking.

There are two basic options when choosing a battery, with pros and cons to each. A traditional lead acid battery is otherwise known as a wet battery, due to the fact that it is filled with liquid battery acid. Wet batteries are perfectly adequate and they are very cheap. The disadvantages are that they are heavy and also must be isolated from the driver, so that in an accident, or if the car becomes inverted, it is not possible for the acid to leak on to the driver. If the battery is located in its original position in the boot, no further action must be taken, as the rear bulkhead would have already been sealed. If a wet battery was installed in the driver's compartment, it would have to be sealed in a leak-proof battery box.

The alternative to a wet battery is a dry cell racing battery. Dry cell batteries don't have liquid acid in them so do not need to be isolated from the driver. The other advantage of a dry cell battery is that they weigh less, but are, however, a little more expensive then their lead

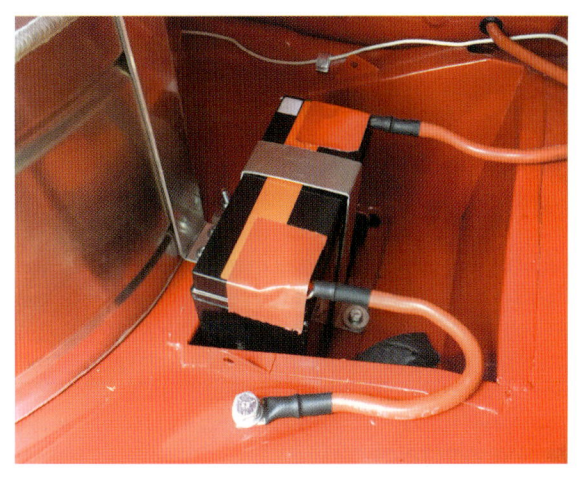

wiring loom, instruments and switch gear, safety, engine electrics

Our dry cell battery mounted in the original location in the boot.

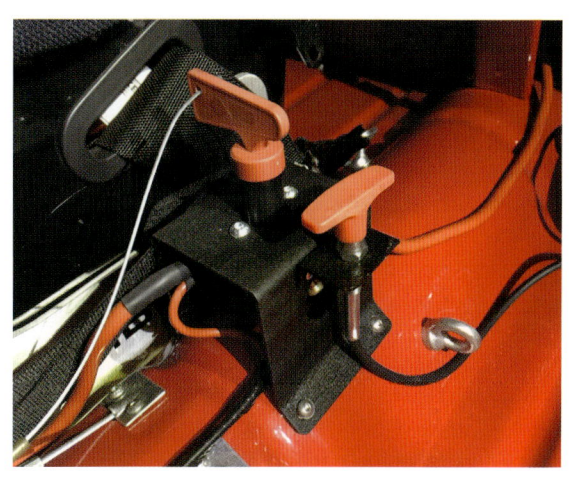

The master switch isolates the battery and cuts the ignition system.

acid counterparts. More recently we've seen lithium ion batteries coming to the market place. They are very light and claim to be powerful and long lasting but they can be very expensive. We have yet to use one so cannot really comment on their effectiveness.

It sounds obvious, but your battery should be fitted securely, be unable to move and unable to short out the terminals. If your battery is strapped in and clamped in place with a metal clamp, be sure to consider the location of the clamp and the terminals in relation to each other and the bodywork. The MSA requires that the earth lead from the battery be identified by a yellow marking. The neatest way to achieve this is the use of yellow shrink-wrap tubing. The regulations continue:

MSA Yearbook 2017 (J) Competitors: Vehicle Electrical Systems

5.14.3 With the exception of racing cars, be equipped with battery, generator, self-starter, side, tail, and brake lights. All this equipment to be in normal working order. Exceptionally when taking part in an event held totally off the public highway, need not comply with DfT Statutory Requirements regarding lighting or horn.

5.14.4 With the exception of racing cars, or cars of Periods A to C, have headlights in normal working order with glasses of minimum 182.5 sq cm each unless SRs permit their removal.

Where the term 'racing car' is used in regulations, it tends to refer to cars that were designed as such, for example single-seaters, sports racing cars and prototypes. The Mini is a production saloon car, so it is not considered a 'racing car' and to comply with MSA standards must be equipped with a battery, generator, starter motor, side lights, head lights, tail lights and brake lights. And like any vehicle being prepared for circuit racing, it must also be fitted with a master switch or external circuit breaker.

FIA Appendix K 2017
5.3 Battery, Circuit Breaker

5.3.2 There must be a general circuit breaker which must cut all electrical circuits (battery, alternator or dynamo, lights, hooters, ignition, electrical controls, etc. – but with the exception of those that operate the fire extinguisher) and must also stop the engine.

MSA Yearbook 2017 (K) Competitors: Safety External Circuit Breaker

8.1 The circuit breaker, when operated, must isolate all electrical circuits with the exception of those that operate fire extinguishers.

8.2 The triggering system for the circuit breaker on saloons should be situated at the lower part of the windscreen mounting, preferably on the driver's side or below the rear window.

8.5 The triggering system location must be identified by a Red Spark on a White-edged Blue triangle (12cm base), and the 'On' and 'Off' positions clearly marked.

When the master switch is turned off it must also turn the engine off. It cannot simply be installed in line with the battery cable. Although it will isolate the battery if installed this way, it will not shut down the engine. The master switch must cut the electricity to the ignition. Typically, the master switch will be installed in a position

wiring loom, instruments and switch gear, safety, engine electrics

that can be reached by the driver whilst seated. It will need to be operated from outside the vehicle by way of a pull cable. The preferable position for the external pull cable is on the front scuttle. Should the vehicle become inverted, the external pull cable must be easily reached by a marshal and clearly marked with a red spark in a blue triangle.

The final piece of safety equipment that must be fitted is a rain light, or 'red warning light'. The regulations state:

MSA Yearbook 2017 (K) Competitors: Safety Red Warning Light

5.1 A rearward-facing red warning light of a minimum of 21 watts, with surface area minimum 20cm^2, maximum 40cm^2, or of 21 watts with a surface area minimum of 50cm^2 and with lens and reflector to EU Standards, must be located within 10cm of the centre line of the vehicle and be clearly visible from the rear. Vehicles fitted with full width bodywork may alternatively use two lights equally located about the vehicle centre line. An alternative light unit of equal or enhanced constant luminosity or LED lights that are either homologated by the FIA or comply with relevant EU Regulations may be used.

5.2 The warning light must be switched on when visibility conditions are reduced, or as detailed within championship and/or event regulations, or when so instructed by the Clerk of the Course.

It sounds simple enough. You must have a red rearward-facing light with a 21W bulb in it. Any period fog light can be used, so long as it has a red lens and 21W bulb. Alternatively, you may use a modern LED rain light; however, if LEDs are used the light must be FIA-approved or EU compliant. The position of the rain light or rain lights (plural) seems to confuse even scrutineers at times, but if a solitary rain light is used, it must be within 10cm (4in) of the centre line of the car. Popular locations on a Mini are the rear valance below the bumper or mounted to the parcel shelf inside the rear window. Alternatively, the regulations state quite clearly that you can use two rain lights equally located about the vehicle centre line. For a saloon car, this means you can potentially fit a 21W light bulb in each of your tail lights if there is room and it does not interfere with the running or brake lights.

ENGINE ELECTRICS

The engine's electrical components are much the same as any other car of the period. There is a starter motor, dynamo or alternator, distributor, coil and spark plugs. Most cars of this age, including the Mk1 Mini, use an inertia-type starter motor. This means that there is an inertia mechanism which throws the pinion gear into the flywheel's ring gear when the starter motor spins up. It is a crude system, which ultimately causes wear to both the pinion and the ring gear. As the high-speed spinning pinion is thrust into the stationary ring gear, the teeth are inevitably worn away. Nevertheless, it gets the job done.

As we have already seen in the regulations, a production saloon car is required to have a self-starter. The original factory-fitted Lucas-type starter motors will generally suffice, but we have had problems with the quality of new reproduction items, so unless you are working to a tight budget we would recommend an aftermarket alternative. For our race-car build, we are using a British-built

Our rain light is mounted beneath the rear bumper.

An original inertia starter motor.

wiring loom, instruments and switch gear, safety, engine electrics

The original Lucas dynamo can prove to be less reliable in a race car.

Original floor start push button repurposed in an auxiliary panel.

tain a steady voltage. By adjusting the spring tension on the switches, it is possible to alter the rate at which they open and close and alter the voltage supply.

If well maintained and adjusted, the control box will work just fine for a road car, but will carry a reasonable risk of unreliability that is best avoided in a race car. The second problem is that in the 1950s and 1960s most road-going engines would rarely see 5,000rpm and would

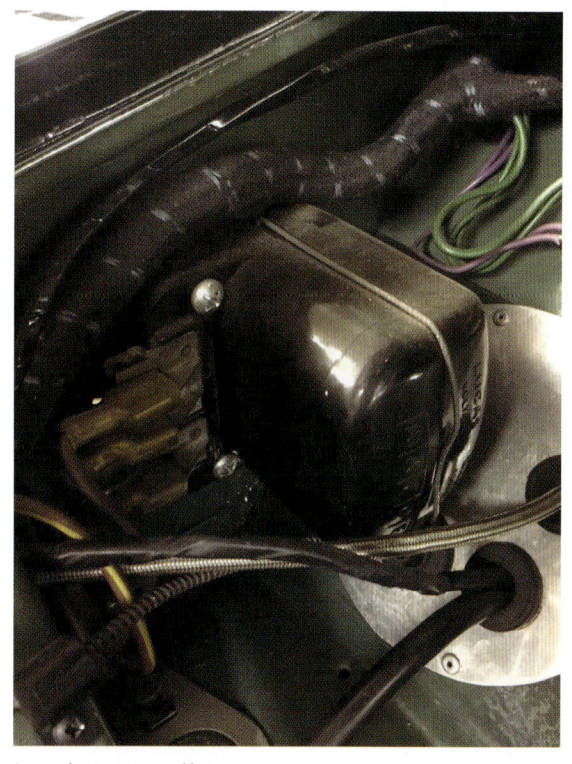

high-torque, geared inertia starter motor from WOSP. WOSP have been producing high-performance starter motors and alternators specifically for motor racing since 1990.

Early cars used a floor-mounted push-button starter solenoid mounted next to the right-hand side of the floor tunnel in front of the cross member. If you have gone to the effort to rewire your car and have run the battery cable inside the passenger compartment rather than underneath, you will no longer have the option of using a floor-mounted starter solenoid. Most high-torque, geared starter motors have a solenoid built in, so there will be no need to use another. If you are really very fond of the floor-mounted push button, it may still be utilized simply as a starter button.

Almost all British cars of the period used a Lucas dynamo and although they were perfectly adequate in their day, they will fall a little short in today's competition engines. The original Lucas dynamos put out around 22amps, which is enough to charge a battery and power an ignition system. The first problem with the dynamo is the regulator or control box. The control box crudely controls the voltage supplied to the vehicle through a pair of contact breakers, which open and close rapidly to main-

Lucas dynamo control box.

133

spend most of their time between idle and 4,000rpm. A competition engine may only be coming 'on cam' at 4,000rpm and will be run up to 7,500rpm for extended periods of times. This is a lot to ask of a dynamo that was not designed to run at that speed. You can compensate to some degree by fitting a larger pulley and slowing it down, but there are still some other downsides. The dynamo is heavy and like the starter motor, the build quality of new items or rebuilt items cannot be guaranteed.

The alternative to the dynamo is of course the alternator. One advantage of an alternator is that it has an electronic regulator built in, which is more reliable than the dynamo's control box. It also weighs less than a dynamo. Fitting an alternator is not a straight swap. The wiring loom is different, so when fitting a new wiring loom in your racing Mini you need to allow for an alternator. The Lucas ACR units were fitted as standard to most British cars in the 1970s. In theory, these alternators should be adequate; however, in recent times we have seen many new and remanufactured items fail after a very short time. As with the starter motor, we would recommend an aftermarket alternative. For our project, we are using a beautifully engineered alternator from WOSP. Made in the UK, this lightweight high-performance alternator is designed to be a straight swap for the Lucas ACR unit and uses the same mountings. These alternators are compact, light and, most importantly, reliable. An alternator mounting bracket will be required if switching from a dynamo. Our one came from Mini Sport (part number SMB158).

IGNITION

If your starter motor or alternator fails, it may not end your race. If your ignition system fails, it most certainly will. As with most other systems, reliable performance is of the utmost importance. The ignition system is comprised of a number of different elements: the distributor; contact breaker points and condenser (or electronic ignition); rotor arm; distributor cap; HT leads; coil; and spark plugs. Any one of these components has the potential to fail and end your race.

FIA Appendix K 2017 Appendix VIII
1. Electrical Devices

1.7 Plugs, ignition coil, condenser and distributor: Makes are free; The number of plugs per cylinder, the ignition coil, condenser, distributor and spark plug types must conform to the manufacturer's specification for the model concerned.

1.8 The addition of an electronic ignition system is not permitted, nor is that of an electronic rev. limiter.

At the centre of the ignition system is the distributor. The 850cc Mk1 Mini was originally fitted with a Lucas 23D4 distributor with vacuum advance and the Mini Cooper S without vacuum advance. Any distributor that is fifty years old is going to be worn out and any road-orientated advance curve is not going to be appropriate. Both the Lucas 23D/25D and the 43D/45D

WOSP make this lightweight alternative to the Lucas ACR.

wiring loom, instruments and switch gear, safety, engine electrics

Your distributor will have a centrifugal mechanical ignition advance mechanism inside. As the distributor spindle accelerates, the centrifugal mechanism throws out the bob weights, which in turn rotates the baseplate and the points, so that the spark plugs fire earlier in the stroke. The rate at which the centrifugal mechanism rotates the baseplate is determined by the weight of the bob weights and the strength of the springs that hold them. Heavier bob weights or lighter springs will throw out more quickly. By changing the springs and the weights, it is possible to alter the rate of ignition advance through the entire rpm range. If you plot a graph to show how many degrees the ignition advances at regular rpm intervals, you would get a curve. This is your advance curve.

The advance curve of a distributor must be tailored to match the performance characteristics of an engine. Generally, road-going engines that produce power from low down will have a gradual advance curve. The ignition will advance slowly over the entire rpm range. A race engine that does not come on cam until 3,000rpm will have an advance curve that increases rapidly from that point and will reach maximum advance as quickly as it can. Because a race engine will be using a high compression ratio and high-octane fuel, it will tolerate a quicker increase in ignition advance and ultimately a higher maximum ignition advance without detonating. If you were to run a race ignition curve on a road engine, you would

Lucas distributor from Aldon Automotive with an advance curve profiled for our racing application.

will work, but you will want a new or remanufactured unit with the correct advance curve and without a vacuum advance. Vacuum advance timing is used in addition to mechanical timing and is generally used to help improve fuel efficiency and drivability.

Ignition timing advance is a critical area of engine tuning. With a high-compression competition engine we will be using as much total advance as we can. More ignition advance means that the spark plug will fire earlier in the stroke, allowing for more of the fuel to be burnt and generating more power. The total amount of maximum advance will be limited by the design of the engine, the compression ratio and the octane of the fuel. If the ignition is advanced too much, the cylinder pressures will be too high, generating extreme temperatures that could melt a hole in the top of the piston. Because the ignition timing is so critical, we want to maintain strict control over it. A vacuum advance makes it much harder to set up the ignition timing accurately, as it will constantly alter the advance depending on vacuum pressure. The last thing you want is to have maximum mechanical advance and the vacuum system advance the ignition even further.

Advance mechanism inside the Lucas distributor.

find that there would not be enough ignition advance at low rpm and far too much advance at the mid- to high rpm range, which would likely cause some damage.

A lot of ignition advance must be accompanied with a higher compression ratio and higher octane fuel. If you have too much ignition advance or low-octane fuel, detonation will occur. Detonation is where the air and fuel mixture in the cylinder combusts too early in the stroke, causing a 'knocking' sound in the engine. The result of this will be greatly increased cylinder pressure and consequently an increase in heat, which will eventually cause fatal damage, such as blowing or melting a hole in the top of a piston or burning the valves. We will look into this again when we cover tuning the engine in Chapter 9, but as a note we never see the need to run more than 28 degrees maximum advance on a historic race A-series. Although the A-series can in theory run more, you need to balance performance with reliability. At the maximum possible advance you may gain 1bhp, but you will lose any safety margin you might have had. If the fuel you are using is a little less than you thought or the race day is very hot, you may run into problems without a degree or two as a safety margin.

As for sourcing a suitable distributor, we in the UK are very lucky. The BMC A-series engine has been around a long time, it was fitted to many vehicles and has been well developed over the years. Consequently, there are people who have already done all the hard work for us. Most good distributor tuners will be familiar with the needs of the A-series engine. They may ask you what camshaft you are using and will profile a distributor's advance curve accordingly. Aldon Automotive Ltd and the Distributor Doctor are both very good at what they do and can provide a distributor to suit your needs. For engines that are less well supported, you may only find the best results through experimentation on an engine dyno.

For FIA Appendix K, you must run contact breaker points and a condenser. You have no choice. No electronic ignition systems or inductive discharge units are allowed and the scrutineers will check. Use the best points you can buy. Good-quality points are available from the Distributor Doctor and from Swiftune. They will cost you a tenner, but they will work. Never try racing on a £4 set of points. Likewise, the condenser should be the best quality you can buy and we always use the Swiftune condenser. It will cost you £25 +VAT, but, again, do not try racing on a £4 condenser. It is not worth losing the several hundred pounds spent on an entry fee for the sake of points and condenser failure. If you choose to race outside of Appendix K, you may be allowed to run an alternative ignition triggering system.

HSCC Historic Touring Car Championship Regulations 2017
5.7.7 Ignition systems
The distributor must remain in the original position and retain its original function, but it may be fitted with an after-market spark triggering system. It must be the sole means of ignition advance and retard and must distribute the high tension spark. No system is permitted which processes intelligent information gathered from the engine and/or the ambient conditions.

Most race organizers who allow electronic ignition specify that the system must be entirely contained within the distributor cap and there are many electronic triggering systems available which do just that. In the years we have been racing we have seen many electronic ignition systems fail or become unreliable. Over the last few years we have been using the Pertronix Ignitor from Aldon Automotive almost exclusively and have found them to be reliable. The Pertronix Ignitor comes with a module to replace the points, which screws to the baseplate and a magnetic trigger that slots over the distributor shaft underneath the rotor arm. There is a red and a black wire

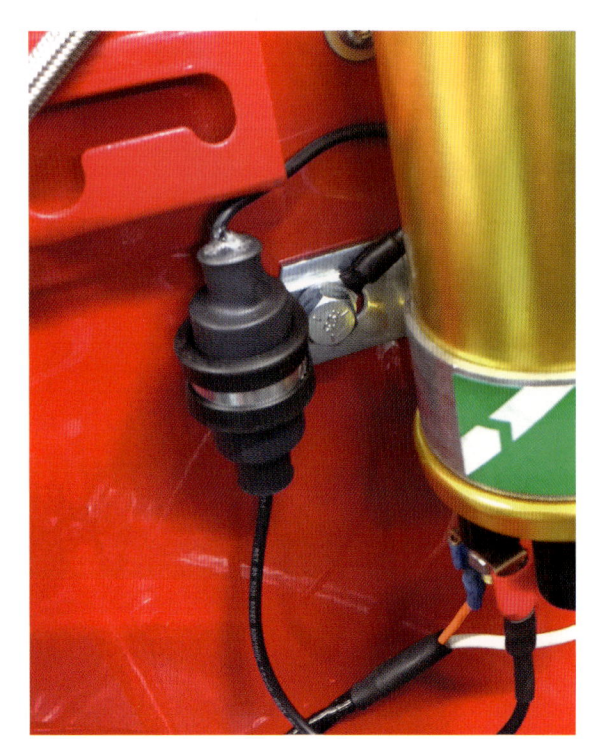

The competition condenser from Swiftune is the best available.

136

wiring loom, instruments and switch gear, safety, engine electrics

which connects to the positive and negative terminals of the coil.

The rotor arm and distributor cap, like the points and condenser, must be the best you can buy. Use only the genuine red rotor arms. These are available from Distributor Doctor, Aldon Automotive and Swiftune and will cost about £7. Do not use a black plastic rotor arm unless it is original new old-stock Lucas. If you have a black plastic one, throw it in the bin now and order a red one. Good-quality distributor caps are also available from the suppliers mentioned. When it comes to ignition, do not buy cheap! You would be surprised how many race cars you see running around with misfires and cheap condensers and rotor arms. These simple items cost very little in the grand scheme of things, but are vital if you want a reliable engine.

Quality HT leads are available from most suppliers ready to fit. 7mm silicone leads will do the job perfectly, but for a period-appropriate look we will often make our own HT leads from the yellow and black copper/PVC leads and plastic NGK plug caps. As for spark plugs, we only use NGK; any other spark plug will go in the bin. Spark plugs are designed to operate in a specific temperature range. The lower the spark plug number, the 'hotter' the plug; the higher the number, the 'colder' the plug. A 'hot' spark plug will heat up quickly, whereas a 'cold' spark plug will resist heating up. A race engine with a high compression ratio will have much greater cylinder pressure and a higher flame temperature and because of this requires a cold spark plug. If you put a hot plug in a race engine, it will likely melt. In a race engine we will usually run a BP8ES or BP9ES spark plug. If an engine is going to be taken out on the road at all, a BP6ES might be used. One thing you should always check is that the threaded cap on the end of a spark plug is tightened before fitting, as these can come loose and cause a misfire.

Finally, you will need a good ignition coil. For simplicity, we only use standard 12V coils on the race cars rather than a ballast system. From the factory, most 1950s and 1960s British cars probably had a ballasted ignition. The ballasted ignition system is designed to provide a bigger spark whilst cranking the engine. This would have been quite clever on a winter's morning in 1962 when you needed to get to work, but for a race engine in 2016 it is not necessary. Coils can and do fail from time to time. You will see in the paddock that most people use the Lucas Sports coil DLB105, which is easily recognized by its golden yellow casing. It is relatively expensive at around £18 +VAT, but has proved to be reliable – and reliability is the key when it comes to race-car electrics.

NGK spark plugs are the only kind we use.

The gold Lucas Sports coil is a popular choice amongst historic racers.

Setting up our Appendix K Mini on the rolling road.

9 setting up, HTP application and race preparation

It may have taken months, or even years, but you have finally finished building your historic Mini race car. You obviously have a patient family. Your electrical systems are tested and working, your engine cranks over and you have high-octane petrol in the tank. You might feel the need to hit the track as soon as you can, but there are a few steps to take to ensure that your engine starts safely and is set up and run in properly before you use it in anger. In this chapter, we look at running the car for the first time, setting up the engine, setting up the handling, applying for an FIA HTP (Historic Technical Passport) and what it is involved in pre-track preparation. None of these vital preparations should be overlooked if you wish to have a reliable racer.

ENGINE SET-UP AND TUNING

It is very important to take care when first running your engine and to be sure it is set up properly before any extended use or high-rev running. If you have built your engine with a static compression ratio of 12:1 or more, it is advisable to use no less than 100RON octane race fuel, probably higher to be on the safe side. We use 101RON octane race fuel from Sunoco in all our race cars. If your

setting up, HTP application and race preparation

Oil pressure at 75psi at idle when cold.

compression ratio is less than 12:1, you may be able to use 98RON unleaded pump fuel with a suitable additive such as Miller's CVL. Remember that higher-octane fuel will give you a safety net from any detonation issues. It is too easy to melt a piston with poor-quality fuel, or too much compression or ignition advance.

There are a few things you need to do before firing up your new race engine for the first time. This is our basic start-up procedure. Check the engine oil level and coolant level in the radiator. Turn on the master switch and fuel pump and allow the fuel system to pressurize. Check all fuel unions very carefully for any sign of a leak. If you find a leak, shut off the pump immediately and attend to it. Fuel leaks obviously lead to fires, so check very carefully. Check every fuel union for moisture; they may not be dripping, but may simply appear wet. Use a coloured paper towel, as the colour will darken when wet, making it easy to spot. Once you are satisfied that there are no fuel leaks, you can set the pressure on the fuel-pressure regulator. For twin SUs, the fuel pressure will need to be around 3.5psi. If you are running a Weber carburettor, it should be no more than 5psi.

Before you start your engine for the first time, or whenever you change the oil or leave it for a long period of time, you will need to build up oil pressure. Filling the oil cooler with engine oil before cranking the engine will help the oil pressure to come up more quickly. Remove all spark plugs, turn off the fuel pump and crank the engine over until you see the oil pressure come up on the oil-pressure gauge. Once you have oil pressure on the gauge, stop cranking and check every oil pipe union for leaks. This includes the capillary to the oil-pressure gauge. A leaky capillary on the back of a gauge can drip engine oil on your shins. Oil lines will need to be checked again once the engine is running and up to temperature.

When you are satisfied that there are no oil leaks, it is nearly time to start the engine. Check the coolant level again. Having cranked the engine over to bring up oil pressure, it may be necessary to top up the coolant as the system circulates and pushes out any air. Refit the spark plugs, connect the HT leads, turn on the ignition and fuel pump and crank the engine. All being well, it should fire up. You may need to adjust the ignition timing by rotating the distributor to get it to fire and idle. Your oil-pressure gauge should be reading around 70–80psi when cold.

Setting ignition timing to 26 degrees BTDC.

setting up, HTP application and race preparation

Keep the first run fairly brief. Check again for fuel and oil leaks and again check the coolant level in the radiator. If all is well, start the engine again. Watch that the oil pressure comes up quickly and keep the revs fairly high at around 1,500–2,500rpm. Do not leave the engine at a slow idle whilst cold, as there may not be sufficient oil reaching the cam followers, which will cause unnecessary wear. Gently blip the throttle repeatedly to around 3,000rpm until the engine reaches 50°C, then shut it off. Check again for any fluid leaks and check all your levels.

You now need to set the ignition timing. On a newly built A-series engine the ignition timing should be set to a safe 24 degrees Before Top Dead Centre (BTDC). Once the engine is run in and the carburettors have been tuned for best fuelling, you will find power gains from further advancing the ignition. 26–28 degrees BTDC usually provides a good balance between power and reliability. There may be additional power at 28–30 degrees BTDC, but your safety margin will be lost. Detonation caused by too much ignition advance and poor-quality fuel can destroy your engine in just a few minutes: 1–2 degrees less ignition advance may just save your engine at the cost of only 1bhp.

If you have bought a complete engine from an engine builder, it will hopefully come fully set up and run in on an engine dyno. If that is the case, there is little more you need to do. Your engine is ready to go. If, however, you have built your own engine, or bought an engine that has not been on a dyno, it will need to be set up professionally. With twin SU carburettors, the needles will need profiling to achieve the optimum air-to-fuel mixture ratio across the entire rpm range. With Weber carburettors, the correct jetting will be needed. Only with the correct mixture will your engine produce optimum power and efficiency. Achieving the correct mixture and the optimum power requires the use of either an engine dyno or a rolling road.

Here at CCK Historic we use a Maha MSR500 rolling-road dynamometer. All of the cars we prepare spend time on the rolling road when new and during the race season for both setting up and monitoring engine performance. The rolling road allows us not only to set up an engine for optimum fuelling, it also allows us to experiment in the quest for performance. We can experiment with carburettor modifications, different intake manifolds or different ignition settings. However, it is not just peak power we are looking for. Getting the power to come in earlier and increasing the spread of power across the whole rev range will bring significant gains on the track.

The dyno works by putting a load on the engine with a brake. The load applied to the engine is designed to mimic the load experienced by an engine when driving on the road. Most modern dynamometers use an electromagnetic brake to provide the load. With the engine

Our Mini on our Maha MSR500 rolling road.

setting up, HTP application and race preparation

Gas analysis during constant rpm test.

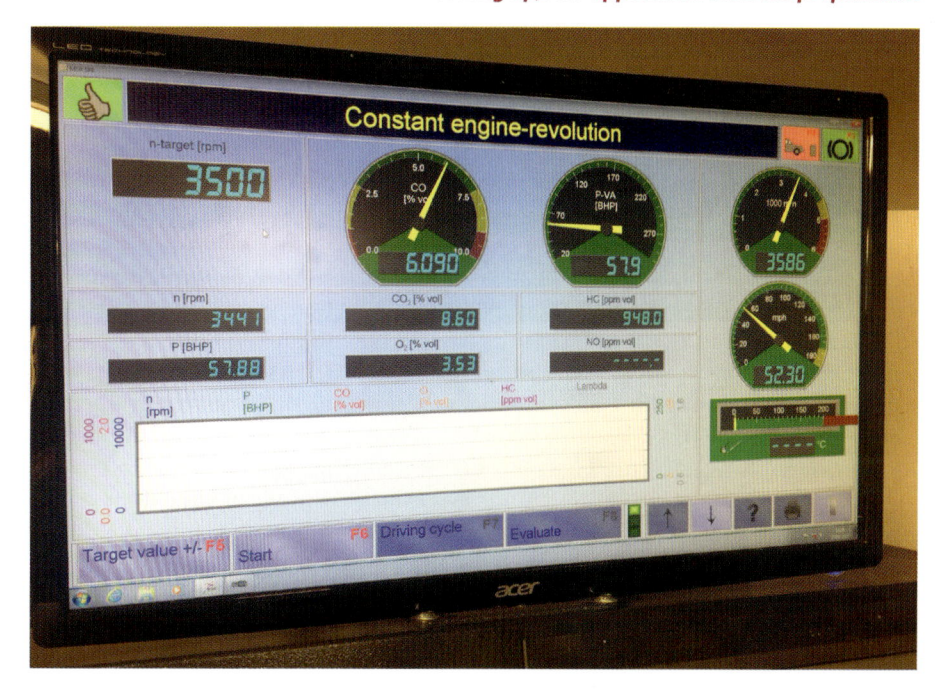

running under load, a gas analyzer is used to measure the gases in the exhaust. It is the percentage of carbon monoxide (CO) that tells us how rich or lean the fuel-to-air mixture is. With a vehicle strapped down on our rolling road, the process we use to determine optimum fuelling begins with a series of constant rpm tests. We set the machine to apply the load and hold the engine at a constant 3,000rpm, for example. The engine is held at a set constant rpm for around 20sec whilst we look at the gas analysis and wait for it to stabilize. We want to see a good fuel mixture at both partial throttle and wide open throttle. Once the gas analysis is made at 3,000rpm we will increase to 4,000rpm, for example, and carry out the same test.

Once we have completed the constant rpm test across the rev range, we can begin to adjust the mixture. With SU carburettors like the pair fitted to our race car, if our tests show that the mixture is getting lean above 4,000rpm, we need to file the end of the needle to allow more fuel to pass through the jet. If the mixture is too rich, we will need to find a leaner set of needles, as we cannot add material to our existing needle to reduce the amount of fuel let through the jet. If you cannot get enough fuel into the mixture without filing the needle into a razor blade, a bigger jet will be needed. Most 1.5in SUs will use a .090in jet at the bottom. For race engines that jet will need to be replaced with a .100in jet or drilled out to .100in if you have an accurate set of jet drills.

Carburettor needle being filed.

This needle has been filed towards the top to allow more fuel in at higher rpm.

141

setting up, HTP application and race preparation

The other part of the SU carb that will have an effect on your fuelling is the dashpot. Within the dashpot is a coil spring and an oil damper. A heavier spring will slow down the rate at which the needle rises and a lighter spring will let the needle rise more quickly. You can further tune the reaction of the needle by changing the oil in the dashpot. A lighter oil will allow the needle to react more quickly.

Once we have got the fuelling to an acceptable level we will do a power run. A power run takes approximately 45sec and will measure the power as the car accelerates up to maximum rpm. We also measure the exhaust gases, which are plotted on the same graph as the power curve. If we see from the graph that the CO percentage is tailing off at high rpm, we would file a little more off the end of the needle. Another power run will produce another graph and show if we have made any power gains. On a brand new engine we will restrict the rpm and the length of time running on the rollers until the engine has been run in. Once the engine is run in, we can utilize the full rpm range and also start to look for power gains by advancing the ignition timing. On our Mini race car, we found a gain of 2bhp and an increase of 300rpm in the power band by advancing the ignition from 24 degrees BTDC to 26 degrees BTDC. We tested the ignition at 28 degrees BTDC, but no further gains were found, so we went back to 26 degrees BTDC.

HANDLING SET-UP

The Mini's handling has been legendary since its inception back in 1959. The racing potential was realized because of its exceptional handling. However, you cannot expect simply to drive out on the track and corner like the best of them without careful consideration to the set-up. The suspension will need setting up if you are to get the most out of each lap. The set-up you use on your Mini will develop as you become comfortable with the car and your skill develops.

Every car handles differently and getting the most from any car on the circuit will depend greatly on its set-up, the geometry of the steering and suspension, the ride height, the shock absorber settings and the weight balance. These settings vary from car to car and from driver to driver, but there are fundamentals you need to understand. We will outline some basic settings here, but the only way you are really going to get the car dialled in is to go testing. If you are building to the FIA's Appendix K, you need to familiarize yourself with the following rules:

FIA Appendix K 2017 Appendix VIII
10 Wheelbase, track, ground clearance
10.1 Wheelbase and track
10.1.1 They must be those homologated or, if the model was not homologated, must conform to the manufacturer's original specification.
10.1.2 The tolerance granted concerning the tracks is +/−1%.
10.2 Ground clearance
All sprung parts of the car must have a minimum ground clearance of 100mm, such that a block of 800mm × 800mm × 100mm may be passed underneath the car from any side, at any time of the compe-

The Mini's exceptional handling helped to make it a legend.

setting up, HTP application and race preparation

Metal shims to level the car.

tition. Ground clearance may be measured at any time during a competition, on a surface specified by the eligibility delegate, and in conformity with the Homologation Manual published by the FIA in 1993.

11. Weight

At all times during a Competition, a car must weigh no less than the minimum weight specified on its HTP.

Measurements taken from the lip on the seal at the front …

Strictly speaking for an FIA Appendix K Mini, none of the suspension can be adjustable. That means fixed length bottom arms, fixed radius arm brackets, fixed tie bars and no adjustable ride-height kit. In reality, things are a little different. If you look around the current crop of Appendix K Minis in the UK, you will find that most are running adjustable ride height and adjustable rear camber brackets. Most of the UK race series are allowing adjustable ride-height kits, but check the regulations first to avoid having a problem on race day. The rear camber brackets tend to be allowed as long as they are fixed with a bolt or by welding them in a fixed position.

The other important area that needs to be mentioned is the front track width. The homologated limit on track width has just been officially widened to 127.5cm from 124.2cm as stated on the homologation form. However, achieving this track width is still a challenge whilst maintaining a decent amount of negative camber.

For an accurate set-up and for accurate measurements, the floor must be totally flat. Our workshop has a flat floor, but if you do not have one you can get your car level using thin metal plates to shim under the tyres.

Starting with the ride height, we will take our measurements from the external lip along the sill just in front of the rear wheel arch and just behind the front wheel arch. At the front you will require a maximum measurement of 230mm (9in). The rear of the car needs to measure about 13mm (½in) higher than the front. We have used Mini Sport's Adjusta Ride kit, which easily allows us to adjust the ride height. Once you start driving the car the suspension may settle down, so checking the set-up and readjusting the ride height may be required.

Camber angle refers to the angle of the wheels when looked at from the front. Positive camber is when the top

… and the rear.

143

setting up, HTP application and race preparation

Adjusta Ride kit on our Mini.

Rear adjustable toe and camber brackets.

of the wheel is further out from the bottom and negative camber is when the bottom of the wheel is further out than the top. Generally, negative camber helps to improve grip. Negative camber at the front of the Mini is not adjustable, unless you are running your car in a series that allows the use of adjustable bottom arms. Those building to Appendix K will be restricted to the fixed 1.5-degree negative camber bottom arms. The amount of negative camber you actually achieve will ultimately be determined by the manufacturing accuracy of the components and the subframe. Small variations in manufacturing tolerances will vary the end result. The front of our car ended up with 1.0 degrees negative camber on the left and 1.2 degrees on the right. The negative camber is achieved by pushing the bottom ball joint outwards.

While we may want negative camber, the downside for those of us building an FIA car is that we also get an increase in front track width. The front track width for FIA Minis needs to be 127.5cm. In order to achieve this, you may have to consider machining the back of your wheels or a small amount from the face of the drive flange to bring that width in. When we measured our car, it was 128.1cm out of the box. That meant finding 3mm to take off each side. We used Mini Sports adjustable toe and camber brackets for the rear radius arms. The rear camber needs to be set between 0–0.25 degrees negative.

Caster angle refers to the angle of the vertical axis of your Mini's steered wheels. Positive caster means the top of the axis, or top of the front hub leaning backwards. Positive caster will help the wheels to self-centre, but most importantly it will give a negative camber gain

Camber angle.

Caster angle.

setting up, HTP application and race preparation

when cornering. This means that as you steer and the car leans away from the apex of the corner, the suspension on the outside wheel compresses, giving a gain in negative camber and increasing grip.

Caster angle is not adjustable on the standard tie rods, which will be required for Appendix K. However, if you use a pair of adjustable tie rods to achieve the desired amount of caster, you can measure the length and modify the standard fixed-length bars to match. If you have 1.5 degrees of negative camber, you should be running 6 degrees of positive caster. If you have less than 1.5 degrees negative camber, you can somewhat make up for it by increasing the caster to up to 7.5 degrees positive.

The toe angle refers to the angle of the wheels when looked at from above. Toe-out is when the front of the wheels angle outwards away from the centre line of the car; toe-in is when they angle in towards the centre line. When the front wheels toe-in, it will improve straight-line stability at the cost of steering response. When the front wheels toe-out, the car will react more quickly to steering inputs. We have set the front of our car to have 20 minutes' toe-out.

The rear of a Mini is quite sensitive to toe angles and finding the balance between stability and cornering speed will depend on your level of experience. On a road car you might set the rear wheels parallel, as this will reduce oversteer. A front-wheel-drive car will have a natural tendency to understeer. On the circuit, we want to counter that tendency by setting up the back of the car to oversteer. How much oversteer will depend on your car-control abilities and your level of experience. For a novice or for someone who is new to racing a Mini, the rear should be set to 0.5 degrees toe-out. With more experience and if you really want to get the back sliding, there can be as much as 2 degrees toe-out. The rear track width should be 120.3cm. Some race series, such as the HSCC's Historic Touring Cars or the CSCC's Swinging 60s, will be less

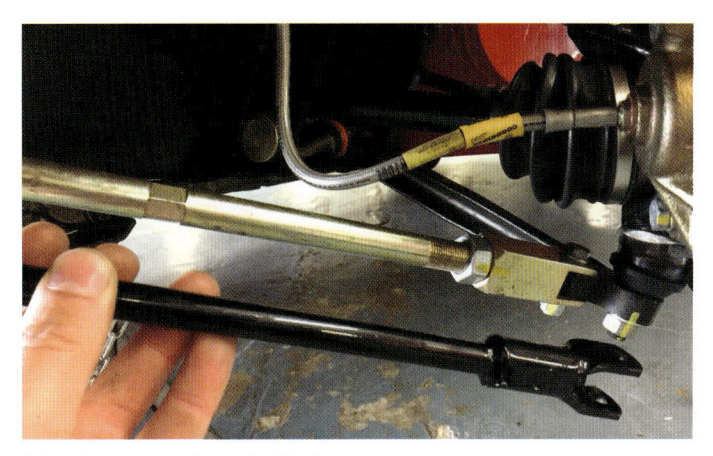

Adjustable tie bar and a standard tie bar.

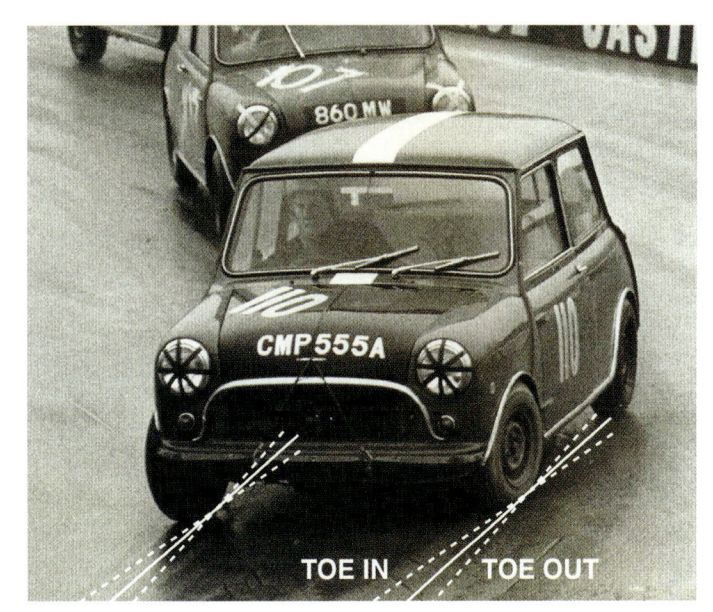

Toe angle.

John Rhodes slides the rear through the corner.

setting up, HTP application and race preparation

Tracking gauge used to check toe angles.

restrictive in their regulations, allowing for wider track and adjustable bottom arms and tie bars, which make set-up adjustments quicker and easier.

Whichever race series you are planning to compete in, you will be using adjustable shock absorbers. Our steel-bodied AVO dampers have a single knob for adjustment. They are simple and inexpensive and do the job reliably. Unless you need to find fractions of a second in your lap times, it should not be necessary to spend a fortune on dampers. Typically we will start out by setting both front and rear dampers to a middle setting and make adjustments during testing. On a Mini, the rear shock absorbers should typically be run harder than the front. Whilst testing with Bill Sollis, we adjusted our rear shocks to their maximum.

Tyre pressures will make a big difference to the handling. With a historic racing Mini on Dunlop CR65 historic tyres, it is typical to run a higher pressure on the back than on the front. A lower tyre pressure will promote better grip. On the front we will start by running 35psi cold and on the rear 38psi. You can adjust the balance of the car by varying the tyre pressures by a degree or two. In the wet we would typically lower the tyre pressure to improve grip.

Corner-weighting a race car involves adjusting the weight over each wheel. The main goal is to achieve an

Checking tyre pressures.

setting up, HTP application and race preparation

Electronic scales show that our car weighs 635kg (1,400lb) with fuel on board.

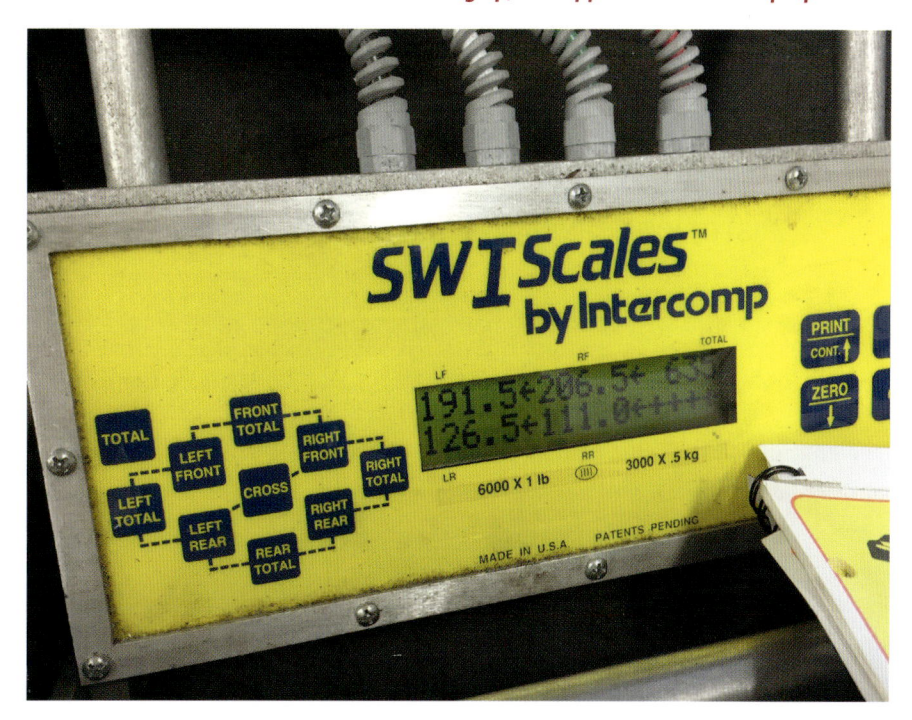

equal balance left to right, with the driver seated and carrying an average fuel load. With a historic Mini there will not be a lot you can do compared to a single-seat racing car with fully adjustable suspension. There are many firms that offer corner-weighting as a service, or if you are a serious competitor you may feel the need to purchase your own set of scales. To balance a car accurately it must be done on level ground. If the ground is not level, you need to use shims under the scales. When corner-weighting a car, it should be done with the driver seated, all fluids and an average amount of fuel for the racing you plan to do.

The biggest advantage can be found if you can manage to build a car that is underweight. Then you can strategically place ballast in the car to bring the weight up and improve the overall weight balance. This is called static weight distribution. When adding ballast, you want to place it as low as possible in order to keep the centre of gravity low. Add ballast to whichever corner helps to achieve better balance between left and right and front and rear. If your car is not underweight and you do not want to use ballast, the only way to balance the car is to move components physically. Heavy objects like the battery are the first to be relocated. However, with the Mini the battery is already in a fairly good location at the back of the car. The fire extinguisher is a good item for strategic placement. Anything that can be mounted on the opposite side to the driver will help left-to-right weight balance.

The final area of corner-weighting is the diagonal. Adjusting the ride height at each corner will adjust the diagonal cross-weight of the vehicle. By raising the ride height on the front left, for example, you will increase the weight of the car at the front left and rear right and reduce the weight at the front right and rear left. Likewise, lowering the ride height at one corner will reduce the weight at that corner and at the diagonal opposite corner. The overall homologated weight for the 1275 Mini Cooper S is 620kg (1,367lb), without driver and fuel. Most cars should be close to this weight. Those cars with lightweight T45 roll cages achieve this quite easily. Those with standard roll cages may come out a little overweight. The finished weight of our car with fuel was 635kg (1,400lb), so the dry weight should be about spot on.

FIA HISTORIC TECHNICAL PASSPORT APPLICATION

When your racing Mini is complete, and if you've built it to the FIA's Appendix K regulations and the necessary homologation form, you may choose to apply for a Historic Technical Passport, or HTP. The process is relatively simple when the subject for inspection is a common and familiar vehicle such as a Mini Cooper S. Most FIA inspectors will have come across plenty of Minis and there are enough out there racing that there exist no real question marks.

setting up, HTP application and race preparation

Red/black dot entries:

HISTORIC TECHNICAL PASSPORT – VALID IN: RACING & -H-CLIMB & - RALLY

This Technical Passport is not a certificate of authenticity, nor does it in anyway verify the history of the car or its constituent parts. It merely confirms that at the date of the inspection, the car appeared to be eligible to compete in FIA-sanctioned events for historic vehicles. Neither the FIA nor the ASN certifies or takes responsibility for the accuracy of the chassis number. The items shown below as "asserted" are those claimed by the owner based upon his best available knowledge.

Issuing ASN: **MSA**   Form Number: Category: **Competition Touring Car**

Period: F - 1962 to 1965   valid to 31.12.2026   FIA Class: CT7

The original of this document was completed in accordance with Appendix "K" to the International Sporting Code, for cars taking part in historic competitions. This certified copy of the original form remains the property of the FIA and, if replaced with a new form, must be returned to the issuing ASN which holds the original. During the whole event the car must conform to all the declarations of this HTP.

APPLICANT'S ASSERTIONS:

Make asserted: AUSTIN   Manufacturer asserted: B.M.C/COOPER CAR CO.

Model asserted: MINI COOPER "S" 1275   Date of original manufacture asserted:

Vehicle chassis / VIN n° asserted:

Year of specification: 1965   FIA identity n°:

Engine type: STR4 OHV   Engine capacity: 1293 cm^3 corrected: cm^3

FIA homologation form number (if applicable): 1300   Number of relevant valid pages of homologation form: 11

Each page of this form, as well as the edge of each photograph, must bear the stamp of the issuing ASN

We, the MSA, have checked the information given on this form and confirm that to the best of our knowledge and belief, the car complies with the period specification of the make and model represented.

Date: Signature and stamp: Name and status of signatory:
ROB JONES, CEO
For and on behalf of the
ROYAL AUTOMOBILE CLUB
MOTOR SPORTS ASSOCIATION

FIA HTP vignette

2013 International HTP

Page 1

This is what the HTP papers look like.

setting up, HTP application and race preparation

FIA holographic sticker is placed on the car by the inspector.

If you are in the UK, the process begins with the MSA. If you are in another country, you will need to contact your local motor-sport governing body. We will describe the process here in the UK, but it will be similar for other countries. First, you need to contact the MSA and pay for your application, otherwise known as purchasing a 'GB number'. The GB number will be your application number and if your application is successful, it will also become your HTP number. The cost of the GB number and the application to the FIA changes from time to time, so contact the MSA for up-to-date pricing. You can purchase your GB number over the phone. Then, with your number in hand, you will need to contact an FIA inspector. Every inspector will have a different speciality. Some will specialize in single-seaters, some in sports racing cars and some in saloon and sports cars. An inspector's proximity may also have a bearing, as you may have to pick up their travel expenses. The MSA will provide a list of their inspectors' contact details. When you organize an appointment for the inspection of your car, the inspector will ask for the GB number. With that number, they will be able to retrieve the holographic sticker from the MSA. This sticker has to be placed on the car by the inspector and will represent your vehicle's FIA identity.

Make sure to be ready before the day of inspection arrives. Be sure that your vehicle conforms to the FIA homologation to your best knowledge. Be sure that the vehicle is accessible and that you have the means to remove the wheels so that the brakes and suspension can be inspected and photographed. The inspector's job is to inspect the vehicle and fill in the application form accordingly. They will answer every question on the form and take the necessary photographs. They will take measurements of the track and the wheel base and record what they find. It is not their place to tell you what you can and cannot do, although if they spot something blatantly obvious they will likely let you know and give you a chance to correct it.

A typical inspection will usually take around three or four hours, after which the inspector will take the information and the photographs home and compile a

HTP photograph of the front suspension.

149

setting up, HTP application and race preparation

formal HTP application. When the application is complete, they will send it to you for your approval and for you to complete and sign a declaration form. If you are happy to proceed, the application will be submitted. All you can do now is to wait for an answer, which may take as little as two weeks but could just as easily take six weeks or more. If any problems are found, the MSA will write to you and give you the opportunity to correct them. For example, you may be told that you have the wrong type of radiator, or that your rear anti-roll bar is unacceptable because it is adjustable. You will need to rectify any issues raised and submit a new photograph showing that the part has been corrected.

When the application has been approved, the MSA will ask you to pay the remainder of the fee. Again, this fee varies from year to year. Once the final amount is paid, the MSA can issue your papers. Under the current rules, your HTP will last ten years before it needs to be renewed. Renewal is the same process as a first-time application, although the MSA does have a tendency to change the process from year to year and adjust the way the fees are structured, so contact your local governing body for the latest information.

Keep your HTP papers safe. They are valuable. If you are racing in a strictly Appendix K class, you will need to bring your papers to the circuit, as you may be asked to produce them. If you are racing at an FIA-sanctioned event in Europe, you will most definitely need to show your actual HTP documents. A copy will not suffice. It is also worth noting that the officials in Europe can be very fastidious and may insist that your vehicle matches the photograph on the cover of your HTP exactly. They may not like it if you have changed any stickers. If you decide to change the colour of your car, you will need to pay to update the HTP.

RACE-CAR PREPARATION

We have all seen race cars break down on track, drop oil, loose a wheel or worse. Perhaps the most fundamental responsibility with any race car, for the good of your competitors, is proper preparation. Before each and every time you head to the circuit or for any competition you *must* prepare the car properly. This is a fundamental safety requirement and must never be overlooked. It is not just for your safety, but also for the safety of the other drivers on track, as well as their respect. If a nut comes loose and something falls off your car or breaks on track, at the least it might cause yellow or red flags as the problem is dealt with by the marshals, but at the worst it could

Mark nuts and bolts with a paint pen during the spanner check.

cause an accident. People spend a lot of time and money going racing and if you cause a session to be red-flagged because of your poorly prepared car, you will quickly make yourself very unpopular in the paddock.

Ensuring that your car is ready for the track begins with a spanner check. Get the car in the air, either on a ramp if you have access to one or on axle stands. You need to spanner-check the whole vehicle. Check that every nut, bolt and screw is tight. We use a paint pen to mark every nut and bolt. It helps you to keep track of your progress, as well as providing a visual indicator if any nut or bolt does come loose as it will break the dot of paint.

In the engine bay check all fluid unions. Water, oil and fuel unions should all be checked for leaks and nipped up to make sure they are tight. Check fluid levels. Check the engine for oil leaks and make sure that your sump plug is tight. We recommend using lock wire on the sump plug, as losing the sump plug and all your engine oil on the circuit is an unforgivable sin and will result in you being ostracized by the paddock. It could also destroy your engine. Inspect the throttle cables for wear and fraying

setting up, HTP application and race preparation

and check that the cable has not slipped and that you can achieve full throttle at the carburettors. If the cable is frayed, it should be replaced. Check that the fan belt is tight and check it for wear. Test that the alternator or dynamo is charging and that all electrical connections are tight, especially the ignition system and master switch. A loose ignition wire can end your race prematurely. Check the spark plugs and HT leads. Ensure that the little threaded ends on the spark plugs are tight. If one of these comes loose, it can cause a misfire.

Check the brake and clutch systems for leaks and bleed them. Remove the brake calipers and drums and inspect the pads and shoes for wear and heat damage. Overheated brake pads and shoes will show cracks or crumbly patches in the surface of the friction material. If you can, use a dial gauge to check whether the brake discs are warped. In the boot, inspect the fuel tank, breather and fuel pump. In the cockpit be sure to check that the seat and harnesses are secure. Check the pedals and the gear selection. Test the emergency pull cables and if they are tight pull out the inner cables and lubricate them with oil or grease.

Check that all of the lights function. You will need headlights, tail lights, brake lights and a rain light in order to pass scrutineering. Test the gauges and warning lights. Test your wipers. Check that the exhaust system is secure and free from any leaks. Ensure that the universal joints and CV joints move freely and are greased. Grease all of the grease points on the suspension and wipe off any excess. Check your ride height, camber settings and tracking before you head to the track each time. Check your shock absorber settings. These may not change very often, but if your last session was in the wet and you softened the shock absorbers, you need to make sure that standard setting has been returned.

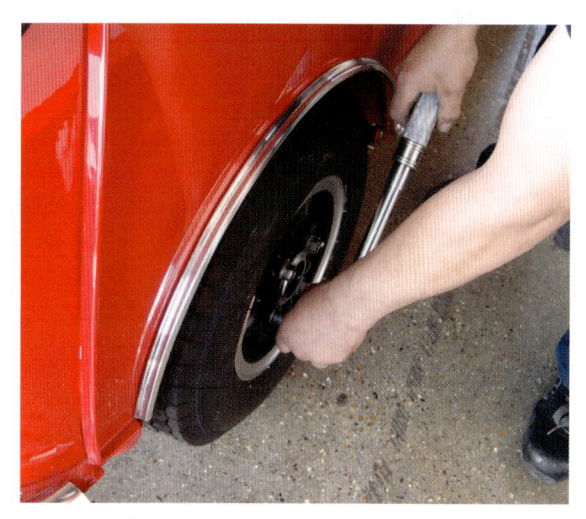

Torque your wheels nuts to 45ft lb.

Check the wheels. Check the threads on the wheel studs and nuts and replace any that look like they may be damaged or stretched. Losing a wheel on the circuit is another unforgivable sin, but you still see it happen from time to time. Check tyres for wear and damage. It is good practice to overinflate tyres by a few psi when prepping the car. When you get to the circuit, it is much easier to let the tyre down to your desired pressure than inflate it if it is low. Finally, you *must* torque the wheel nuts with a calibrated torque wrench when prepping the car and before every single session of your race weekend. For a Mini with the standard $3/8$in UNF wheel studs the torque setting is 45ft lb.

Failing to prep your race car thoroughly before every track day, test day or race weekend is not acceptable. For your sake and those around you, never head out on track in a poorly prepped vehicle.

151

Our Mini's first test at Brands Hatch.

10 testing and racing

It is not advisable to take your freshly built Mini racing car and enter it straight into a race. As skilled a mechanic as you may be, it is likely to end in a DNF (Did Not Finish) and a waste of your time and money. You need the chance to shake the car down. All the new components need a chance to bed in. You need to start pushing the brakes and the engine slowly whilst looking for any shortfalls or problems. All being well, your car will perform satisfactorily straight out of the box, but you will inevitably find some issues, such as an engine running hot and a need for more cooling or perhaps a set-up issue with the suspension or handling. You might even find that one of the brand new parts bolted to the car has already decided to fail.

If you are an experienced racer, you should be familiar with much of this chapter already, but for those who have not raced before in any vehicle this chapter will aim to outline some important points. It will take a good few races before you get to grips with it and many more to hone your race craft.

SHAKEDOWN AND TESTING

We chose Brands Hatch for our shakedown as it is our local circuit, we know it like the back of our hands and we love it. It was also the venue for our Mini's first race. We booked a track day over the phone and reserved a garage alongside experienced Mini racers Nick Paddy and Bill Sollis. Nick and Bill were getting in some practice in their own Appendix K Mini Cooper S ahead of the same race we had entered. Bill Sollis is well known in the Mini

152

testing and racing

Brands Hatch garage with Bill Sollis and Nick Paddy setting up in the background.

racing fraternity and is one of the most experienced and successful competitors. Bill very kindly agreed to test our car for us and help set it up for the race

The day of your test or track day has arrived and you have successfully made it to the circuit with your race car in tow. When you first arrive at the circuit, you need to find a convenient spot in the paddock or find your garage, if you have booked one. As a driver, you will need to sign on and if it is a track day you will need to attend a driver's briefing before being allowed out on track. Test days require a race licence and do not usually have a briefing. Your car needs fuel. This may sound obvious, but you would be surprised by how many people run out of fuel on track and have to be recovered. You will need to bring your fuel with you and if your engine requires the use of a higher-octane race fuel, it will need to be ordered ahead of time as there is unlikely to be any race fuel available at the circuit unless it is the Friday before a big race weekend, in which case there may be a lorry full of race fuel in attendance. Check your tyre pressures and adjust if necessary, then check that your wheel nuts are torqued. For a Mini, that needs to be to 45lb/ft.

The engine needs to be properly warmed up a good 30min before heading out on track. Start the engine and gently blip the throttle to approximately 3,000rpm until the water-temperature gauge reads around 70ºC. If the weather is particularly warm, it is advisable not to warm the engine quite as much. When the desired temperature has been reached, shut off the engine, as you need to allow at least 15–20min for the heat to soak evenly through the engine.

Before they let you out on track, your car will have to pass a noise test. There will be a dedicated zone in the paddock or in the garages where the noise testing will take place. Drive to the noise-test zone and await instructions. The testers will tell you to hold the engine at a constant rpm, usually at two-thirds of your maximum rpm, while they measure how loud your car is. If you pass the noise test, they will put a sticker on the windscreen and you will be free to head out on track. If you fail the noise test, you will not be let out. You will have to make your car quieter and have it retested before you will be allowed on track.

We keep a selection of mufflers with us that attach to the end of the tailpipe and do a decent job of knocking a

testing and racing

Set-up advice from Bill Sollis' test session.

testing and racing

couple of decibels off a car's noise level. You will find that not all noise tests are equal – for example, on one day at one circuit the result may be 102db, while on another day at another circuit it might be 106db. Some noise testers can be very rigorous. One trick that is worth remembering is to drive your car around the paddock until it is good and hot, then go to noise testing. When the car is hot, it tends to be a little quieter, which can make all the difference. It is also worth noting that your engine may be louder or quieter at certain rpms – for example, you may find that when you rev it to 4,000rpm it produces 106db, but if you rev it further to 5,500rpm, the noise level actually comes down to 105db.

When you book a track day or a test day, the circuit will advertise the noise level. A lot of track days will be limited to 98db, which will be fine for a road car, but not for your racing Mini. If you take your racing Mini down to the circuit on a 98db day, it will probably fail the noise test and will not be allowed out on track unless you have an extra muffler. Test days and some track days will have a noise limit of 105db. This is the standard noise limit in the UK for almost all motor racing, so most race cars and exhaust systems are built to meet this noise level.

If it is a track day, you will probably be required to do two or three sighting laps before being free to lap at full speed. This involves following a course car at a moderate speed so that you can familiarize yourself with the circuit and see where the marshals and the flags are located. When on a track day, rather than testing, you are not allowed to time your laps. You will also notice that some days are labelled as having an open pit lane. These days will usually have fewer cars out on track and you will be free to head out on track whenever the track is live and complete as many laps as you like. If it is not an open pit lane day, the day will be divided up into sessions. Groups of just five to ten cars will be allowed out on track for a limited amount of time, maybe 20min per period.

Once you are free to go at your own pace, keep your first session in a new car relatively short, maybe three laps. Build up your speed slowly, test the brakes and monitor the feel of the brake pedal, watch your engine temperature and oil pressure and get a feel for the handling of the car. Bring the car into the pits and take a short break.

If this is the very first time the car has been out on track, give it a quick visual inspection, check fluids, check for leaks, torque the wheel nuts to 45lb/ft and head back out for another five to ten laps, if allowed. Again, keep a close eye on temperature and oil pressure, brake pedal feel and biting point. After this short session, it is worth taking the wheels off to check and clean the brakes. As

testing and racing

Noise test at Brands Hatch.

your brand new brakes bed in, they will create a lot of dust. Clean the dust with brake cleaner. Check that the pads are bedding in properly and that the discs and pads have not glazed up. If they have glazed, you will need to scuff them with a coarse abrasive paper; 40–60grit aluminium oxide will do the job. Check the rear brakes, too. If the drums or shoes have glazed, they will also need to be scuffed. With the brake drums back in place, the brake shoes will need to be adjusted. New brake shoes will likely need to be adjusted throughout the day as they continue to bed in. Poorly adjusted brake shoes will result in a long pedal. Put the wheels back on the car and do not forget to torque the wheel nuts to 45lb/ft.

When heading out on your next session, again, you want to build the speed slowly, building up brake and tyre temperature with the gradually increasing speed. Keep an eye on the engine temperature, oil pressure and brake pedal feel. Start pushing the car a little and if all is well stay out for a few more laps. After five to ten laps, bring the car in for a break and record the tyre pressures. Keeping a record of the changes in tyre pressure will tell you which tyres are doing the most work. As a tyre's temperature increases, so does its pressure. If, for example, the front left tyre pressure has increased by 2psi over the right after a session on track, let some air out to compensate. You want to aim to have equal pressures between the left and the right tyres when they are hot. We keep a notebook with our car for recording this data. You can take note of the air and track temperature and your tyre pressures. Being able to look back at this data will help you in setting up the car in the future.

The temptation for many drivers will be to get out on track and rack up as many laps in the day as possible. However, this practice is counter-productive and will result in you wearing out both the car and yourself. You need to take breaks throughout the day to give yourself a chance to relax and cool off, while your brain absorbs the information it is getting on track. You will learn the circuit and improve your lap times more quickly if you take breaks. It is also very important that you keep hydrated. A lot of moisture is lost through sweat when driving.

The main difference between a track day and a test day is that for a test day you must have a valid racing licence and lap timing is allowed. On a track day, you only need a road licence and lap timing is not allowed. When booking track time, it is worth asking the organizers what

Out on track for the first time.

Heading into the pits.

157

testing and racing

Cleaning the brakes during testing.

other vehicles will also be out on track. Silverstone, for example, is a very fast circuit with many top-level professional teams in the area and will often have some very fast machinery out testing. If you are out in your 1960s Mini for the first time, the last thing you want is to have sports racing prototypes bearing down on you at 180mph.

FURTHER DEVELOPMENT

Once you've gained some experience, competed in a few races and proved your car works, then testing your car will change its focus from the simple shake down and preliminary setup to a more focused pursuit of lap times. There are two areas to focus on when testing: your driving and your car's setup. The former requires practice, experience and driver tuition. Most of the major circuits in the UK will have tuition available, and there is a great number of freelance driving tutors and professional racing drivers who can be employed to tutor your driving. However good you think you are I would always recommend getting some tuition from time to time. It is always good to have an independent view of your driving: they can pull you up on any bad habits you may have developed as well as providing insights into the fastest lines at any particular circuit. They can show you where you are fast and where you can find more time. Ultimately the point of tuition is to improve your driving and your lap times.

The other purpose of testing is to fine to your car's setup. With subtle changes you can fine-tune it's handling and lower your lap times. This process can be a matter of trial and error, or you can seek some help from a professional or an experienced Mini racer to find what changes will result in lower lap times. These may include, but are not limited to, changes to geometry, ride height, weight distribution, shock absorber settings and, if you are really serious, final drive or drop gear ratios.

RACING

You have finally finished the build and the car has been shaken down and tested successfully. You should already have an idea of which club you wish to go racing with, as you would have built your Mini race car to the necessary regulations. Most clubs have membership requirements and some clubs give you the option of day membership

Testing at Brands Hatch.

testing and racing

if you want to try them out rather than commit straight off to a whole year. Whichever club you have chosen to race with, the process of entering a race and the format of the race events are much the same. Most clubs will aim to publish their calendars in January.

When you have chosen a race to enter, contact the club and ask for an entry form. All entry forms are much the same. They will ask for your contact details and an emergency contact, plus details of your vehicle, race licence number and transponder number. If you do not have a transponder and plan to hire one from the circuit, you can leave that part blank. The entry form will also contain the race entry fee and payment details. Most clubs will accept debit/credit card or cheque. Email is the easiest way to submit an entry form, but the post works just fine too. It is worth a telephone call to the club to confirm they have received your entry and that you have made the grid. A lot of races are oversubscribed, so it is always worth getting your entry in early. If the race is oversubscribed, you will be placed on a reserve list. Most races will have a couple of cancellations or a couple of entries that do not show, so the first couple of drivers on the reserve list will usually get a race.

Before the big day arrives you will be sent final instructions, an event timetable, an entry list and a paddock plan. The final instructions will usually contain race-specific instructions for the event, including: access hours for the circuit and paddock; details about signing on and driver briefings; details on scrutineering; noise limits, driver change rules for two-driver races; pit lane rules; the race format; and a list of officials who will be overseeing the event. The entry list will show you who and what you are up against, what class you will be running in and what your race number is. You need to ensure that your car is fitted with suitable race numbers on each door and on the bonnet. The official option is to have white roundels with black numbers. Some scrutineers will turn their noses up at black roundels, or at roundels and numbers of other colours such as red, blue or green. The official line of the MSA is:

MSA Yearbook 2017 Competitors: Vehicles (J) Competition Numbers

4.1 Numbers must be displayed in a durable manner and be black, of a minimum size of 23cm high with stroke width of a minimum of 3.8cm on a white oblong background measuring not less than 48cm × 33cm which must extend at least 5cm beyond the outline of the numbers. Alternatively, the numbers may be displayed on a white circular background provided that the background extends at least 5cm beyond the outline of the numbers.

4.1.1 If on a white vehicle a background of the dimensions in 4.1. must be delineated by a continuous black line, except for cars of period A to E.

4.1.2 Numbers must be displayed on each side of the vehicle (front doors, alongside the cockpit or on rear wing end plates) and on the foremost part of the nose.

The paddock plan is a map of the paddock showing designated areas for each club or each race. You will need to identify where in the paddock you should be. Some people get a little grumpy if you set yourself up in the wrong place, plus you will most likely want to fraternize with your fellow competitors and club members to get the most out of the event. Most people arrive at the circuit the night before, but it is not compulsory as long as you arrive in good time. Signing on and scrutineering usually take place fairly early in the morning, so if you are not at the circuit the night before you may have an early start on race day. Signing on and scrutineering will usually commence between 7:00–8:00am, but be aware that there is often an early morning ban on noise from race engines. Check your final instructions for details. The noise ban may be in place until 8:30 or 9:00am and it may be different from Saturday to Sunday.

Most race events will have a fuel supply, but not always, so check before you go. One of the main race fuel suppliers in the UK is Anglo-American Oil Company, which supplies Sunoco race fuels at most of the big events. Most race events will also have a tyre supply; HP Tyres attend most events with a supply of Dunlop historic racing tyres. If you are likely to need tyres, be sure to call them before the weekend to ensure that they have your tyres on the truck.

If you are a new or novice driver on a National B licence, you will need to affix a sticker with a black cross on a yellow background to the back of your car. The black and yellow cross will remain on your car for your first six races (or five races if you choose to marshal for one race). After each of your first six races, provided that you have behaved yourself, driven safely and finished the race, you will collect a signature from the Clerk of the Course. In the MSA's Yearbook is a tear-out upgrade card. Your photograph will need to be attached to the upgrade card and it is on this card that you then collect the signatures. Once you have six signatures, submit your card to the MSA and upgrade to a National A licence. Some high-profile events, such as those held at Goodwood, require

testing and racing

In the paddock under our awning.

a National A licence. Full details on licences can be found in the *MSA Yearbook*.

Scrutineering

Scrutineering is an important part of each race meeting. The process involves the inspection of every race car and every driver's race wear and helmet. Without passing scrutineering, you will not be racing. Scrutineering will take place in either a designated scrutineering bay or in a garage in the pit lane. Note that if you head to the scrutineering bay early in the morning, before the race engine running ban has been lifted, you will have to push your car there.

The scrutineers will be looking to ensure that your vehicle and race wear adhere to the regulations set out in the MSA Yearbook. The scrutineers will need to be satisfied that your vehicle is in good condition and is safe to race. They will be looking for any signs of damage, wear and tear, or in the case of historic vehicles they will also have to consider any corrosion or fatigue. They will not be

A black and yellow cross lets other drivers know you are a novice.

testing and racing

concerned with eligibility to any given race or club. They are simply there for safety. The scrutineers will not care if you have the wrong radiator for your club's regulations, or if your carburettors were not homologated by the FIA. Eligibility to any given race series, championship or club will be handled by eligibility scrutineers provided by the club. If you are at a strictly FIA event or in an FIA race, you may face an FIA inspector, who will be looking to ensure that your car meets its homologation. If you are racing an FIA vehicle, you must bring your actual FIA papers to the race meeting, not a copy, as you may be asked to produce them. At European circuits, such as Spa-Francorchamps or the Nürburgring, the FIA inspectors can be very strict.

The safety scrutineers will look for any fluid leaks, as leaving oil on the track is seriously frowned upon. They will open the bonnet and boot for a visual inspection. They will look at the throttle return springs and throttle cables; they will look at the steering and may check the brake pedal. They will check the function of the cut-off switch and the external pull cables, and that the fire extinguisher and harnesses are in date. They will check that the roll cage is secure and meets the regulations and that the bulkheads are sealed from the engine, fuel tank and battery. They will look at the fuel tank, filler cap, spill tray and roll-over valve. They will check the function of

Our Mini in the scrutineering bay.

The scrutineer inspects Shaun's race suit.

testing and racing

the lights, specifically the headlights, brake lights and rain light. All being well, they will pass your car and put a sticker on it to show that they have done so. They will also check that your helmet and race wear is in date and in good condition.

If your car fails scrutineering for something major, then it is your own fault and you should learn what is expected and come back better prepared next time. If it fails for something minor, don't panic. Provided that you have adequate time before your qualifying session, you can rectify the issue and re-present for scrutineering once resolved. If you have not got the means to fix it yourself, don't be shy. Everyone in the paddock will have to go on the scrounge at some point in their racing career, so do feel comfortable about approaching other competitors or race teams to ask for something. Most people will be more than happy to help.

Qualifying

Once you have been successfully scrutineered, you will need to prepare your car for qualifying. The car needs fuel and you must set your tyre pressures and make sure your wheel nuts are torqued. Our basic tyre-pressure settings for a Mini on Dunlop CR65 historic tyres is 35psi on the front and 38psi on the rear while they are cold. Torque your wheel nuts to 45lb/ft. You will use less than 1ltr of fuel a minute, but there is no real need to risk running out. If your qualifying session is 20min, put at least 20ltr of fuel in the tank.

For each session of your race weekend, there will usually be somebody to call you up either in person or over a tannoy. They should announce that you have qualified at least 20min before you need to be in the assembly area. We recommend you start getting ready 1hr before your

Marshal in the assembly area.

testing and racing

Shaun makes sure that his harness is tight.

session is due to begin. You need time to prepare yourself, get dressed and warm up your engine. To allow heat to soak in, your engine needs to be warmed up 30–45min before the session, unless there is an early morning ban on engine running. Gently blip the throttle up to 3,000rpm until you start to build some temperature. Around 70°C is fine. You can then shut it off and wait to be called up to the assembly area. Remember that race meetings are often running ahead or behind time, so do not expect your session to be at exactly the published time. Be prepared for an early session. You need to be fully prepared and dressed in your race suit when they call you up. It is good practice to place your helmet and gloves in the car so that you don't forget them.

If you have never competed at the circuit before, it is a good idea to familiarize yourself with the assembly area, pit lane and parc fermé before your first session. There may or may not be a driver briefing before qualifying, so check your final instructions. When called up, drive down to the assembly area. Sometimes you will be stopped on your way into the assembly for a noise test. Your scrutineering sticker will also be checked. There will be a marshal in the assembly area who will line you all up appropriately and there should be another marshal who will check that the safety pin has been removed from your fire extinguisher.

Shut your engine off, as it can often be a 15–30min wait until your session begins. A marshal will come around a few minutes before your session and gesture to put your helmet and gloves on and get into your car. Make sure your harnesses are tight! Drivers have died because of loose belts. They are not there for your comfort. It is good to have someone to assist you. They can make sure that your harness is tight, check that the pin has been removed from the extinguisher and double-check that all of your doors, boot lid and bonnet are securely fastened.

The marshal will blow a whistle and signal when it is time to start the engine and you will be directed out of the assembly area one at a time on to the circuit. Often you will be directed down the pit lane, then on to the circuit. In this instance, the normal pit lane exit rules apply. Do not cross the white line. If you are running the heater to keep the engine cool, and you probably will, make sure that you open some windows. If you open the front window on the driver's door and the rear window on the other side you can channel the air to help keep you cool.

On your out-lap, take the time to warm up the tyres and the brakes and build your speed slowly. Look for where the marshals are posted. They should be waving green flags, and if you can, spot where the slip roads off the circuit are. If you have a mechanical issue on track and cannot make it back to the pit lane, finding a slip road or a marshal quickly can cut down the loss of time for recovery quite significantly. If a session is yellow- or red-flagged because you abandoned your broken race car at the exit of a high-speed corner and it took the marshal 10min to recover your vehicle, you are not going to make too many friends. In order to qualify for your race, you must complete three laps. If you do not get three laps

testing and racing

MSA RACE LICENSE

In order to compete in circuit racing in the UK you will have to have a race license. Just like your road license you will take both a written and a practical test. In order to get started you must purchase a 'Go Racing' starter pack from the MSA; the easiest way to do this is through their online shop. The starter pack will come with everything you need including all the necessary forms, a copy of the MSA year book, and a DVD. Once you studied the information then you will need to book your ARDS (Approved Racing Drivers School) test. Most of the major circuits in the UK will run ARDS courses, usually during track days. The easiest way to book is over the telephone. The average cost of the ARDS test in 2017 is about £250.

On the day of your ARDS test you should arrive at the circuit in good time as you will need to sign in. There is a written exam, covering such things as identifying flags, which you must pass. You will also be taken out on track where your driving will be observed by a qualified ARDS instructor.

Once you have successfully passed your ARDS course then your examiner will stamp and sign your license application. To get your first race license you need to fill in the form and submit it to the MSA with the necessary fee. If you are over 18 you will also need to have a medical examination by a GP. Most GP's can do this for you but they usually charge for it. The costs seem to range between £40 and £100 for a sports medical examination.

The first licence you receive will be your National B. When racing with a National B license you must affix a novice cross sticker to the back of your race car. The novice cross is a black cross on a yellow background. In order to remove the novice cross and upgrade to a National A license you must accrue six signatures from the clerk of the course on your upgrade card. Any MSA yearbook will have an upgrade card you can tear out. You will need to permanently affix a passport photo to your upgrade card and bring it with you to your race meetings. In order to get a signature on it you need to drive respectfully and finish your race safely. If you like you can race five times for five signatures and spend a day on a marshal's post to get your sixth signature. Once your upgrade card is completed you can submit it to the MSA along with the appropriate form and fee to upgrade to your National A. Once you have received your National A license you can remove the novice cross from your race car and be you'll be eligible to compete in higher-profile events.

Unless you plan to compete internationally then you will not need to upgrade again. You will however, need to renew your license every year. To renew your license you will need to complete a form, pay a fee and if you are under 45 you need a medical self declaration. If you are over 45 then you will need an annual medical examination with your GP.

Qualifying at the Brands Hatch Mini Festival.

testing and racing

in before the race, you will not be allowed to race. It is good practice to get three laps in before you start pushing harder. If you are qualifying for a two-driver race, it is required that both drivers complete three laps.

You need to pay close attention to the flags when on track. We will not go into too much detail here as you would have covered flags in depth during your Association of Racing Drivers (ARDS) course, but it is important to act when you see them. Most commonly you will see blue and yellow flags.

When out on track it is easy to forget about your gauges. Check the temperature and oil pressure regularly. The engine should run at less than 90°C. Because a Mini only has a small radiator mounted to the side of the engine, it has a hard time keeping cool. You will probably have to run the heater whilst on track to help. If the temperature goes over 95°C, you may need to back off and let it cool down. If you slow down and the temperature does not drop, you will need to bring the car in and shut it off, as either something is broken or you simply have insufficient cooling. Your oil pressure will run at around 60–70psi at full chat. At idle, when the oil is hot it may drop to as low as 20–30psi. Pay close attention to your oil pressure, as spotting a drop in pressure early can save your engine from catastrophic damage. If you notice the oil pressure slowly dropping during the session, head straight into the pit lane and shut off your engine. If you wait until your warning light comes on at around 20psi, fatal damage may have already been done. If you have a problem and cannot make it back to the pits, find the most sensible place to stop the car so that time is not wasted recovering you.

When you are on track qualifying, find a bit of space from your fellow competitors and concentrate on putting together clean, consistent laps. Remember that this is not a race, so don't worry about fighting for position with another driver, as it will only slow you down. Be observant and look in your mirrors. It is good practice when on the straights routinely to check your gauges and mirrors. If a faster car is approaching from behind, let them pass. You will not be popular if you are lapping unaware of those around, if you are holding people up, or, worse, turning in front of fast approaching vehicles. If you wish to let somebody pass, hold your line and give them room to get by. It is the responsibility of the car behind to get past the slower car in front safely. The most important thing is not to make any sudden or unpredictable manoeuvres.

It is quite common for most amateur drivers to lap a couple of seconds slower in qualifying than they do in a race. The heat of competition in the race will often push a driver to knock a few seconds off their qualifying lap time. When the qualifying session is over, you will be shown the chequered flag. Take your in-lap relatively slowly, get some air through the engine and let everything cool down a little. There will be a marshal to direct you off the circuit either into the parc fermé or directly into the paddock. Always follow the marshal's instructions. Once you are back to your spot in the paddock, shut off the car, get out and drink some water. It is important to keep yourself hydrated. You lose a lot of fluid in a race car through sweat, especially in a Mini with the heater running. Our Mini has a small electric circulation pump plumbed in next to the heater. Running this pump after the engine is switched off circulates the water and helps to prevent any hot spots in the engine. Take a note of your hot tyre pressures and adjust if necessary.

You will probably have a few hours before your race so it is best to get changed and relax. Soon after qualifying there will be printed result sheets available, so you can check your qualifying position and your best lap time.

Assembly area ahead of the race.

testing and racing

Once the car has cooled down you will need to check it over prior to the race. Provided that nothing went wrong during qualifying you should not have a lot of work to do before your race.

The Race

You will need to perform another basic preparation before the race. It is worth getting the car up on axle stands and taking the wheels off. We will usually remove the brake drums to scuff them and the shoes with some coarse sandpaper to remove any glazing. The same can be done at the front with the brake discs and pads. Clean the brakes with brake cleaner and reassemble. Give the car a once-over and check that nothing has come loose or started leaking. If all is well, refit the wheels and lower the car back down to the ground. Torque the wheel nuts to 45lb/ft and check the tyre pressures. Check all fluids and top up if any are low.

The general procedure for the race session will be similar to qualifying. Warm up the engine 30–45min ahead of your race. Make sure that you are ready for your race session when it is announced. Again, we would recommend being with your car 1hr before your race. There may be a driver's briefing before you are called up to the assembly area, so check your final instructions. When you are called up, you need to head to the assembly area.

There will be marshals in the assembly area who will organize you according to your grid position and again you may have a 15–20min wait before the signal to start engines. You will get the signal to put your helmet on and get in your vehicle. Make sure that you are safely strapped in, that your extinguisher pin has been removed and that all of your vehicle's closing panels are secure. If you are running the heater to keep the engine cool, make sure that some windows are open for ventilation. When the race is ready to begin, you and your fellow competitors will be directed on to the circuit and lined up in the appropriate grid position.

You will have at least one formation lap, or green flag lap. Use this lap to familiarize yourself again with the location of the marshals and to warm up your brakes and tyres. Knowing where the marshals are is an important safety concern and will reduce stoppage time if you can find them quickly when needed. You can weave from side to side to warm up your tyres, but never take up more

Druids hairpin at Brands Hatch.

testing and racing

Shaun on the outside at Druids.

than 50 per cent of the track width when doing so. A good way to warm up the brakes is to accelerate on the straights to make some space, then take a few stabs on the brake pedal with your left foot, being sure to check your mirrors.

You may have seen that some Mini racers will spin up the front wheels before they reach their starting position on the grid. It is important that you do not stop before getting to your grid position and that you do not waste any time. The cars at the front of the grid will be waiting for you. When you get back to the starting grid, you may be directed to your starting position by a marshal, or there may not be a marshal and you might be required to remember your position and line up yourself. Once lined up, you could be shown a board or series of boards indicating the time left until the start. This might be 30sec, or it might be less. Some grids get going very quickly with no time shown, so be observant and keep your eye on the gantry lights. The starting lights on the gantry will illuminate red and the race will begin when the lights go out. If the race is started with a flag, the race will begin the moment the flag drops. If the starting grid is on a hill, such as at Brands Hatch, do not forget to take your handbrake off. Racing with it on will blow up your rear brakes pretty quickly.

If you have a problem and fail to pull away for the green flag lap, you must immediately raise an arm in the air out of your window and keep it there until a marshal comes to you. If you get going and manage to catch up to the pack, you can find your place but only if it is safe to do so. In motor sport it is often common sense that rules. If you cannot safely return to your grid position before the pack reaches the grid, you will have to start from the back of the grid. If you fail to get going, the marshals will push you into the pit lane. If you manage to sort the problem, you will have to start from the end of the pit lane. A marshal will signal once the grid has cleared and it is safe to exit the pit lane.

With the race under way, you need to be aware of other cars in front and behind. The first couple of corners on the first lap will always be a challenge, as there are so many cars vying for the same piece of track and you will all be heading in with cold tyres and cold brakes. Concentration is key. Try to place your car in the safest position.

As you make it through the first few corners, the pack will spread out a little. You can begin to gauge your pace

testing and racing

The marshal waves a yellow and red striped flag to indicate a slippery track.

against those cars around you. You will start to get a feel for your strengths versus those of your competitors and you can begin to line up those cars in front that you think you can overtake. If you are a novice driver, do your best to keep it clean, stick to your line and do not make any unpredictable manoeuvres. Be observant and check your mirrors. If you need to defend your position, you can only make one manoeuvre on the straight. Do not do it in the braking zone and do not make any erratic moves.

When you complete your lap and are passing the pit wall, give a wave to your supporters to let them know you are all right. If there is a big speed differential between you and the leading pack, they will catch up with you in five or six laps and they may come up quickly. There might be as many as six cars in the leading pack, so check your mirrors and be sure not to get in their way.

In the heat of the race, it can be easy to forget about the gauges. You need to keep a regular eye on the oil pressure and the temperature, as, in the event of a mechanical problem, spotting a drop in oil pressure or a rise in temperature early on can save you an expensive rebuild. If you see that the temperature is rising, you may be able to avoid a DNF if you back off a little and manage the temperature. If the oil pressure begins to drop, you will have no choice but to call it a day.

You must pay close attention to the marshals' flags and respond immediately whenever flags are shown. If you are shown a blue flag, you will need to let the car behind you pass. Do not make any sudden or unpredictable moves to pull out of the way or slow down. If you back off a little and leave space, the driver behind will find his way past safely. The rules for yellow flags are the same, but if the Clerk of the Course deems it necessary, the 'SC' board will be shown and the Safety Car will be deployed. When the Safety Car is deployed there is of course no overtaking and all cars must line up behind it, following at the same speed with no more than five car lengths between you and the car in front. Do not pass the Safety Car unless signalled to do so. In order to pick up the leader, the Safety Car may signal you to come past by waving an arm out of the window. If you are signalled past, you must continue at reduced speed and hopefully pick up the back of the pack. Once the issue has been resolved the Clerk of the Course will bring the Safety Car in and the race will resume when the green flag is waved. When you see the

The chequered flag.

Mini being inspected following a race.

testing and racing

green flag you may increase your speed immediately, but you must not overtake until you cross the start/finish line.

There will be driving standards officials watching. The black and white flag will be shown for suspect driving behaviour and if you are shown the solid black flag your race is over. There will be a system of penalties that can, and will, be applied. What penalties and how they are applied will depend on the race organizer or championship officials, but may include: a stop and go penalty in the pit lane; a drive-through penalty in the pit lane; or a time penalty added at the end of the race. The Clerk of the Course will be responsible for dishing out the penalties and if you get any you will need to report to them for a slap on the wrist. If your driving has been deemed to be dangerous, then as well as a penalty in your race you may also be given points on your race licence and a fine. Points on your race licence are much like points on your driver's licence. If you accrue twelve points, your licence will be taken away.

If you have entered a single-driver race, your race will likely be between 15–30min. If it is a two-driver race, it could be as long as 30min to 1hr, with a mandatory pit stop. The pit window is the time that the pit lane is open for the driver change. It will be in the middle of the session and will last around 15–20min. Within this time, you will have to pit and swap drivers. If you do not have a second driver, your club will have published a set of pit-stop rules. Learn these rules or risk getting a penalty. It might be that you have to stop in the pits and wait for 1min, or it might be that you have to get out of the car, shut the door, do a little dance and get back in again. If you miss the pit window and come in when the pit lane is closed, you will also get a penalty.

At the end of the race, the chequered flag will be waved at the start/finish line. After crossing the finish line, you need to back off and let the car cool down before coming into the parc fermé at the end of the lap. Some events or championships may use parc fermé rules and assemble all cars together after the race. The race organizers may choose to bring the first three finishers or a random selection in for further inspection, weighing or to inspect HTP papers. This is to check that competitors are not cheating and to help deter them from doing so. You will otherwise be free to return to the paddock and relax. Get changed out of your race suit and rehydrate. If this was your only race of the event, you can either enjoy the rest of your day or go home. If you have another race, you will need to repeat your pre-race prep once the car has cooled down.

There is so much that can only be learned through experience, so take this chapter as nothing more than a simple guide. If you have never raced before, it will probably pay off to make friends with a more experienced racer who can help guide you. It takes many years to hone your race craft, so don't expect too much too soon and don't push yourself too hard. Motor racing is full of highs and lows. You will have weekends of total elation and other weekends of total despair where nothing seems to go your way. This is the nature of the sport and the reason we love it, although during the lows it can be hard to remember the highs. Don't forget that racing should be fun. Always use common sense, drive safely and you will earn the respect of your fellow competitors.

useful contacts

ACW Motorsport Plastics – Polycarbonate windows for motor sport
Avonhouse Unit 1
Blackfriars Road Trading Estate
Blackfriars Road
Bristol BS48 4DJ
United Kingdom
Tel: +44 (0)1275 546 008
Website: www.acwmotorsportplastics.co.uk
Email: tony@acwmotorsportplastics.co.uk

Aldon Automotive – Ignition parts and distributors for road and race
Breener Industrial Estate
Station Drive
Brierley Hill
West Midlands DY5 3JZ
United Kingdom
Telephone: +44 (0)1384 572553
Website: www.aldonauto.co.uk
Email: info@aldonauto.co.uk

AVO UK Ltd – Shock absorbers for all applications including bespoke service
Caswell Road
Brackmills Industrial Estate
Northampton
Northamptonshire NN4 7PW
United Kingdom
Tel: +44 (0)1604 708101
Website: www.avouk.com
Email: sales@avouk.com

CCK Historic – Race preparation and support, restoration and service of classic vehicles
Rosehill Farm
Burnt Oak Road
Uckfield
East Sussex TN22 4AE
United Kingdom
Tel: +44 (0)1825 733060
Website: www.cckhistoric.com
Email: info@cckhistoric.com

Concept Racing – Aluminium Mini fuel tank and motor-sport fabrication
Unit 5C Alton Road Business Park
Alton Road
Ross-on-Wye
Herefordshire HR9 5BP
United Kingdom
Tel: +44 (0)1989 763777
Website: www.conceptracing.co.uk
Email: info@conceptracing.co.uk

Corbeau Seats/LUKE Harnesses – Leading manufacturer of racing seats and harnesses
17 Wainwright Close
Churchfields Industrial Estate
St Leonards-on-Sea
East Sussex TN38 9PP
United Kingdom
Tel: +44 (0)1424 854499
Website: www.corbeau-seats.com
Email: sales@corbeau-seats.com

Demon Tweeks – Race preparation parts supplier
75 Ash Road South
Wrexham Industrial Estate
Wrexham
North Wales LL13 9UG
United Kingdom
Tel: +44 (0)1978 664466
Website: www.demon-tweeks.co.uk
Email: sales@demon-tweeks.co.uk

Distributor Doctor – Best-quality Lucas ignition components
Unit 8
Old Brewery Road
Wiveliscombe
Somerset TA4 2PW
United Kingdom
Tel: +44(0)1984 629540
Website: www.distributordoctor.com
Email: martin@distributordoctor.com

useful contacts

Fédération Internationale de l'Automobile – Motor sports' international governing body
8 Place de la Concorde
75008
Paris
France
Tel: +33 1 43 12 44 55
Website: www.fia.com

Gary Hawkins – Motor-sport Photographer
Tel: 07956 409952
Email: g.hawkins1963@ntlworld.com

HP Tyres Ltd – Supplier of Dunlop historic racing tyres
Units 5 & 6 Broad March Trade Park
Long March Industrial Estate
Daventry
Northants NN11 4HE
United Kingdom
Tel: +44 (0)1327 301887
Website: www.hptyres.com
Email: office@hptyres.com

Kent Auto Developments (KAD) – Appendix K anti-roll bar and other performance Mini parts
Brooker Farm
Newchurch
Romney Marsh
Kent TN29 0DT
United Kingdom
Tel: +44 (0)1303 874082
Website: www.kentautodevelopments.com
Email: sales@kentautodevelopments.com

Lifeline Fire & Safety Systems – Motor-sport fire-extinguisher systems
Falkland Close
Charter Avenue Industrial Estate
Coventry
West Midlands CV4 8AU
United Kingdom
Tel: +44 (0)24 7671 2999
Website: www.lifeline-fire.co.uk
Email: sales@lifeline-fire.co.uk

Mini Sport Ltd – Leading parts supplier for the classic Mini since 1967
Thompson Street
Padiham, Lancashire BB12 7AP
United Kingdom
Tel: +44 (0)1282 772043
Website: www.minisport.com
Email: sales@minisport.com

M-Machine – The best place for Mini body panels
Unit 6 Forge Way
Cleveland Trading Estate
Darlington
County Durham DL1 2PJ
United Kingdom
Tel: +44 (0)1325 381300
Website: www.m-machine.co.uk
Email: sales@m-machine.co.uk

Motor Sports Association – Motor sport's governing body in the UK
Motor Sports House
Riverside Park
Colnbrook
Berkshire SL3 OHG
United Kingdom
Tel: 01753 765000
Fax: 01753 682938
Website: www.msauk.org
Competition licences: 01753 765050
For HTP documents, ask for MSA Historic Technical department or email: htp@msauk.org

Piper Cams – Camshafts, valve springs, valve caps and timing gears
Units 5 & 6 Bowles Well Gardens
Folkestone
Kent CT19 6PQ
United Kingdom
Tel: +44 (0)1303 245300
Website: www.pipercams.co.uk
Email: sales@pipercams.co.uk

Play Mini – International automotive export agents
13 & 14 Faygate Business Centre
Faygate Lane
Horsham
West Sussex RH12 4DN
Tel: 01293 851944
Website: www.playmini.co.uk

useful contacts

Questmead Ltd – Competition brake pads and shoe lining
The Lodge
Meadowcroft Mill
Off Bury Rd
Bamford
Rochdale
Lancashire OL11 4AU
United Kingdom
Tel: +44 (0)1706 363939
Website: www.questmead.co.uk
Email: sales@questmead.co.uk

Swiftune Ltd – Omega pistons, competition condenser and other competition Mini components
High Chimney Farm
Biddenden Road
St Michaels
Tenterden
Kent TN30 6TA
Tel: +44 (0)1233 850843
Website: www.swiftune.com
Email: sales@swiftune.co.uk

WOSP – Racing starter motors and alternators
Find your nearest dealer on their website: www.wosperformance.co.uk

index

8-port   15
11 studs   90

alternator   133–134
anti-roll bar   65, 66
ARDS test   164, 165

balancing   96
battery   20, 51, 130–131
big-end bearings   102–103
body   27–38
body panels   30–38
   boot floor   32, 36
   door skin   38
   floor   30–31
   front panel   34
   quarter panel   31
   rear panel   32, 36
   rear seat panel   32
   rear valance   32, 36
   scuttle   34
   sills   30–31, 35
   stiffener   36
   subframe mounting panel   37
   wheel arch   36
   wings   34
bodywork   19, 27–38
bonnet   38, 54
   bonnet fastening   54
boot lid   38, 54
bore   19, 88
brake bias valve   69
brake fluid   71
brake lines   21, 71
brake master cylinder   71
brakes   67, 71, 156, 158
bulkheads   21, 31, 36–38
bumpers   35

camber   143–147
camshaft   92–93, 99–105
   camshaft bearings   99–100
   camshaft followers   92–93, 103
   camshaft timing   94
carburettors   19, 118–123, 140–142
   tuning   138–142
caster   143–147
centre main strap   89, 101
circuit breaker   20, 51, 131–132
club racing   25–26
coil   110, 137

compression ratio   91
condenser   136
connecting rods   93, 94, 99–103
corrosion   20, 27, 30–36
crankshaft   94–95, 99–106
   crankshaft damper   95–96
crown wheel & pinion   79–80
CSCC   26
CV joint   82–83
cylinder head   90–91, 103, 106
   valves   90–91, 103
   valve springs   91–92

differential   18, 78–79
distributor   134–137
door pocket   45
driveshafts   82
drop bracket   67
drop gears   81–82
dynamo   133–134

electrics   124–137
engine   85
   assembly   98–106
   electrics   132–137
   installation   106–107
engine block   87–90, 98–106
   main caps   89, 100–102
exhaust   97–98

FIA   11, 16–25
   Appendix K   11, 16–23
   Appendix J   17–18
   Appendix VIII   17
   Appendix IX   17
final drive   79–80
flywheel   95–96
front bulkhead   32–33, 37, 38, 121–122
front brakes   68
front subframe   37, 59–64
fuel   19, 135–136, 138–139, 153, 159, 163
fuel line   21, 115–117
fuel pump   111, 117
fire extinguisher   20, 21, 49–51, 163
fireproof bulkhead   21, 37–38
fuel tank   18, 21, 111–115
   fuel tank foam   21, 115
fuse box   127

gear lever   31
   remote   31, 83–84

index

gauges   128–130
gearbox   75–80
geometry   143–147
Group 2   15, 17
Group 5   15

HANS device/FHR   48–49
Hardy Spicer joint   82
head gasket   103, 106
headlights   56
heater   109–110
helmet   53, 162, 163
homologation   11, 16–19, 23–24
HRDC   26
HSCC   25–26
HTP   23, 138, 147–150, 162
hydrolastic   16, 18, 58, 60, 64

ignition coil   110, 137
ignition system   134–137
ignition timing   135–136, 139–140
inlet manifold   120–123

license   104
LSD   18, 78–79

main bearings   100–104
master switch   20, 51, 131–132
Masters   25
mirrors   21, 55
MSA   11–25

noise test   153, 156, 163

oil catch tank   21, 55, 56
oil cooler   106–108
oil pressure   139, 155, 165, 168
oil pump   96–97, 103

pistons   93, 94, 99–103
preparation   35, 37, 150–151, 166
pull cables   51, 131

qualifying   162–165

race entry   159
race numbers   159
race suit/overalls   52–53, 162
race wear   52–53, 162
racing   158–170
racing licence   159
radiator   106–110
   hoses   110
rain light   55, 132
rear brakes   69
rear bulkhead   31, 36–38

rear subframe   37, 59, 60, 63–65
regulations   14–25
ride height   142–144
rocker gear   91–92
roll cage (ROPS)   22, 39–46
   welding   27, 28
   reinforcement plates   27, 28, 41, 44
rolling road   140–142
rubber cone   58, 61
rust   20, 27, 30–36

safety   19, 34, 37, 39–56
safety car   168
safety harness   23, 40, 47, 163
scrutineering   18, 159–162
seam welding   28, 35–37
seat   46
shock absorbers   37, 146
spark plugs   137
starter motor   132–133
steering   66–67
steering wheel   21, 67
stroke   19
subframes   37, 57–65
suspension   57–66
   setup   142–147
switch gear   125, 126–127, 128

tachometer   128–130
temperature   106–110, 140, 155, 163, 165, 168
test day   153
testing   152–159
tie rods   62, 63
timing gear/vernier   93, 105
toe   143–147
tolerance   19
towing eye   55
track day   153
track width   19, 60, 142
tuning   138–142
tyres   72–74
   tyre pressure   146, 156, 163, 165

U2TC   26
valve   90, 103

warning lights   128–130
water pump   96–97
weight   143, 147
welding   28–38
wheel nut torque   151
wheelbase   19, 60, 142
wheels   71–72
windows   51, 54
windscreen   21, 51
wiring loom   126–127

RELATED TITLES FROM CROWOOD

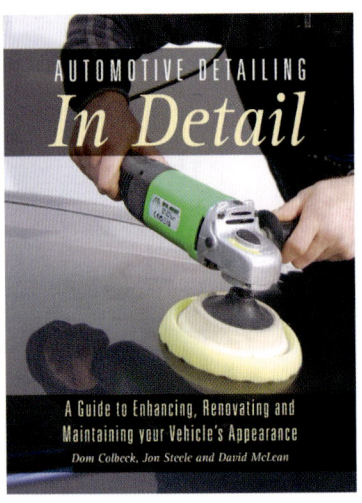

Automotive Detailing – In Detail
DOM COLBECK
ISBN 978 1 78500 242 7
300 illustrations, 272pp

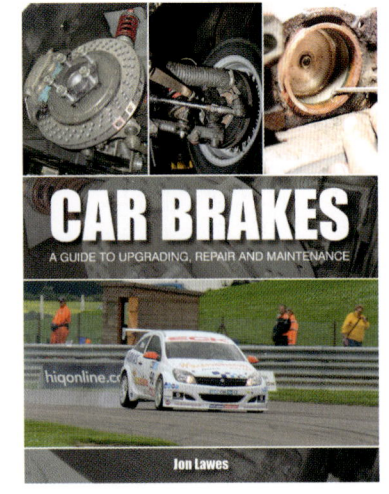

Car Brakes
JON LAWES
ISBN 978 1 84797 674 1
120 illustrations, 96pp

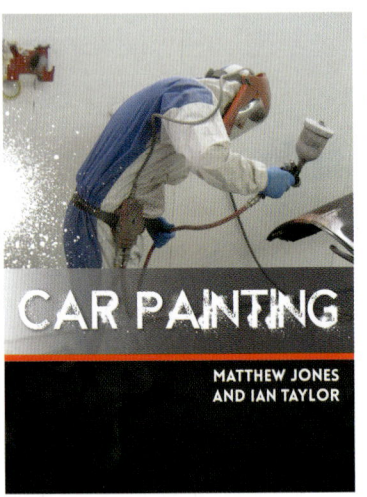

Car Painting
MATT JONES
ISBN 978 1 84797 947 6
200 illustrations, 144pp

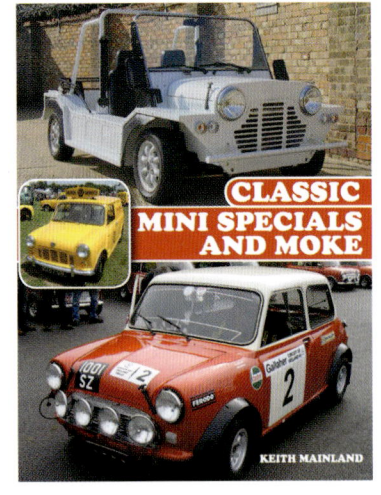

Classic Mini Specials and Moke
KEITH MAINLAND
ISBN 978 1 78500 001 0
300 illustrations, 192pp

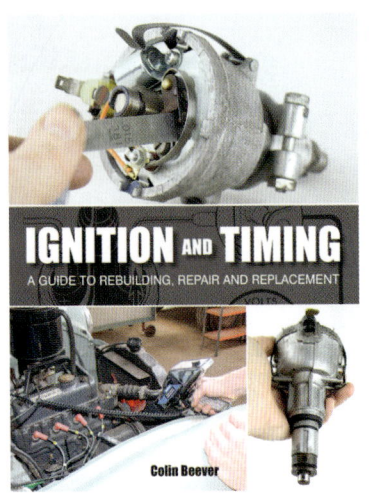

Ignition and Timing
COLIN BEEVER
ISBN 978 1 84797 973 5
90 illustrations, 96pp

In case of difficulty ordering, please contact the Sales Office:

**The Crowood Press
Ramsbury, Wiltshire SN8 2HR
UK**

Tel: 44 (0) 1672 520320
enquiries@crowood.com
www.crowood.com